GRUESOME SPECTACLES

GRUESOME SPECTACLES

Botched Executions and America's Death Penalty

Austin Sarat

with

Katherine Blumstein
Aubrey Jones
Heather Richard
Madeline Sprung-Keyser

STANFORD LAW BOOKS
An Imprint of Stanford University Press
Stanford, California

Stanford University Press
Stanford, California

Sarat, Austin, author.
  Gruesome spectacles : botched executions and America's death penalty / Austin Sarat.
    pages cm
  Includes bibliographical references and index.
  ISBN 978-0-8047-8916-5 (cloth : alk. paper)
  1. Executions and executioners—United States—History. 2. Capital punishment—United States—History. I. Title.
  HV8699.U5S268 2014
  364.660973—dc23
                              2013043599

ISBN 978-0-8047-9172-4 (electronic)

Typeset at Stanford University Press in 10.5/15 Adobe Garamond

To Ben with gratitude
for his sweetness and sparkling wit

Contents

"There is no law that is not inscribed on bodies. Every law has a hold on the body. . . . Every power, including the power of law, is written first of all on the backs of its subjects."

—Michel de Certeau, *The Practice of Everyday Life*

"Make a good job of this."

—William Kemmler, first person electrocuted in the United States, 1890

"Do they feel anything? Do they hurt? Is there any pain? Very humane compared to what they've done to our children. The torture they've put our kids through. I think sometimes it's too easy. They ought to feel something. If it's fire burning all the way through their body or whatever. There ought to be some little sense of pain to it."

—Mother of a murder victim on being shown the planned death by lethal injection of her child's killer

"People who wish to commit murder, they better not do it in the state of Florida because we may have a problem with our electric chair."

—Robert Butterworth, Attorney General, State of Florida, remarking on a malfunction that caused a fire during an electrocution

"Though our brother is on the rack . . . our sense will never inform us of what he suffers. . . . By the imagination we place ourselves in his situation, we conceive ourselves enduring all the same torments, we enter as it were into his body, and become in some measure the same person with him."

—Adam Smith, *The Theory of the Moral Sentiments*

CHAPTER 1

The Mere Extinguishment of Life?

Technological Efficiency, Botched Executions, and the Legitimacy of Capital Punishment in the United States

On September 28, 1900, the state of North Carolina hanged Art Kinsauls for a murder committed in Sampson County. Born in that county in 1865, Kinsauls had lived there his entire life, marrying a local girl, Posunnie Gibsy Bass, in 1896. Even though Art weighed only 110 pounds, he was said to be "tough as iron."[1] He had the unfortunate habit of getting into violent arguments and carried on a long running feud with John C. Herring, his neighbor. One night when Kinsauls was in Art Vann's Store at Beaman's Crossroad, an argument began and then a fight broke out. "Kinsauls reached into the meat box and got a sharp butcher knife and stabbed young Herring to such an extent that he died during the night."[2]

Kinsauls was arrested a few days after Herring's death and taken to the county jail in Clinton. With the help of a group of his friends, he soon escaped, and avoided capture for nine months. The sheriff and a posse only recaptured him after a gunfight at his farm, which left him seriously wounded. Brought to trial in October 1899, Kinsauls was found guilty of murder and was sentenced to hang.

On the surface at least, there was nothing remarkable about North Carolina's plan for the Kinsauls execution. Hanging had been the primary method of execution in the United States since the founding of the American colonies. It was an inexpensive, low-tech way of putting people to death. Hangings could be handled at the local level, and did not require elaborate execution protocols.[3]

Kinsauls refused to go quietly. He tried to kill himself twice, first with an overdose of sleeping pills and later by using a tin lid to cut his throat. Both attempts failed, but each resulted in a postponement of his execution. In the meantime, North Carolina governor Daniel Russell received many requests for a reprieve from influential Sampson County citizens, each of which the governor refused.

On the day of the hanging, hundreds of people traveled from all over the county to witness it. The gallows was erected near the jail where Kinsauls had originally been held. As in all its executions, Sampson County used a stepladder as its gallows, but in this instance it failed to do its job. The drop height proved insufficient to break the condemned's neck. With Kinsauls suspended at the end of the rope, the attending physician quickly determined that he was still alive.

Compounding the problem was the fact that his neck had only partially healed from his last suicide attempt. As a result, when Kinsauls fell from the stepladder, the rope ripped open his neck wound and left him bleeding profusely. The assembled crowd of friends and neighbors nearly rioted. Undaunted by the failure of their first execution attempt and the increasingly chaotic, bloody scene, officials cut him down, forced him up the ladder again, and repeated the drop. This time the execution succeeded and Kinsauls died. His was the last public hanging in Sampson County.[4]

Newspapers all over the country took note of the Kinsauls execution. Headlines in the *Atlanta Constitution,* the *New York Times,* the *Washington Post,* and the *Republic* (St. Louis, Missouri) announced that it had not gone as planned. For example, the *Washington Post* titled its article "Murderer Hanged Twice."[5] The stories, in turn, used vivid language to convey the horror of Kinsauls's last minutes on earth. The *Post* described a "Ghastly Gallows Scene,"[6] and the *Virginian Pilot* called it a thoroughly "revolting execution."

Almost a century later, in March 1997, American newspapers carried stories of another botched execution—the electrocution of Pedro Medina, a thirty-nine-year-old Cuban immigrant convicted and condemned for stabbing a Florida high school teacher to death.[7] After the current was turned on, as one newspaper put it, flames "leaped from the head" of the condemned. "'It was horrible,' a witness was quoted as saying, 'a solid flame covered his whole head, from one side to the other. I had the impression of somebody being burned alive.'"[8] Another reporter wrote, "The electrocution of Pedro Medina on Tuesday was the stuff of nightmares and horror fiction novels and films. A foot-long blue and orange flame shot from the mask covering his head for about 10 seconds, filling the execution chamber with smoke and sickening witnesses with the odor of charred human flesh."[9]

Yet news reports also conveyed the "reassuring" reaction of Dr. Belle Almojera, medical director at Florida State Prison, who said that before the apparatus caught fire Medina already had "lurched up in his seat and balled up his fists—the normal reaction to high voltage. . . . 'I saw no evidence of pain or suffering by the inmate throughout the entire process. In my professional opinion, he died a very quick, humane death.'"[10] The Florida Supreme Court found that "Medina's brain was instantly and massively depolarized within milliseconds of the initial surge of electricity. He suffered no conscious pain."[11] And others defended his botched electrocution by noting that it "was much more humane than what was done to the victim."[12]

Despite these attempts to contain adverse public reaction, the Medina execution, like the Kinsauls execution before it, made headlines because it suggested that the quest for a painless, and allegedly humane, technology of death was by no means complete. Both botched executions remind us of the ferocity of the state's sovereign power over life itself. At the same time, these news stories also offered capital punishment's supporters a hint of relief. Most stories treated Medina's electrocution as a mere technological glitch rather than as an occasion to rethink the practice of state killing itself. Florida's Fort Lauderdale *Sun-Sentinel* opined, for example, that the state "is justified in imposing the death penalty. . . . But it has no justification for retaining a method . . . that is so gruesome and violent and sometimes flawed."[13] What might have been a challenge to the legitimacy of the killing state was quickly written off as Florida's failure to keep up with the technology of the times.

Botched executions, like those of Kinsauls and Medina, have been, and remain, an important part of the story of capital punishment in the United States. From the beginning, American execution practices have been designed to differentiate law's violence from violence out-side the law—to sharply set capital punishment apart from the crimes the law condemns. This was especially true in the twentieth century, when enormous efforts were made to put people to death quietly, in-visibly, and bureaucratically.[14] The course of the last century is littered with various technologies—hanging, firing squad, electrocution, the gas chamber, lethal injection—used in a continuing effort to find an appar-ently humane means by which the state could take life.[15] Executions, in this system, are not supposed to make headlines.

Headlines today tell of a remarkable transformation in America's death penalty. Over the course of the last decade, death sentences and executions have both fallen dramatically.[16] We now impose fewer death sentences and execute fewer people than at any time in a quarter cen-tury. These changes have been driven by concerns about the reliability of the death penalty system in fairly adjudicating guilt and innocence, and in differentiating those who deserve a death sentence from those who do not. In addition, today the state's dealing in death is linked to a concern for technological efficiency. We are invited, following Dr. Almojera, to imagine the body as a legible text, readable for what it can tell us about the capacity of technology to move us from life to death, swiftly and painlessly[17]—to ensure that execution is nothing more than "the mere extinguishment of life."

But why should the state care about the suffering of those it puts to death? Painful death might be more just and more effective as a de-terrent than a death that is quick, quiet, and tranquil. Because justice would seem to demand equivalence between pain inflicted in the crime and the pain experienced as part of the punishment, there is something unsettling and paradoxical about the state's constant search for a painless way of killing those who kill. As Arlene Blanchard, a survivor of Timo-thy McVeigh's 1995 bombing of the Alfred P. Murrah Federal Build-ing in Oklahoma City, in which 168 people were killed, explained after McVeigh's death sentence was handed down, "death by injection is 'too good' for McVeigh." She said he should be put in solitary confinement for life or simply hanged from a tree. "I know it sounds uncivilized, but

I want him to experience just a little of the pain and torture that he has put us through."[18] Or, as William Baay, an emergency worker who helped remove bodies from the Murrah building, put it, "I don't think conventional methods should be used. They should amputate his legs with no anesthesia . . . and then set him over a bunch of bamboo shoots and let them grow up into him until he's dead."[19]

Even as capital punishment seeks to do justice and/or satisfy the public desire for vengeance, the state has countervailing concerns. It must distinguish execution from the acts to which it is a supposedly just response. The state must also find ways of killing in a manner that does not allow the condemned to become an object of pity, or to appropriate the status of the victim. But despite determined claims to the contrary, capital death never simply means death. Rather, since its inception, it has been inextricably tied to the instruments used to carry it out. The legitimacy of state killing depends largely on execution method. Technology mediates between the state and death by masking physical pain and allowing citizens to imagine that execution is clean, efficient, and painless.

When executions go wrong, they signal a break in the ritualization and routinization of state killing. Such mishaps can turn the organized, state-controlled ritual into torture. Solemn spectacles of sovereign power morph into horrible events and critical attention gets focused on the evolving execution technologies—and, even more intently, on their failures.

Gruesome Spectacles: Botched Executions and America's Death Penalty examines the history of botched executions in the United States from 1890 to 2010, a period in which approximately 3 percent of all executions were botched.[20] Botched executions occur when there is a breakdown in, or departure from, the "protocol" for a particular method of execution. The protocol can be established by the norms, expectations, and advertised virtues of each method or by the government's officially adopted execution guidelines. Botched executions are "those involving unanticipated problems or delays that caused, at least arguably, unnecessary agony for the prisoner or that reflect gross incompetence of the executioner."[21] Examples of such problems include, among other things, inmates catching fire while being electrocuted, being strangled during hangings (instead of having their necks broken), and being administered the wrong dosages of specific drugs for lethal injections.

Of approximately nine thousand capital sentences carried out in the United States from 1890 to 2010, we know of 276 that were botched—79 from 1900 to 1919, 70 from 1920 to 1949, 23 from 1950 to 1979, and 104 from 1980 to 2010 (see Appendix A).[22] This book describes the problems that have plagued the technologies of state killing in an effort to understand those numbers as well as how and why things go wrong during executions. It tells the story of America's death penalty through the eyes of those whose executions have gone terribly wrong (see Appendix B).

The book focuses on 1890–2010, which was a crucial period in the transformation of America's capital punishment from its traditional to its more modern form. It was, in addition, a critical period in what death penalty historian Stuart Banner calls "the continual centralization and professionalization of punishment,"[23] and in the development of new technologies of execution. In this context, one might expect that botched executions would have undermined the death penalty's legitimacy. As Chris Greer argues,

> Botched executions are of particular interest for at least two obvious reasons. First, they represent a direct challenge to the state's desired presentation of capital punishment as quick, clean and painless. Secondly, by making the violence inherent in capital punishment clearly visible, and raising questions about the suffering of the condemned, they present abolitionists with an important opportunity to mobilize support against the continued use of the death penalty.[24]

Yet despite Greer's reasonable expectation, throughout the twentieth century botched executions played only a minor role in efforts to end the death penalty in the United States. This book considers why they have not played a larger role in the efforts of abolitionists to end the death penalty.

The twentieth-century search for ever more invisible, "humane" methods of state killing depended upon certain assumptions about the legibility of pain in the journey from life to death. But the legal construction of state killing, while it appears to reveal an assumed empathy or identification between the state and those it kills, works primarily to differentiate state killing from murder. In these efforts, we are collectively invited to search for a way of taking life that signals our superiority and that marks the distinction between state violence and violence outside the law, between a death we call capital punishment and a death we call murder.

Doing Death Silently, Invisibly

The recent history of state killing in the United States reads like a story of the triumph of progress applied to the technologies of death.[25] From hanging to electrocution, from electrocution to lethal gas, from electricity and gas to lethal injection, the law has moved, though not uniformly, from one technology to another.[26] With the invention of new technologies for killing or, more precisely, with each new application of technology to killing, the law has proclaimed its own previous methods barbaric, or simply archaic, and has tried to put an end to the spectacle of botched executions. Thus, as one judge said about electrocution, "Execution by electrocution is a spectacle whose time has passed—like the guillotine or public stoning or burning at the stake. . . . Florida's electric chair, by its own track record, has proven to be a dinosaur more befitting the laboratory of Baron Frankenstein than the death chamber of Florida State Prison."[27] Responding to the advent of lethal injection, another judge characterized the continuing use of hanging as "an ugly vestige of earlier, less civilized times when science had not yet developed medically-appropriate methods of bringing human life to an end."[28] Nothing but the best will do in the business of state killing.

This search for a technological fix contrasts markedly with the execution practices of another era. As historian and social theorist Michel Foucault notes, in the past executions were "[m]ore than an act of justice"; they were a "manifestation of force."[29] They were always centrally about display, in particular the display of the majestic, awesome power of sovereignty to decide who suffers and who goes free, who lives and who dies. Public executions functioned as public theater but also as a school for citizenship.[30] Selecting the right method to kill was a matter of sovereign prerogative. Execution methods were chosen for their ability to convey the ferocity of the sovereign's vengeance.

In the past, state killing produced a sadistic relation between the executioner, the victim, and the spectators. The pleasure of viewing, as well as the instruction in one's relation to sovereign power, was to be found in witnessing pain inflicted. The excesses of execution and the enthusiastic response of attending audiences blended the performance of torture with pleasure, creating an unembarrassed celebration of death as one person's sovereign will materialized on the body of the condemned. The display of violence—of the sovereignty that was constituted in killing—was designed to create fearful, if not obedient, subjects. Gruesome spectacles simply accentuated the fearsome lesson.

The act of putting someone to death contained a dramatic, awe-inspiring pedagogy of power. "The public execution," Foucault explained,

> has a juridico-political function. It is a ceremonial by which a momentarily injured sovereignty is reconstituted. It restores sovereignty by manifesting it at its most spectacular. The public execution, however hasty and everyday, belongs to a whole series of great rituals in which power is eclipsed and restored (coronation, entry of the king into a conquered city, the submission of rebellious subjects). . . . There must be an emphatic affirmation of power and its intrinsic superiority. And this superiority is not simply that of right, but that of the physical strength of the sovereign beating down upon the body of his adversary and mastering it.[31]

Capital punishment was precisely about the right of the state to kill as it pleased, and sovereignty was known in and through the very act of taking life. Executions were designed to make the state's dealings in death majestically visible to all. Live, but live by the grace of the sovereign; live, but remember that your life belongs to the state. These were the messages of executions in an earlier era.

Without a public audience state killing would have been meaningless. As Foucault put it, "Not only must the people know, they must see with their own eyes. Because they must be made afraid, but also because they must be witnesses, the guarantors of the punishment, and because they must to a certain extent take part in it."[32] According to this understanding of punishment, the people were, at one and the same time, fearful subjects, authorizing witnesses, and lustful participants.

Today, execution, with some notable exceptions, has been transformed from dramatic spectacle to cool, bureaucratic operation, and the role of the public is now strictly limited and strictly controlled. Modern executions are carried out behind prison walls in what amounts to semi-private, sacrificial ceremonies in which only a few selected witnesses are gathered in a carefully controlled environment to see and, in their seeing, to sanctify the state's taking of the life of one of its citizens.[33]

Capital punishment has become, at best, a hidden reality. It is known, if it is known at all, by indirection. Hugo Bedau, a distinguished philosopher and ardent abolitionist, noted that "The relative privacy of executions nowadays (even photographs of the condemned man dying are almost invariably strictly prohibited) means that the average American literally does not know what is being done when the government, in his name and presumably on his behalf, executes a criminal."[34] What was public is now private. What was high drama has been reduced to a matter of technique.

Whereas the technologies of killing deployed by the state were once valued precisely because of their gruesome effects on the body of the condemned, today we seek a technology that leaves no trace. While in the past technologies were valued as ways of making sovereign power awe-inspiring and terrifying, today the process of state killing is medicalized; it is less about sovereignty than science. Executions

> were progressively stripped of their ritualistic and religious aspects. . . . [A]s Americans developed a keen dread of physical pain, medical professionals teamed up with . . . engineers to devise a purportedly "painless" method of administering the death penalty. . . . The condemned man. . . . had now become simply the object of medico-bureaucratic

technique—his body read closely for signs of pain. . . . The overriding aim of the state functionaries charged with conducting executions nowadays is to "get the man dead" as quickly, uneventfully, impersonally, and painlessly as Nature and Science permit.[35]

Since the earliest recorded execution in America in 1608, the state has put approximately 17,000 men and women to death.[36] "We've sawed people in half, beheaded them, burned them, drowned them, crushed them with rocks, tied them to anthills, buried them alive, and [executed them] in almost every way except perhaps boiling them in oil."[37] Today, however, five methods of execution are legally available: firing squad, hanging, lethal gas, electrocution, and lethal injection. Lethal injection is an authorized method of execution in thirty-two states. The firing squad is legal only in Oklahoma (but only if lethal injection and electrocution are declared unconstitutional), while New Hampshire and Washington allow death by hanging in addition to lethal injection. Four states (Arizona, California, Missouri, and Wyoming) allow the use of lethal gas and nine more permit electrocution.[38]

This array of methods stands in stark contrast to the end of the nineteenth century when hanging was America's primary method of execution. In 1888, when New York became the first state to substitute death by electrocution for hanging, it did so because an expert commission found it to be "the most humane and practical method known to modern science of carrying into effect the sentence of death."[39] States that eventually followed New York's lead "viewed (electrocution) as less painful than hanging and less horrific than having the condemned swing from the gallows."[40] In time, states that rejected hanging in favor of the gas chamber viewed the latter as "more decent" than electrocution since it seemed less violent and did not mutilate the body.[41] The original legislation authorizing the use of gas stipulated that the condemned was to be put to death "without warning and while asleep in his cell."[42]

Similar concerns about decency have been echoed in the most recent development among the technologies of state killing. Upholding the constitutionality of lethal injection, a federal district court recently noted that "There is general agreement that lethal injection is at present the most humane type of execution available and is far preferable to the sometimes barbaric means employed in the past."[43] This is hardly the language of the survivors and families of the victims of the Oklahoma City bombing or the awe-inspiring sovereignty about which Foucault wrote. It begs the question, What exactly is at stake when the state imagines itself executing decently, painlessly, humanely, and flawlessly?

On the Invisible Body of the Condemned

Cases challenging the constitutionality of particular methods of execution are regularly, though not frequently, brought before courts in the United States.[44] In the first two cases to reach the United States Supreme Court, it first upheld the use of firing squads[45] and then electrocution as methods by which the state could take life.[46] In the latter case, the Court proclaimed that no method of execution could be used that would "involve torture or a lingering death."[47] It went on to say that the state could kill so long as it used methods that did not impose "something more than the mere extinguishment of life."[48]

In a single remarkable sentence, the Court casually purports to limit sovereign prerogative. The juxtaposition of the word "mere" with the phrase "extinguishment of life"—an awkward circumlocution for death—seemingly acquiesces in the view that this "mere" death at the hands of the state gives no grounds for complaint. With this declaration, the Court leaves no room for mishaps that very often make execution something more than merely extinguishing life. It condemns excess, "something more," as if state-imposed death itself was not already an excess that marks the limits of the state's sovereignty over life.[49]

The state can spare life, or extinguish it, but it cannot require its victims to "linger" between life and death. Law stands ready to police the work of sovereignty, but it still grants sovereignty its due. The sovereign domain extends to deciding who shall die and how they die; law is left to regulate only the technologies through which the state takes life.

Sometimes, however, even this jurisdiction has seemed more than the law could, or would, handle. Indeed, more often than not, the law has restrained itself from intervening in the face of allegations about the excesses of the state's dealing in death or about executions gone wrong. Perhaps the most famous instance of such inaction occurred in *Francis v. Resweber*,[50] a case in which the Supreme Court allowed the state of Louisiana to electrocute a convicted murderer a second time after the first attempt was botched.

As the Court recounted the relevant facts, "Francis was prepared for execution and on May 3, 1946 . . . was placed in the official electric chair of the State of Louisiana. . . . The executioner threw the switch but, presumably because of some mechanical difficulty, death did not result."[51] Sometime later Francis sought to prevent a "second" execution by contending that it would constitute cruel and unusual punishment.[52] Justice Reed, writing for a majority, responded to these claims in what initially appears to be a rather unusual way. For him, the cruelty of Louisiana's plan had little to do with Francis,[53] and any pain he might have suffered during the first execution or his painful anticipations of the second. The Constitution, as Reed understood it, clearly permits "the necessary suffering involved in any method employed to extinguish life humanely."[54] In Reed's formulation, then, some suffering, suffering deemed "necessary," is fully compatible with humane killing. Something more than the mere extinction of life is permissible so long as that excess inheres in the "method" and so long as it is impossible for the state to kill without it.

If Francis were to undergo a second, more lethal dose of electricity, it would be because the law, not the judges, allowed it. According to that law, the fact of the first, unsuccessful execution would not "add an element of cruelty to a subsequent execution."[55] The constitutional question, as Reed saw it, turned instead on the behavior of those in charge of Francis's "first" execution, those authorized to unleash state violence. Their acts and intentions were decisive in determining whether a second attempt at execution would be unconstitutionally cruel.

From the facts as he understood them, Reed found those officials to have carried out their duties in a "careful and humane manner" with "no suggestion of malevolence"[56] and no "purpose to inflict unnecessary pain."[57] The fact that the execution was botched had no independent constitutional significance.

Justice Reed described diligent, indeed even compassionate, executioners frustrated by what he labeled an "unforeseeable accident . . . for which no man is to blame," and concluded that the state itself would be unfairly punished were it deprived of a second chance to electrocute Francis.[58] Indeed, when Reed does consider the effect the first attempt had on Francis, he suggests, again relying on the image of the first electrocution as an accident, that Francis could only have suffered "the identical amount of mental anguish and physical pain (as in) any other occurrence, such as . . . a fire in the cell block."[59] While Reed described Francis as an "accident victim," the issue from Francis's perspective was the future as much as the past. What was constitutionally significant was the connection between the violence inflicted on him during the first execution attempt and the violence the state, with the Supreme Court's blessing, proposed to inflict on him in a second electrocution.

The Court's interest in the pain Francis had already experienced and would again experience was so remote, as was the singular and individual death it was condoning, that only late in the dissenting opinion of Justice Burton was any reference made to the effect of the first execution attempt on Francis. There we are told that his "lips puffed out and he groaned and jumped so that the chair came off the floor."[60] Nonetheless, even here the significance of Francis's pain and impending death is deferred. References to that pain, taken from affidavits by witnesses to the first electrocution, were included solely to point out a "conflict in testimony,"[61] which made it impossible, in Burton's view, to determine whether any electricity had actually reached Francis during the abortive execution attempt. The conflict to which Burton refers arose when those in charge of the electrical equipment testified that "no electrical current reached . . . (Francis) and that his flesh did not show electrical burns."[62]

Burton did worry about the number of botched executions the majority might tolerate before declaring subsequent attempts to be cruel and unusual. Yet while he labeled the state's desire to carry out another attempt "death by installments,"[63] most of his opinion was devoted to careful scrutiny of Louisiana's death penalty statute. Death itself was not the object of attention. Instead Burton affirmed the possibility of law's mastery over death, as well as law's fidelity to its own rules for taking life. A proper execution is one whose occasions and procedures are prescribed by law, just as a proper judgment is one governed by the law and the law alone.

Since the statute made no provision for "a second, third or multiple application of (electric) current,"[64] a second execution attempt should not be permitted. Though he differed as to the correct outcome, Burton joined Reed in severing the connection between their own acts of judgment and the fate of Willie Francis. The Court acted as if the state's behavior was constitutionally significant, while it ignored the experience and prospective death of the state's intended victim.

The way Burton and Reed proceeded in *Francis* seems, in the end, all too familiar and yet, from the perspective of the reactions to the Kinsauls and Medina executions, somewhat strange. In *Francis*, death and the fact of an execution gone wrong is the heart of the matter. But it has only a shadowy presence, barely acknowledged. Where it is, as it were, inadvertently glimpsed, Francis's return date with electrocution is presented as the implementation of some abstract, impersonal set of written rules; the judge's own hand is stayed. In Burton's and Reed's opinions, both death and the event of the state's failure to get it right become strangely absent subjects. This book seeks to reverse the perspectives of Burton and Reed by bringing the experiences of those whose executions have been botched into the history of America's death penalty—by telling the stories of the people whose deaths involved something much more than the "mere extinguishment of life."

The "Body in Pain"

Today death remains the absent subject when courts confront challenges to the state's technologies of death. However, since the *Francis* case, where the question of pain was almost completely elided, courts faced with these challenges now focus, almost obsessively, on that question.[65] Sometimes they treat the body as a legible text. Evidence that the state's method of taking life imposes something more than the mere extinction of life can be read on the body of the condemned, they assume. At other times, however, courts seek to read pain indirectly, hardly mentioning the body at all. That said, the law's increasing obsession with pain is much more about the way it appears to those who serve as witnesses, real or imagined, to executions. The experience of execution by its witnesses—their "suffering"—fuels the search for painless death.

Three late-twentieth-century examples serve to highlight this continuity and difference. All of these cases try to identify the line between an acceptable use of a technology of execution and a botched execution. The first, *Campbell v. Wood,*[66] decided in 1994, dealt with the constitutionality of hanging; the second, *Fierro v. Gomez,*[67] decided later that same year, dealt with execution by lethal gas; the third, a 1999 decision of the Florida State Supreme Court, *Provenzano v. Moore,*[68] concerned the constitutionality of electrocution. The first upheld the use of hanging; the second prohibited California from using gas to kill; the third found that death in the electric chair did not violate the Constitution.

Campbell v. Wood

In 1976, Charles Campbell was sentenced to forty years in prison for assaulting and sodomizing Renae Wicklund in her home two years earlier. After five years of "good conduct," he was transferred to a work release facility in Everett, Washington. A few months later, Renae Wicklund, her eight-year-old daughter, Shannah, and her neighbor Barbara Hendrickson were found brutally murdered in Wicklund's home. All three were strangled, slashed at the throat, and had bled to death. Campbell was convicted on three counts of aggravated first-degree murder on November 26, 1982, and sentenced to death.[69]

From March 1985, when the Snohomish County Superior Court first issued a death warrant, to the Ninth Circuit's remand for an evidentiary hearing concerning the constitutionality of hanging on May 1,

1993, Campbell filed a total of four appeals, three habeas corpus petitions, and six other various motions.[70] Along the way, hanging was put on trial.

In one of Campbell's appeals Judge John C. Coughenour, of the federal district court in Seattle, conducted a three-day evidentiary hearing in order to determine whether execution by hanging constituted cruel and unusual punishment in violation of the Eighth Amendment. While the state attempted to prove the mathematical precision and painlessness of hanging and its compatibility with the ideals of the modern liberal state, Campbell's lawyers fought against this abstracted scientific construction and "domestication" of the noose. They argued that "what the law essentially is cannot be dissociated from the hood placed over Campbell's head, the shackles fastened around his ankles, the oversized eyehook securing the rope that ends in a noose encircling his neck."[71] They tried to expose hanging as a barbaric anachronism. Campbell's case rested, in effect, almost entirely on the history of botched executions.

At first, Campbell's attorneys' task might not seem difficult at all. Throughout the course of the twentieth century, jurisdiction after jurisdiction in the United States and around the world had rejected hanging precisely because it was deemed excessively and irreconcilably "barbaric." By 1973, only seven states still permitted it. However, from the outset, Campbell's challenge faced two formidable obstacles. First, although hanging was used in each of the seventy-three executions carried out in Washington's history, the state admitted that it had no records, of any kind, of judicial hangings occurring prior to January 1993.[72] Moreover, the district court held that any evidence Campbell offered concerning past hangings was irrelevant unless it met certain, practically unobtainable criteria. An impressive compilation of evidence documenting 170 botched judicial hangings performed in the United States between 1622 and 1993 was excluded because Campbell's lawyers (understandably) could not specify (1) the executed person's weight, (2) the exact height that person dropped, and (3) the width of the rope.[73]

In short, the court deemed every execution conducted before Washington's adoption of its present protocol irrelevant. During the evidentiary hearing, Walla Walla State Penitentiary's superintendent acknowledged that the *Field Instruction Manual* prepared by the Department of Corrections in 1992, outlining the state's "new" hanging procedures, had been copied verbatim from a 1959 manual of army regulations titled *Procedure for Military Execution.* When Campbell's leading attorney asked superintendent Tana Wood why the state specifically chose to adopt the army's protocols, she responded, with a shocking lack of pretense, "Because it came from the military."[74]

In fact, as Campbell's lawyers pointed out, the military manual based its procedure on a mathematical table correlating the weight of the condemned and the length of the rope, measurements produced by a British investigative committee in 1886 (see Table 1). British Home Secretary Richard Asshelton Cross had appointed the committee and charged it with inquiring into "the existing practices as to carrying out of sentences of death, and the causes which in several recent cases have led either to failure or to unseemly occurrences." The table was generated out of the committee's research using a dynamometer and hundreds of sacks filled with varying amounts of sand.

The 1993 evidentiary hearings revolved around the state's contention that the table "may be fully depended upon to produce instantaneous

TABLE 1. Scale of Drops

Weight (lbs.)	Drop	Energy developed (ft.-lbs.)	Weight (lbs.)	Drop	Energy developed (ft.-lbs.)
98	11'5"	1,119	196	6'5"	1,258
112	10'0"	1,120	210	6'0"	1,260
126	9'6"	1,197	224	5'7"	1,251
140	9'0"	1,260	238	5'3"	1,250
154	8'2"	1,258	252	5'0"	1,260
168	7'6"	1,200	266	4'8"	1,241
182	6'11"	1,259	280	4'6"	1,260

Source: Report of the Committee to Inquire into the Execution of Capital Sentences (1886). Kaufman-Osborn, *From Noose to Needle*, 88.

loss of consciousness and the speedy death of even the most robust."[75] As Kaufman-Osborn observes, "In a nutshell, whereas the state's attorneys must render persuasive the table's implicit claim to eliminate the possibility of error and so guarantee a death that entails no detectable suffering, Campbell's attorneys must seek to trouble these claims by undermining the table's pretense to practical certitude and so rendering the body a site of possible pain."[76] In the words of a prison spokesperson, Campbell's imminent execution would be, like "any given hanging," nothing more than a simple "math problem."[77] And yet, despite such official confidence, history emphatically demonstrates that hanging human bodies "without risk of failure or miscarriage of any sort" has always been, and continues to be, an unrealizable dream.[78]

This was the context of Campbell's appeal to the Ninth Circuit Court of Appeals and his claim that hanging violated the Eighth Amendment ban on cruel and unusual punishment. According to Judge Beezer, writing for the *Campbell* majority, the court had to decide "whether hanging comports with contemporary standards of decency."[79] He noted that while few states used hanging, no court in the United States had ever found execution by hanging to violate the Constitution. As Beezer argued, the question of whether hanging was acceptable depended on "the actual pain that may or may not attend the practice."[80]

Determining the constitutionality of this method of execution required the court to read the body of the condemned for what it reveals of its suffering as it moves from the world of the living to the world of the dead. Beezer took note of the fact that the district court had heard extensive expert and eyewitness testimony concerning the pain associated with hanging.[81] He wrote confidently about the court's ability to know the pain of the condemned even as he noted that pain itself would not render hanging invalid. A method of execution, he claimed, relying on *In re Kemmler*, an 1890 case in which the Supreme Court upheld electrocution, and *Francis*, is unconstitutional if it "involves the unnecessary and wanton infliction of pain."[82]

With this as the standard, Beezer offered an extended discussion of the methods used in hanging, contrasting in particular the so-called "long-drop" with the "short-drop" method.[83] Several factors, he found, contribute to making death by hanging "comparatively painless"[84]; for example, the length of the drop, the selection and treatment of the rope, the positioning of the knot. The state of Washington's use of the long-drop method, he said, is designed "to ensure that forces to the neck structures are optimized to cause rapid unconsciousness and death."[85] The result of that method, Beezer argued, was that "unconsciousness and death . . . occur extremely rapidly, that unconsciousness was likely to be immediate or within a matter of seconds, and that death would follow rapidly thereafter."[86] He ended his opinion by reiterating that "Campbell is not entitled to a painless execution, but only one free of purposeful cruelty."[87]

Here Beezer seems to return us, at least partially, to the world of *Francis* in which attention moves from the executed to the executioner, from the body in pain to the intentions of state officials. But there is a crucial difference: unlike in *Francis*, where the subject of pain is almost completely avoided, in *Campbell* determining the pain associated with one or another technology of death is a necessary, though not sufficient, first step. If such a determination suggests that the condemned is subject to pain, the court must then, but only then, inquire into the purposes of the state in imposing death through that method. Evidence of pain attendant to a routine or a botched execution is significant as a sign of barbarism on the part of those who take life. Pain is thus the dangerous supplement of death, signaling as it does excess or sadistic pleasure associated with the willful taking of human life.

Judge Reinhardt dissented from Beezer's view in *Campbell* because it seemed to equate the Eighth Amendment's "evolving standard of decency" jurisprudence solely with an inquiry into pain and its purposes. In Reinhardt's view the development of "new and less brutal methods of execution, such as lethal injection . . . as well as the risks of pain and mutilation inherent in hanging" make the latter constitutionally defective.[88] The fact that by the time of *Campbell* all but a few state legislatures had abolished hanging provided, for Reinhardt, a crucial indicator of its incompatibility with contemporary standards of decency. Moreover, if the reduction of needless pain were to be taken as the exclusive measure of a technique's constitutionality, "barbaric and savage" forms of punishment, such as the guillotine, would not be constitutionally impermissible.

In the end, even if the Constitution were to mandate only an objective inquiry into pain and its purposes, and even if every hanging were carried out in a flawless manner, judicial hanging would still, in Reinhardt's view, be unacceptable because it is "a crude, rough, and wanton procedure, the purpose of which is to tear apart the spine. It is needlessly violent and intrusive, deliberately degrading and dehumanizing. It causes grievous fear beyond that of death itself and the attendant consequences are often humiliating and disgusting."[89] Reinhardt focused too on the prospect of a botched execution as he contemplated a "high risk of pain far more than is necessary to kill a condemned inmate. If the drop is too short, the prisoner will strangle to death, a slow and painful process . . . [if the drop] is too long the prisoner may be decapitated."[90]

A punishment can be cruel, Reinhardt contended, even if it is not painful. Cruelty can arise "from the relatively painless infliction of degradation, savagery, and brutality. . . . Indignities can be inflicted even after a person has died."[91] The Constitution *obligates* the state, when it chooses to kill, to "eliminate the degrading, brutal, and violent aspects of an execution, and substitute a scientifically developed and approved method of terminating life through appropriate medical procedures in a neutral, medical environment."[92] Where science makes available technologies for ending life that serve the same goals, but with markedly lower risk of imposing pain, the Constitution *requires* that the state follow science. On Reinhardt's reading, the state is not master of technology; it is instead subservient to it. Whereas Beezer imposed few limits on the sovereign's choice of methods of execution, Reinhardt would eliminate much, if not all, of the sovereign's discretion.

While Beezer and Reinhardt differ on the sufficiency of pain and the significance of the risk of a botched execution as a standard in determining the constitutionality of a method of execution, both assume that they can know the pain of another and that they can represent it faithfully in their opinions. As Reinhardt put it, "There is absolutely no question that every hanging involves a risk that the prisoner will not die immediately, but will instead struggle or asphyxiate to death. This process, which may take several minutes, is extremely painful. Not only does the prisoner experience the pain felt by any strangulation victim, but he does so while dangling at the end of a rope."[93]Although neither Beezer nor Reinhardt may know, or be able to accurately represent, death, they write with no hesitancy about their ability to know the pain that precedes it.[94]

Fierro v. Gomez

The apparent displacement of death, as well as this same confidence in the court's ability to read and represent pain, reappear in *Fierro*. Judge Patel notes, early in her opinion, that while lethal gas had been California's execution technology of choice since 1937, in the mid-1980s Warden Vasquez of San Quentin revised the state's execution protocol. This statement takes on significance later in her decision when it is linked to the kind of technological imperative hinted at in Reinhardt's opinion in *Campbell*. As Patel put it, neither the warden nor his staff "consulted scientific experts or medical personnel in formulating the execution protocol nor did they examine records from previous California executions."[95] The result is characterized as an "unscientific, slapdash" execution protocol.[96]

When sovereignty today exercises its power over life and death, it is no longer free to kill in a gruesome way in order to instill awe and fear in the citizenry. The availability of lethal injection, which Patel characterized as "more humane than lethal gas as a method of execution," renders the latter "antiquated" and suddenly incompatible with the Constitution.[97] Taking *Campbell* as governing authority, Patel characterized it as making "clear" that the "key question to be answered in a challenge to the method of execution is how much pain the inmate suffers."[98] *Campbell*, she argued, "dictates that a court look first to objective evidence of pain."[99] After providing an elaborate description of the gas chamber and the procedures used during an execution by lethal gas, Patel reviewed contradictory expert testimony concerning the effects of lethal gas and the precise ways it brings about death.

According to her summary, the basic disagreement between plaintiff and defense experts is "whether unconsciousness occurs within at most thirty seconds of inhalation, as defendants maintain, or whether, as plaintiffs contend, unconsciousness occurs much later, after the inmate has endured the painful effects of cyanide gas for several minutes."[100] To resolve this conflict, she reviewed extant scientific literature and determined that while "plaintiffs' theory of death through cellular suffocation has traditionally been the accepted viewpoint,"[101] the scientific community was neither uniform nor clear in its conclusions.

Next Patel reviewed two types of eyewitness accounts of execution by lethal gas. The first type, contemporaneous observations and records of physicians who attended every execution by lethal gas, reads like an obsessive archive of death. In those records physicians note when, during the course of an execution, each of the following events occur: "'Sodium Cyanide Enters'; 'Gas Strikes Prisoner's Face'; 'Prisoner Apparently Unconscious'; and 'Prisoner Certainly Unconscious' and 'Last Bodily Movement.'"[102] Second, she also considered the observations of lay witnesses.

Patel prefaced her discussion of all this evidence by noting that "neither consciousness nor pain is easy to gauge. Actions that appear volitional or appear to be a reaction to pain may in fact be unconscious and non-volitional."[103] Yet these cautions did not inhibit her interpretation of the observational testimony. Pain, while difficult to measure, could be read on the surface of the body, by untrained people as well as by medical personnel. Their observations provided the basis for constitutional judgment.

In California's two most recent executions, physicians observed that "certain unconsciousness" did not occur until three minutes after the gas hit the face of the condemned. Records of California's earlier executions contain similar results. Taken together, the expert testimony, the scientific literature, the physicians' records, and eyewitness statements "compel" and "unmistakably" point,[104] according to the judge, to the conclusion that during a period of consciousness following the dispensing of lethal gas, "inmates suffer intense, visceral pain, primarily as a result of lack of oxygen to the cells."[105] This shows that, in contrast to its advertised virtues, execution by lethal gas is frequently botched. The result, Patel asserted, moving from calm balancing of evidence to vivid imagery, is "akin to the experience of a major heart attack, or to being held under water."[106] Resorting here to analogy, Patel conjures imagined horrors somewhat closer to the average citizen's experience than the particular horrors of death in the gas chamber.

Patel, like Beezer and Reinhardt in *Campbell*, foregrounds the question of what the journey from life to death might be like under a certain execution technique. She too focuses on the risk of executions gone wrong and the presence of pain as she carefully constructs a narrative from different strands of evidence. Her opinion textualizes pain, at times by focusing on the body of the condemned and at other times by reading through it to understand consciousness and its limits. She insists that the state kill as flawlessly, as softly, as gently, as painlessly as the innovations of men and women allow.[107]

Provenzano v. Moore

The majority in *Provenzano*, which began by taking the fact of botched executions seriously, focused on problems in the execution of another Florida inmate, Allen Lee Davis, though it claimed that his execution was not botched. "Allen Lee Davis," the court claimed, "did not suffer any conscious pain while being electrocuted in Florida's electric chair. Rather he suffered instantaneous and painless death once the current was applied to him."[108] The *Provenzano* majority cautioned against misreading the body, saying, "The nose bleed incurred by Allen Lee

Davis began *before* the electric current was applied to him, and was not caused whatsoever by the application of electrical current to Davis."[109] It noted that "the record in this case reveals abundant evidence that execution by electrocution renders an inmate instantaneously unconscious, thereby making it impossible to feel pain."[110] Because it is painless, the court concluded, death by electrocution is not cruel, and because it is not cruel, it is not unconstitutional.

In his dissent Justice Shaw agreed, at least in part, about the centrality of pain, though he reached strikingly different conclusions about its presence when electrocution is used. Like Reinhardt in *Campbell*, he insisted that the courts should not focus exclusively on pain as the sole indicator of cruelty. Taking botched executions as his template, he insisted the court should attend to the question of what he labeled "violence, mutilation, and disgrace."[111]

Choosing the guillotine as his example, Shaw expressed a breezy confidence in his ability to read pain when he noted, "while beheading results in a quick, relatively painless death, it entails frank violence (i.e. gross laceration and blood-letting) and mutilation (i.e. decapitation), and disgrace . . . and thus is *facially cruel*."[112] Pain as well as violence, mutilation, and disgrace, he claimed, accompany electrocution. "Not only was every execution in Florida accompanied by the inevitable convulsing and burning that characterizes electrocution, but further, three executions were marred by extraordinary violence and mutilation. In two . . . , smoke and flames spurted from the headpiece and burned the heads and faces of the inmates. In the third execution, the inmate bled from the nostrils and was at least partially asphyxiated by the restraining devices; and he too was burned."[113]

Shaw's opinion goes on for pages providing elaborate, detailed, and graphic descriptions of those three executions, paying particular attention to the third, the Davis execution. But in a truly extraordinary gesture, he appended to his opinion "post-execution color photos of Davis before he was removed from the electric chair. These photos . . . provide a vivid picture of a violent scene . . . [and] show a ghastly postexecution scene."[114] While he provided a description of what those photographs show ("a stream of blood pours from his nostrils, flows over the wide-leather mouth-strap, runs down his neck and chest, and forms a bright red pool . . . on his white shirt"[115]), the photographic evidence was meant to speak for itself and, in so doing, to capture the brutal reality of an execution gone awry.

Appending such images to a judicial opinion transgresses convention in such a way as to ensure that they will be the subject of considerable attention and commentary. Photographs shock and appeal to a different register of understanding. They make pain and the violence associated with state killing into a matter of sight. Because they are so "vivid," Shaw assumed that they would convey reality in a way language never could. Thus the presence of the photos is not only an almost unprecedented judicial effort to make state killing visible, it also provides a stark reminder of the limits of language when it ventures to speak about physical violence and physical pain.

Pain, literary theorist Elaine Scarry observes,

> has no voice. . . . When one hears about another's physical pain, the events happening within the interior of that person's body may seem to have the remote character of some deep subterranean fact, belonging to an invisible geography that, however portentous, has no reality because it has not yet manifested itself on the visible surface of the earth.[116]

According to Scarry, "Whatever pain achieves, it achieves in part through its unsharability, and it ensures this unsharability through its resistance to language."[117]

"A great deal is at stake," Scarry herself suggests, "in the attempt to invent linguistic structures that will reach and accommodate this area of experience normally so inaccessible to language."[118] Judicial opinions on methods of execution surely confirm this view. Yet Scarry reminds us that the courts' capacity to understand and to convey to their readers the pain of the person being executed is quite limited.

Scarry invites us to consider *Francis*, *Campbell*, *Fierro*, and *Provenz-*

ano for what they tell us about the use of language to comprehend and represent violence and pain. She invites us to consider how we can understand what happens to the condemned when executions are botched. However, she suggests that in law, as elsewhere, the language available to capture that understanding is quite limited. "As physical pain is monolithically consistent in its assault on language," Scarry writes, "so the verbal strategies for overcoming the assault are very small in number and reappear consistently as one looks at the words of the patient, physician, Amnesty worker, lawyer, artist."[119]

Those verbal strategies "revolve (first) around the verbal sign of the weapon."[120] We know pain, in the first instance, through its instrumentalities, for example hanging or lethal gas. Second, we know it through its effects. Here violence and pain are represented in the "wound," that is, "the bodily damage that is pictured as accompanying pain."[121] But as Scarry suggests, these representations cannot provide certain or reliable grounding for a jurisprudence that seeks to govern the technologies through which the state puts people to death. Yet it is precisely those representations that play a central role in the way we understand botched executions.

If Scarry is right, then when judges, journalists, and scholars confront the fact of botched executions, they face epistemological and interpretive as well as legal and political problems. By deferring the question of death and foregrounding the question of pain, they are required to take seriously the empirical world of the body and its suffering even as they necessarily run up against the limits of their capacity to know that world and to translate that knowledge into language.[122] Yet again, we are driven back to the question of why the issue of pain and the search for efficient, reliable, and painless execution play so large a part in the law's effort to regulate execution and to police the boundary between an acceptable and a botched execution.

The Hand of Punishment, Humanely Applied?

Even as the United States seems to be on the road to abolishing death as a criminal punishment, we remain committed to the effort, when we do execute, to execute gently—to impose no more pain than is necessary. That the law requires the state to kill in this manner seems, in a way, counterintuitive; it may precipitate one kind of crisis of legitimacy by distancing the state from the voices of victims and the demands of vengeance and, in so doing, by raising questions like those raised by the mother of a murder victim quoted in one of the epigraphs of this book: "Do they feel anything? Do they hurt? Is there any pain? Very humane compared to what they've done to our children. The torture they've put our kids through. I think sometimes it's too easy. They ought to feel something. If it's fire burning all the way through their body or whatever. There ought to be some little sense of pain to it."

Perhaps this strategy is less counterintuitive than it might seem. Legal scholar Alan Hyde argues that the requirement that the state kill humanely "follows a common pattern in which the humanistic, sentimentalized body in pain emerges as a site of empathy and identification" in the nineteenth and twentieth centuries.[123] Sentimentalizing the body of the condemned, Hyde notes, establishes a bridge between the criminal and the public. The criminal, no matter how horrific his deeds, is like us in his body's most basic "amenability to feeling."[124]

The concern that punishment not inflict physical pain and the empathy which pain enables and expresses, Hyde observes, "lies behind the curious search in American legal history for painless methods of execution."[125] In an endlessly repeating ritual, he says, "electrocution, gas chambers, lethal injections are each introduced with tremendous fanfare as a painless form of death, until each is revealed to promote its own kind of suffering on the way to death."[126] Yet as Hyde himself recognizes, execution marks the limits of empathy, reminding citizens of the ultimate disconnection between themselves and the condemned, a disconnection that seeks to operate at the moral level.[127]

Thus the problem of botched executions and the search for painless death might be better understood as one way of keeping sentimental, simplifying narratives of criminal and victim intact by not allowing the condemned to assume the status of victims of outmoded technologies of death. Law imposes on sovereignty the requirement that no matter how heinous the crime or how reprehensible the criminal, we not do death as death has been done by those we punish. We give them a kinder, gentler death than they deserve to mark a boundary between the "civilized" and the "savage," rather than to establish a connection between citizens and murderers. We kill humanely, not out of concern for the condemned but rather to vividly establish a hierarchy between the law-abiding and the lawless.[128]

We may not be able to know death, or comprehend its possibilities or its horrors, but where law requires the killing state to kill efficiently and reliably, it seeks legitimacy in an image of the hand of punishment humanely applied. It may be death we are doing, but it is a death whose savagery law insists it can, and will, control. Botched executions would seem to complicate that effort and to turn executions into the kind of gruesome spectacles that marked the premodern era.

For the judges in *Campbell, Fierro,* and *Provenzano,* botched executions threatened to erode the boundaries between the state's violence and its extralegal counterpart. As Judge Shaw observed, "The color photos of Davis depict a man who—for all appearances—was brutally tortured to death by the citizens of Florida. . . . Each botched execution cast[s] the entire criminal justice system of this state—including the courts—in ignominy."[129] Botched executions generate for Shaw, and others like him, an anxious questioning about the ways state violence truly differs from the violence to which it is, at least in theory, opposed. The effort to kill softly, gently, painlessly, humanely is one response to that questioning, one way of trying to show that the state, though born of the violent disruptions of the existing order of things, can transcend the violence of its origins.[130]

As a response to this anxious questioning, courts insist on policing the technologies of death and work hard to ensure that sovereign power responds to scientific progress, that ferocity gives way to bureaucracy. State killing, guided by the restraining hand of law, in this view should be rational, purposive, and proportional; the violence to which it responds is, in contrast, imagined to be irrational, anomic, and excessive. In the face of scientific "progress," the forms of legal procedure cannot condone archaic displays of sovereignty like those demanded by the survivors and families of the victims of the Oklahoma City bombing.

The chapters that follow take up each of the major methods of execution used during the twentieth century,[131] in each case first examining how the technology was linked to the effort to kill painlessly and efficiently. These chapters describe the kinds of things that have gone wrong with those technologies, and tell the stories of some of the men and women who have died when those technologies misfired. Schooled by Scarry about the limits of representation, this book nonetheless takes up the metric of pain. It does so precisely because of its centrality within the contemporary jurisprudence of capital punishment, and to show how that metric works in popular culture as well as judicial opinions. This is done to foreground the question of whether the state can even superficially live up to its commitment that execution should involve no more than "the mere extinguishment of life."

The book also investigates how botched executions propelled changes in methods of execution over the course of the twentieth century. Although at times they have occasioned challenges to particular execution methods, botched executions have contributed little to the effort to end capital punishment itself. This is so because they have been understood, to borrow the language of political theorist Judith Shklar, as misfortunes rather than injustices. The book will conclude by describing how, during the twentieth century, the cultural reception of botched executions helped to insure that they did little to undermine the legitimacy of America's death penalty.

CHAPTER 2

A Clumsy, Inefficient, Inhuman Thing

Death by Hanging

In "Earth's Holocaust," an allegorical short story set in the American Midwest, Nathaniel Hawthorne has his fictional reformers throw society's instruments of capital punishment—"those horrible monsters of mechanism . . . which lurked in the dusty nooks of ancient prisoners, the subject of terror-stricken legend"—into their great redeeming bonfire along with the other "condemned rubbish" of the world.[1] The "old implements of cruelty," the halters, axes, and guillotines, are all successively destroyed. When, in 1844, Hawthorne wrote this story, a death sentence meant judicial hanging: to hang by the neck until dead.

For the bulk of human history, states have relied exclusively on the gallows to do their killing. During the two centuries following the Glorious Revolution, when a judge at Old Bailey in London imposed a death sentence he would traditionally don a black cap and print the Latin abbreviation *sus per coll* next to the name of the recently condemned. *Suspendatur per collum*, let him be hanged by the neck.[2] In Hawthorne's tale, it is the gallows' threatened destruction that draws the greatest interest from the surrounding crowd.

At the foot of the fire, Hawthorne stages a debate. "Stay, my brethren!" a particularly bold defender of capital punishment cries out at the sight of the gallows in peril. "The gallows is a heaven-oriented instrument!" the man warns, "Bear it back, then, reverently, and set it up in its old place; else the world will fall to speedy ruin and desolation!" In reply, a "leader in the reform" commands without hesitation, "Onward, onward! . . . Into the flames with the accursed instrument of man's bloody policy! How can human law inculcate benevolence and love while it persists in setting up the gallows as its chief symbol? One heave more, good friends."[3] In the end, the reformers manage to "convince mankind of the long and deadly error of human law" and the gallows is fed to the flames.

Finally, in the twenty-first century, it appears that hanging is indeed near extinction. Congress rejected it as a punishment for federal crimes in 1937 as did the army in 1986, and the vast majority of states no longer use hanging as an execution method. At the turn of the twenty-first century only four states still allowed it, and today just two states, New Hampshire and Washington, continue to permit death by hanging.[4]

The United States inherited its hanging technologies from England. Although the exact date is unclear, we can safely surmise that hanging was first introduced to England by the Germanic tribes who invaded the isle around the middle of the fifth century. Throughout much of its early history, hanging coexisted with other unquestionably brutal forms of execution. Hanging dates back to a time, that is, when torturous methods of execution, such as burning and boiling alive, drowning, stoning, disemboweling, drawing and quartering, and gibbeting were the norm.[5]

By the seventeenth century in England, hanging had replaced most of those other methods of execution. So important was it that Brian Bailey calls the noose and the cross the founding symbols of English society,[6] and in Charles Duff's sharply satirical *A Handbook on Hanging*, he similarly quips, "With the English the hangman is like the dog: the friend of man."[7] Until the 1830s, hangings were the most frequent and firmly embedded rituals in English metropolitan and provincial urban life.[8]

Tying a rope around a man's neck in a slipknot, passing that rope over the bough of a particularly sturdy tree, and hoisting him to the sky turned out to be an invention that would stand the test of time. That said, in the beginning, it was still considered a more disgraceful way to die than beheading or shooting.[9] Until the end of the eighteenth century, the basic method of hanging remained essentially unchanged and relatively simple. In its most rudimentary form, victims "launched into eternity" from tree branches were left to die of asphyxiation caused by strangulation, although disruption of oxygen and blood flow to the brain, combined with structural damage to the neck, certainly played a lethal role as well.[10]

Progress came slowly to the hangman's craft. Eventually, crossbeams were manufactured to supplement the often unreliable natural structure of trees. By the twelfth century at least, although perhaps earlier, literal "hanging trees" were being replaced by manufactured uprights in some English communities.[11] In what Gatrell refers to as the distinctly "medieval way" of hanging, the condemned—noose already fastened around his neck—was required to climb several rungs of a ladder placed against the gallows, at which time the hangman's assistant would tie the rope's far end around the crossbar and the hangman below would twist the ladder, "turning off" the victim as he was suddenly deprived of support.[12] Although ostensibly more refined, "turning off" allowed the condemned to fall only a few inches, insufficient to cause cervical dislocation, so the principal cause of death remained slow asphyxiation. Thus, corpses were customarily not cut down for at least an hour after the drop, not only for the purposes of drama and edification but also to foreclose any possibility of recovery after "death."[13]

Traveling through England in 1698, M. Mison described an execution scene at Tyburn, just outside London:

> They put five or six in a Cart . . . and carry them, riding backwards with the Rope about their Necks, to the fatal Tree. The Executioner stops the Cart under one of the Cross Beams of the Gibbet, and fastens to that ill-favour'd Beam one End of the Rope, while the other is round the Wretches Neck: This done, he gives the Horse a Lash with his Whip, away goes the Cart, and there swing my Gentlemen kicking in the Air: The Hangman does not give himself the Trouble to put them out of their Pain; but some of their Friends or Relations do it for them. They pull the dying Person by the Legs, and beat his Breast, to dispatch him as soon as possible.[14]

England's most primitive hanging practices were transported—along with many of its capital criminals—to the American colonies. While today we have witnessed the "virtual demise of state-sponsored hangings," in the centuries preceding the electric chair's introduction in the late nineteenth century, the gallows was the primary, and often exclusive, apparatus of capital death in the colonies and then in all of the United States.[15]

This is not to say that the art of hanging has been perfected in the United States. While the earliest American criminals were, like their English counterparts, hanged from tree branches, most colonial communities made the transition to other devices shortly after settlement. The ladder would remain the most common method of hanging, despite obvious shortcomings, until the end of the 1600s. Stuart Banner reports that a fall from the ladder was often too gradual or too short to be fatal. Removed horizontally, Banner explains, the ladder allowed prisoners to let themselves down slowly. In a particularly strange incident, Dorthy Talbye, hanged in Boston in 1639, was able to catch the ladder with her legs as she swung and break the force of her own drop. After another Massachusetts woman "was turned off and had hung a space she spake, and asked what did they mean to do."[16] The gallows cried out for reform.

As Banner explains, by the beginning of the eighteenth century—although the innovation came a bit earlier in England—executions were more typically carried out by means of the horse-drawn cart. And as Mison recounted, the new method was not without its own set of irresolvable problems. In 1738, near Williamsburg, Virginia, Anthony Dittond was hanged twice by the cart. When the hangman found Dittond still alive several minutes after the initial drop, he began to pull on his legs. In this case, however, the executioner's well-intended efforts broke the rope, and Dittond, not yet dead, crashed to the ground.[17]

While the cart did away with the complications caused by prisoners either unwilling or unable to climb the ladder of the medieval gallows, and while it made it possible to carry out several hangings at one time, it was still removed horizontally and at a relatively slow speed.[18] What's more, the fall was also still only a few inches. "If anything," Gatrell remarks, "death was more prolonged than hitherto, since at least you could jump off a ladder and break your neck."[19] In other words, because it was even less likely that the condemned would "lapse into unconsciousness at rope's end," deployment of the cart "often extended the duration of visible suffering."[20]

At this point in hanging's history, however, technological improvements were intended to promote efficiency more than painlessness. The gallows was an obvious and undeniable "site of physical pain." "[N]obody doubted," Gatrell writes, "that hanging was a slow and painful way of killing people."[21] Kaufman-Osborn describes a number of types of recurring misadventures at Tyburn in the eighteenth century—ranging from "snapped ropes, to necks that slipped out of nooses, to decapitations, partial and total, to post-hanging revivals of the supposedly dead"—that would persist, remarkably, for centuries to come.[22]

Dissatisfaction with the efficacy of both ladders and carts prompted further innovation. In 1759, Tyburn's infamous "Triple Tree" was torn down and replaced by a portable gallows outfitted with a trapdoor. Now the condemned could simply stand on a trapdoor built into the floor of a raised platform, or scaffold, until its supports were pulled away. In England, the scaffold was first used in the execution of Lord Ferrer. The drop through the trapdoor, however, failed to kill him, and the "time-honored method of pulling on his legs was employed to finish him off." After this initial deployment, the trapdoor was abandoned for a time, not because it was ineffective but rather because, according to London mayor Sir Peter Laurie, it was "too aristocratic a mode for common vagabonds." The basest of England's criminal class deserved the "tortured asphyxiation" of Tyburn's cart.[23]

In the American colonies, the use of the scaffold appears to have predated its first deployment in England by several decades. Boston, for example, had such a device as early as 1694. The scaffold also seems to have caught on more quickly; that is, in the United States scaffolds were already in common use by the beginning of the nineteenth century. Yet problems persisted.

The force of the drop and the actual cause of death in judicial hangings remained impossible to predict or control. Ropes ripped apart as prisoners lurched abruptly downward, and drops were often too short to kill. Even more frequently, the condemned continued to die hard upon the scaffold. Before the introduction of the long drop in the latter part of the nineteenth century, "the agony of slow suffocation without loss of consciousness could last up to twenty minutes."[24] In 1774, Doctor Alexander Monro, a professor of anatomy at Edinburgh, likewise wrote that "the man who is hanged suffers a great deal; that he is not at once stupefied by the shock . . . a man is suffocated by hanging in a rope just as by having his respiration stopped by having a pillow pressed on the face."[25]

By the late eighteenth century, capital punishment became the subject of extensive public conflict in England. In 1783, hangings were moved from Tyburn to a more controlled site just outside the walls of Newgate prison, and it became the custom to drape a white hood over the head of the condemned as he stood on the scaffold. The famed twentieth-century hangman, Albert Pierrepoint, would later claim that the hood was adopted to "mask the contortions of slow strangulation, which were considered too horrible even for the ghoulish British public to witness."[26] Thus, even in this small innovation, it is quite clear that mounting apprehensions about the sanctity of the noose were focused not on the "agony of slow suffocation" suffered by the condemned, but rather on the effect of the *sight* of that pain on spectators crowded before the scaffold.

As the eighteenth century came to a close, calls for reform—both for a decrease in the number of crimes punishable by death and for total abandonment of the gallows—reached unprecedented volumes. And "[n]owhere," American cultural historian Louis Masur writes, "was the debate over the death penalty and the drive to find alternative punishments more compelling than in the United States."[27] Kathryn Preyer explains, "It was easy in America to identify reason and humanity, the watchwords of the Enlightenment, with the successful republicanism of the new nation," and consequently, "to find imprisonment the ideal embodiment of these new goals."[28]

Reform of capital punishment was understood by some to be a mark of the new nation's progress. Benjamin Rush, a prominent physician and signer of the Declaration of Independence, became the first great spokesperson for the anti-gallows movement in the United States when he gave an address in 1787 advocating the total abolition of capital punishment.[29] Then, borrowing from Cesare di Beccaria's renowned essay *On Crimes and Punishments*, Rush responded to critics in 1792 with his *Considerations on the Injustice and Impolicy of Punishing Murder by Death*.

Rush's treatises exemplify—in their strong religious undertones and emphasis on the incongruity of capital punishment with the ideals of republican government—the fact that the antebellum critics of the American death penalty were not primarily concerned with the welfare of the condemned. On the contrary, "arguments against capital punishment centered on the corrupting example of public hangings and on the social guilt of depriving an individual of his inalienable right to live."[30] Rush was not worried about the potential cruelty of hanging—or of the penitentiary for that matter. Capital punishment, he claimed, "lessens the horror of taking away human life and thereby tends to multiply murders."[31] The reform impulse was driven by concern for the "ghoulish public" and their new republican state. The persons killed by that state—the thousands of criminal bodies struggling at the end of the rope—remained, for the most part, absent subjects in the escalating debate.

Furthermore, with no alternative method of execution in prospect, problematizing the "black, giant-like" gallows necessarily meant critiquing the very institution of capital punishment.[32] Banner notes that the small number of capital offenses relative to the English criminal code became a "point of pride" for Americans in the late eighteenth century.[33] After stalling in the first decades of the new century, the spirit of reform peaked from the 1830s through the early 1850s as social organizations such as New York's and Massachusetts's Societies for the Abolition of Capital Punishment were formed.[34] In the North, state after state decapitalized lesser felonies like rape, burglary, and arson, while no state added to its list of capital crimes. By the mid-1850s, three states—Michigan in 1847, Rhode Island in 1851, and Wisconsin in 1853—had abolished the death penalty.[35]

Significantly more successful than efforts to abolish capital punishment completely, however, were legal reforms that relocated the gallows. To take but one example, the hanging of John Lechler on October 15, 1822, triggered the Pennsylvania legislature's initial interest in ending public hangings. This interest arose, however, not because the hanging itself was botched. Rather, the editor of the *Yorktown Gazette* reported that "What has taken place at Lancaster would lead one to believe that the spectacle of public execution produces less reformation than criminal propensity."[36]

Somewhere between fifteen and forty thousand spectators gathered to watch Lechler die on the gallows at Lancaster common. Until the late nineteenth century, hangings were conducted before crowds numbering in the thousands, as part of a larger ritual which included a procession from the jail to the gallows, a sermon, and usually a speech by the condemned.[37] As the burglar Levi Ames is supposed to have said on the morning of his execution in 1773, dramatic spectacle was the objective:

> Ah! what a Spectacle I soon shall be
> A Corps suspended from you shameful Tree.[38]

By the 1820s, critics began to see public hangings as "festivals of disorder" that, as Rush had warned, "subverted morals, increased crimes, excited sympathy with the criminal, and wasted time."[39] Crowds drawn to the gallows, larger than crowds gathered for any other purpose, threatened public order. These early charges of barbarism were not directed at hanging per se, "but at the crowds whose attendance was now construed not as the assertion of a collective political right, but as the expression of an unseemly appetite for sordid amusement."[40] An 1835 New York committee report described spectators as "that class of citizens whose reason is to be convinced, or whose animal feelings are to be excited."[41] One month after the report was published, New York abolished public hanging.

The legislatures of Connecticut, in 1830, and of Pennsylvania, in

1834, also ended public hangings.[42] By 1845, all the states in the New England and Mid-Atlantic regions had eliminated public executions in favor of quasi-private hangings.[43] Throughout the nineteenth century, legislatures around the country followed suit in taking hanging day away from the public.

As the country edged towards civil war, the movement to abolish the death penalty itself faded. Barton summarizes the situation of the anti-gallows movement in the late 1850s: "Largely due to the impending Civil War, however, the inevitable violence associated with the effort to abolish slavery, a movement with which the reformation of capital punishment was intimately connected, death penalty abolitionism lost its momentum, not fully to return to the public spotlight until the turn of the twentieth century."[44] With war raging between North and South, Martin Bovee expressed a shared abolitionist sentiment: "It is useless to talk of saving life when we are killing by the thousands."[45]

And yet, from midcentury on, the privatization of judicial hangings was accompanied by technological innovation in both England and the United States. Hanged at Newgate in 1868, Fenian Michael Barrett died after repeated convulsions, his "protruding tongue and swollen distorted features discernible under the thin white cotton covering, as if they were part of some hideous masquerading."[46] The privatization of executions did not put an end to the potentially preventable, and thus suddenly problematic, painful death by asphyxiation at the gallows. By then, technological change and the general advancement of knowledge in the medical sciences made it possible to minimize human pain and suffering. And so officials began tinkering once again with the design of the gallows and the techniques of the drop.

On the Search for More Efficient Methods of Hanging

An early nineteenth-century innovation was the "upright jerker." This technology, unique to the United States, used a pulley system in which weights fixed at the end of the rope were released by officials, to jerk the condemned up into the air rather than dropping him as was done in other methods of hanging. The upright jerker was engineered to guarantee the sudden application of a force to the neck greater than that supplied by the weight of the prisoner alone. Local officials in counties across the country, searching for a surer means of conducting painless hangings, adopted the new device.

While the upright jerker was already the standard gallows used in New York City by 1845, it spread more gradually to other regions over the next three decades.[47] Despite its intermittent popularity, it never fulfilled its promise of quick and painless execution. Rather, inexperienced executioners continued to struggle with procedure, and far too often the device simply failed to sever the spinal cord, leaving prisoners to die by slow asphyxiation. Critics began to long for the return of the old-fashioned, yet "more certain and humane method of the 'drop.'"[48]

The most important technical improvement of the period was the invention of what eventually came to be known as the "long drop," that is, a fall whose explicit purpose was "to cause a quicker death by dislocating the uppermost cervical vertebrae, thereby separating the spinal cord from the brain stem."[49] The long drop, in other words, was designed to ensure death by the elusive "hangman's fracture," rather than by strangulation.[50] Its basic engineering rationale was similar to that of the upright jerker: a longer drop would allow the condemned to fall at a greater velocity and thus generate a greater force on the neck.

In Ireland, where the technique was first employed, drops typically ranged from ten to seventeen feet; unfortunately, such lengths tended to hasten death by causing decapitation rather than cervical dislocation.[51] The trial and error efforts of William Marwood, who served as Great Britain's executioner from 1874 to 1883, are credited with the "perfection" of the long drop method. He experimented with various locations for the knot (occipital, subaural, and submental) and worked to calculate the optimal distance of the drop with more precision. His tireless experimentations, in turn, would ultimately drive the conception of the mathematical table discussed in Chapter 1.[52]

Nevertheless, as the resurgence of the American reform impulse at the end of the nineteenth century would attest, disturbing uncertainties survived the supposed scientific rationalization of the noose. The standardization of drop length did not automatically eliminate the characteristic variability of death by the rope. Besides knowing the height and weight of the condemned, the hangman had to take age, physical condition, and musculature into account.[53] Furthermore, in practice, the difference between a painless and an excruciating death depended on a wide range of external conditions, including rope elasticity, the position of the knot, the weather, and not least the skills of the hangman.[54]

As Koestler notes, "like any other operation," the "efficacy of breaking a neck depends entirely on the skill of the surgeon."[55] In this sense, the intrinsic unpredictability of hanging was only exacerbated in the United States, where unlike in England and elsewhere in Europe, death sentences were not carried out by professional hangmen. Instead, the responsibility for executions—everything from raising the gallows, tying the noose, and pulling the lever, to the disposition of the corpse—fell to county sheriffs, who, unwilling and unable, tended to delegate these responsibilities whenever possible, often to amateurs even more incapable than themselves.[56] "This diffusion of responsibility to nonprofessionals," Banner argues, "would contribute, in the late nineteenth and early twentieth century, to the United States assuming the lead in developing alternatives to hanging."[57]

While technological innovation slowed at the turn of the century, the duration and degree of pain, and even the cause of death, associated with judicial hanging remained essentially indeterminable. As a medical examiner from San Francisco once explained, "Hanging in itself is a very general term"; it "represents a gamut of effects upon the neck and the structures, leading to some type of neuro or cardiogenic shock."[58] The "hangman's fracture" has always been, and remains, incredibly rare.

An early study of sixty-five hangings conducted in the United States from 1869 to 1873 reported only six complete cervical fractures and four partial fractures. After performing a mass autopsy of murderers executed in England between 1883 and 1945, a more recent study similarly found that only six of the thirty-four bodies exhumed exhibited cervical fractures.[59] A 2009 study, in turn, listed injuries ranging from spinal shock, brain stem damage, vascular and artery occlusion, to asphyxia, strangulation, and general head trauma among the potential causes of death by hanging.[60] Thus, when a doctor was asked, "What, in your opinion, will be the cause of death in a judicial hanging in accordance with the Washington state policy?" his simple-minded response was symptomatic: "Well, the cause of death is the injury that leads to death, so the cause of death is hanging."[61]

Regarding the pain of hanging, British neurobiologist Harold Hillman found that contrary to popular belief, even the comparatively sophisticated English long-drop procedure does not immediately arrest respiration and heartbeat. While both may *start* to slow immediately and breathing often stops within seconds, the heart may beat for up to twenty minutes after the drop.[62] Moreover, in any given case, Hillman told the *Guardian* in 1990, "The victim is likely to suffer severe pain from stretching the skin, strangulation and dislocation of the neck, and is unable to cry out because the rope is pressed around the vocal cords. If the person has strong neck muscles, or is very light, death may take some time. . . . It is not known how long a person feels pain."[63] All this suggests, according to Kaufman-Osborn, that "what the introduction of the long drop accomplished was not instantaneous death, but rather the immediate appearance thereof."[64] Anyway, this result—soothing sights and muted sounds from the death chamber—was what the late-nineteenth-century public had come to demand.

The Gallows in Question

By the end of the nineteenth century, American distaste for the gallows greatly increased. This growing aversion might be explained in four interrelated ways: first, a newly sensitized and class-conscious middle class recoiled from hanging as something base and offensive; second, the middle class developed an aversion to death in general as it was removed from the cadence of everyday life; third, the structural parallels between judicial hanging and the intensified violence of lynchings in the postwar South troubled both state and citizen; and lastly, as already seen, the scientific revolution of the Gilded Age made the creation of new, painless and palatable execution methods—and the ultimate move away from hanging—possible.

An example of the middle class recoiling from hanging is found in reactions to the 1889 executions in Ozark, Missouri, of Dave Walker, his son William, and John Matthews, who had been "noted bald-knobbers," or vigilantes, operating in the southern part of the state of Missouri.[65] The headline of the *Philadelphia Inquirer* front-page report ran, "A Gallows Butchery," and the first sentence recounted that "The execution today was a horrible piece of butchery owing to the blunders of the sheriff."[66] The *Dallas Morning News* likewise headlined its account of the hangings, "A Horrible Execution."[67] The description it provided to its readers is detailed and extensive:

> The stretch of the rope let all fall to the ground. The rope broke in the case of William Walker and fell loose around him as he lay struggling and groaning. He talked for three minutes when he was taken up by the sheriff and deputies and again placed on the scaffold. Dave Walker was drawn up and died in about fifteen minutes. Matthews lived about thirteen minutes and died with his feet off the ground. The scene was horrible in the extreme. Matthews and Dave Walker were cut down at 10:10. The trap was again adjusted and William Walker lifted on it helpless and groaning and gurgling, and almost insensible. . . . The scenes on the gallows were ghastly when the three men dropped through the trap. The feet of Dave Walker and John Matthews touched the ground. In less than a minute the rope around Bill Walker's neck broke, and he fell to the ground crying: "Oh Lord, I hope no man will ever suffer as I have, dying!" He was carried back to the gallows spitting up blood, and was left in his agony until Dave Walker and John Matthews were pronounced dead. The noose was again adjusted and Bill Walker dropped through the trap a second time. His last words were, "Oh, Lord; Oh, Lord."[68]

A newly sensitized middle class, particularly concerned with differentiating itself from the lower classes, came to desire even more distance from such brutalities. Banner, commenting on this emerging sensibility, writes, "the people we would today call the middle class began to see great differences in the realm of taste and manners between themselves and those they considered less refined. Respectable people placed a new emphasis on etiquette and gentility, matters that had once been the province of the rich."[69] Nurturing this new sense of their own superiority, the middle classes refused to see themselves as part of the cheering hanging day mobs. They refused to involve themselves with the vulgarity of "Gallows Butchery."

By the end of the nineteenth century, death itself had become more of a stranger to the American middle class. Instead of families caring for the sick and dying at home, hospitals were now the primary site for medical treatment. Cemeteries were also moved out of public view.[70] And the violence of the Civil War further shaped the middle class's "new relationship with death."[71] The brutality of public hangings came to eerily resemble the mutilation and destruction of the war.

Medical advances of the late nineteenth century both defamiliarized death and, as Annulla Linders argues, made "the elimination of pain not only possible but also desirable."[72] By midcentury, "brutality had become a liability and visible pain a sign of failure."[73] The cause of the transformation, Banner claims, was, finally, "an intensified public focus on the suffering of those who were executed."[74] Scenes of the body in pain were no longer fearsome representations of sovereign majesty, but they were fearsome in the sense of signifying the ugly realities of state-operated vengeance to the public at large.

The middle-class "culture of refinement," coupled with "squeamishness about physical violence and suffering," meant that hanging was associated with the "barbaric" execution methods of the past.[75] Execution crowds were viewed as immoral and disorderly, but also inhumane. Building on an earlier trend, the execution performance was increasingly isolated behind prison walls. Now, even in parts of the South, the past "spectacle of the gallows" was transferred into new public court-rooms: "the ceremonial focus of punishment had shifted from its inflic-tion to its imposition."[76]

Outside the courtroom this distinction was sometimes lost. On the night of May 27, 1889—the same month that the bald-knobbers stran-gled to death atop the Ozark gallows—Albert Martin was lynched by a "masked mob" in Port Huron, Michigan. Two weeks earlier, Martin had "brutally outraged Mrs. John Gillis, the wife of a farmer." At two o'clock in the morning on May 27, the *Kansas City Star* reported,

> [a] noose was quickly made in a long rope which the lynchers carried and it was slipped over his neck while he was yet in bed. The other end of the rope reached out to the street, where it was held by not less than fifty willing hands. With a blood-curdling yell the mob started on a run. Martin was unable to regain his feet and he was dragged through the sheriff's office out to the street.[77]

On the way to the Seventh Street Bridge, "The noose on the rope had loosened and slipped over the wretch's chin and into his mouth. It was then tightened until his lower jaw was pulled down upon his neck in a manner which must have caused the victim terrible suffering." After Martin had been "swung off," his body was left hanging and, "with a few parting shots," the mob quit the scene.[78]

At the turn of the century, lynchings remained purposefully "savage" and "carnivalesque."[79] Moreover, post-Reconstruction "public torture lynchings" generally occurred in broad daylight before large crowds, not unlike the most spectacular public hangings of the early 1800s.[80] Adopting the form of judicial hangings, local lynching mobs attempted to usurp the role of fearful rule enforcer. In the 1890s, the number of lynchings skyrocketed in the South: between 1882 and 1940 approxi-mately four thousand were recorded.[81] The rampant gruesomeness of lynchings played a significant role in the privatization of hanging as the law tried frantically to distinguish itself from virulent mobs.

Also in May 1889, the *Omaha Daily Herald* ran a report entitled,

"A Gallows Expert Talks." The rather lengthy article detailing an interview with Daniel T. Blakely, a well-known Kansas City hangman, was
aptly subtitled, "He Tells Where the Ozark Men Made Their Mistake in
Strangling the Walker Bald-Knobbers—The Proper Mode Described."[82]
Blakely is quoted directly: "Yes, that Ozark job was a horrible botch,
but it might have been safely predicted." He explains away the Ozark
botching by assuming the perfectibility of his craft in the hands of an
artist. He goes on, "You couldn't expect a man who was never had any
experience in the business to do a correct and artistic piece of work."
A "bad bungle" ought to have been anticipated. "It is not every man,"
he explains, "who can conduct an execution without any friction or
unpleasing effects."

Blakely then describes, in painstaking detail, the exact manner in
which he constructs his gallows and his preferred trap mechanism: "I
once saw a man's head almost knocked off by a returning trap. It was
very annoying. I don't like the spring attachment; it is too bunglesome
and noisy for artistic effect. I always pad the bottoms of my traps so
they will move back noiselessly."[83] He went on to discuss the most significant technical innovations of the century: calculation according to
height and weight, attention to the condemned person's physique, drop
length, rope material and width, the importance of greasing and stretching the rope preemptively, knot-tying technique, knot size, and finally
knot placement.

The *Daily Herald* reporter describes how Blakely showed him a used
noose, "a coil of dirty, greasy looking three-quarter inch rope," after
pulling it nonchalantly out of a drawer, and how he later "slopped the
noose over his head and drew the knot up taut under his left ear" in order to make a point. In a particularly sensationalistic moment, he relates
how "the hangman clasped his cold hand about this reporter's throat" in
order to estimate a hypothetical drop length.[84] Even at its most professional and precise, the hangman's art is a strange and chilling business.

The rest of this chapter examines that strange and chilling business
by taking a close look at several types of botched hangings in the twen-

tieth century and by recounting the stories of men and women bleeding and struggling at the end of their respective ropes. During that time, the lives of 2,721 people were ended by hanging. Eighty-five of them (approximately 3%) were the "victim" of a mishap as their death sentence was carried out. Some were dropped and hanged more than once, some were hoisted manually by prison guards, some died hard by upright jerker, some strangled to death, and some lost their heads.

The first case is that of George Robinson, who in 1902, in Virginia, was hanged twice. More than ten years later, John Harris's first drop also failed to kill him quickly, and he was strangled to death at the hands of desperate officials. In 1908, an upright jerker in Powell County, Montana, failed to follow through on its promised innovation and George Rock and William Hayes died after long minutes of labored strangulation. Finally, we discuss Eva Dugan's botched hanging in 1930. Eva, only the twenty-seventh woman to be legally executed in the United States, was decapitated.

George Robinson

Today Wise County, Virginia, calls itself the "Safest Place on Earth."[85] Back in August of 1902, however, George Robinson, a black man, was hanged twice in a dramatically violent fashion at the county courthouse before a crowd of well over one thousand onlookers. "It is hard to conceive of a more horrible spectacle," a reporter wrote, "than a half-dead man being hung," a man hanged twice, "inside the short space of fifteen minutes."[86]

Little is known about George Robinson's life. He was, however, listed on the 1900 Virginia state census as living in Big Stone Gap and employed as a blacksmith. A 2006 retrospective article on hangings in the *Clinch Valley Times* also reported that Robinson had killed his wife, Hortense, at Big Stone Gap on the day of another hanging. Allegedly, he ran her down, caught her in the middle of a stream, and cut her throat with a razor.[87]

Even before Robinson's death on the gallows, his time in prison was plagued by peculiar tragedy. Soon after Robinson went to jail, smallpox broke out among the prisoners. The deputy sheriff, Wilson Holbrook, living in the jail at the time, contracted the disease and died. Sick prisoners, including George Robinson, were moved to a poor farm, and the others were removed to the Scott County jail at Gate City. The ex-deputy sheriff, C. W. Renfro, recalled that on the way back to Wise County, Robinson told him that he killed his wife because she called him a vile name.[88]

Robinson was not a large man. At the time of his arrest, he weighed only around 165 pounds. Despite Robinson's small stature, the deputy sheriff—at the suggestion of the county physician—decided to give him a longer drop. Looking back, Renfro described the disastrous consequences that followed as the "most nerve-racking experience of [my] life."[89]

On Friday, August 8, George Robinson was led by the deputy sheriff to the veranda in front of the courthouse at 11:00 in the morning.[90] There, he turned and faced the crowd of—by some reports—between three and four thousand people. Standing in front of the scaffold, Robinson made a speech of about twenty-five minutes, admitting to the crowd that he was a "bad man" and was getting what he deserved.[91] He also announced that he had killed his brother-in-law but had been acquitted. He called himself a drunkard, a gambler, and a robber.[92]

Robinson was led back inside where he ate a "hearty dinner."[93] At 12:50 P.M. he was conducted once more to the foot of the gallows. Kneeling on the trapdoor, head bowed almost until it grazed the damp wood, Robinson said a quick prayer. The deputy adjusted the rope and cap, and the drop fell at 12:57.[94]

Shortly after Robinson fell downward, the crowd heard what "sounded like the sharp crack of a whip" as the frayed end of the rope recoiled.[95] The rope, made of ranch sea-grass, snapped in two almost halfway between the beam and Robinson's neck, "as if cut with a knife."[96] Robinson struck the ground and rolled over against the wall, blood streaming from his mouth and nose. A bloody ring was cut into his neck by the rope.[97] He cried out in pain while someone ran across the street to Flannary's store to purchase another rope.[98]

After briefly lying unattended on the ground below the sprung trap, Robinson was half carried by prison officials back to the top of the scaffold.[99] Back in the shadow of the noose, now double-tied for good measure, the "poor wretch" crouched down in a corner and watched as officials prepared to hang him a second time. As blood continued to ooze from his nose and mouth, it "seemed as he was trying to press his body through the wall."[100] Nonetheless, Robinson remained "conscious throughout the whole of this remarkable ordeal and did not show the faintest sign of collapse."[101]

"Let me live just as long as possible," he pleaded raspingly. Robinson never uttered another word. With admittedly "hurried hands," Renfro slipped the black cap over his head once more, secured his arms and legs, and adjusted the noose. The new rope stiffened to a straight line as Robinson was "again hauled into space." He was pronounced dead thirty-five minutes later from strangulation.

John Harris

Robinson's case was by no means unique. Hanging not only often kills hard but also often fails to kill at all—and under conditions even more excruciating for the condemned.[102] A decade after George Robinson was, finally, strangled to death, John Harris met a similar fate in Pennsylvania.

Harris was a tall, lanky man and the rope used to hang him was far too long. When he dropped, fast and heavy, he dropped hard. However, with his feet—and then his knees—touching the ground, John Harris did not die quickly. According to the *Washington Post*, the rope that the executioner looped around Harris's neck should have been about three feet shorter. This would have prevented the condemned man from ending up on his knees.[103]

Harris remained motionless in that position for several minutes,[104] and then tried to rise. He screamed and, desperate now, tried to loosen the rope that dug into his neck. For several minutes onlookers just watched, immobile, before the sheriff and his deputies climbed onto the scaffold, where they grabbed the end of the rope tied to the crossbeam and pulled his body back into the air until neither his knees nor feet touched the floor. For eighteen minutes they kept Harris hoisted in the air well above their heads, his legs swinging madly, while he struggled[105] and attempted to climb the rope that was hanging him.[106] Finally, Harris dangled lifelessly at the end of the rope. According to newspaper reports, throughout his ordeal Harris appeared to be in tremendous agony.[107]

This was not the kind of execution that Uniontown sheriff M. O. Keifer and his men had been expecting.[108] At the time, Harris's botched hanging was referred to as "one of the most ghastly executions in the history of Pennsylvania," and with reason. The story of local law enforcement officers hoisting the writhing man over their heads until he choked to death was told and retold in newspapers across the nation.[109] One paper even went so far as to explicitly characterize Harris's hanging as a kind of torture, captioning the piece, "Prisoner Tortured Through Bungling at a Uniontown, Pa., Execution." The paper alleged that someone involved in the execution had intentionally botched the job by adjusting the rope to be far too long for someone of Harris's height, weight, and build.[110]

Before his execution was so badly "bungled," to borrow a term from a Trenton newspaper,[111] Harris had been just another condemned killer. The African American man was convicted of murder for the shooting death of another black male, and subsequently sentenced to death by hanging. The murder itself received no national attention.[112] Harris's execution, only the twelfth in the history of Fayette County, would change that.[113]

The hanging was memorialized as a "particularly revolting" affair by the Associated Press, which blamed Harris's excruciating end on the officers assigned to carry out the execution. The AP condemned them for failing to execute their responsibilities effectively.[114] Because of their mistake, Harris's death did not comport with the humanity that, according to the *Washington Post*, was supposed to characterize hanging. Instead, officers of the law had been forced to hang him—literally—with their own hands.[115]

George Rock and William Hayes

George Rock and William Hayes were cell mates in the Montana State Prison at Deer Lodge.[116] Hayes had been sent to the penitentiary to serve ten years for robbing a saloon.[117] Rock was serving a ninety-nine-year sentence for the murder of Ed Curl, a man who lived in his eating house.[118] In March 1908, Rock and Hayes, with the help of two other inmates, Oram Stevens and C. B. Young, planned a prison break.[119]

At 8:15 in the morning of March 8, the four convicts entered Warden Frank Conley's administrative office, where it was common practice for him to hold "court." Every morning he saw inmates who had broken rules, or he listened grudgingly as they aired their grievances. Inmates would either be called forth to the court or leave a note for a guard asking to see the warden regarding a complaint.[120] On that fateful morning, the four men and a number of other prisoners were taken to a holding room outside the office. They were to be seen one by one.

Warden Conley first met with an inmate by the name of Howell, followed by another prisoner, W. W. Brown. Just as Brown left the office, Conley heard strange noises coming from the holding room. Before he could investigate, Hayes entered the room, jumped the railing separating the prisoners from the warden's desk, and went right up to Mr. Conley.[121] He put a firm hand on the warden's shoulder and said simply, "I want to get out of here," to which Conley replied with equal bravado, "Over my dead body."[122]

When Hayes, flashing a knife, threatened to cut the warden's head off, Conley grabbed his revolver and shot Hayes in the head.[123] Hayes fell to the floor, but was not severely injured. He got up and lunged at the warden's neck, slicing him from ear to collar bone, barely missing the jugular vein.[124] Conley took two more shots at Hayes, but the prisoner continued to swing at the warden with his knife. As he fell to the floor from his bullet wounds, Hayes slashed Conley's leg, leaving him with a deep, long cut.[125]

Meanwhile, in the outer room, George Rock and Deputy Warden John A. Robinson, who was the assigned guard for the morning's court session, were entangled in a parallel fight to the death. Rock, however, had been more successful at attacking his target. Robinson stumbled into the office covered in blood: "My God, Frank," he mumbled to the warden, "They've got me."[126] As Rock entered the room behind the deputy warden, Conley yelled for his friend to get out of the way, and shot at the convict. The struggle continued.

Hayes got off the floor again, cutting and slashing at the warden. Conley attempted once more to shoot him but realized he was out of bullets. With what was left of his strength, he picked up Hayes and threw him into the hall. Conley then grabbed the prisoner's knife and went back into the office to help Robinson.[127]

There the warden succeeded in pulling Rock off of Robinson as the inmate continued to stab at him wildly; using a chair, Conley hit him on the head, knocking him down. However, Robinson, who had been cut deeply, was fatally injured.[128] Knowing Robinson was almost dead, Rock moved onto Conley, slashing at him as Hayes had done.[129]

Minutes earlier, a prisoner working near the office had overheard the violent commotion in the next room. He ran to inform the nearest guards. When they arrived at the office, the door was locked shut. Throwing their weight against the door, they broke in. Deputy Warden Robinson was lying in the corner in a pool of his own blood, hacked and stabbed to death. Warden Conley, also covered in blood, was crouched over George Rock beating him with his gun, his swings growing increasingly weak, as he had sustained over fifty stab wounds.[130] The guard pulled the warden off the prisoner to safety and then hit Rock decisively on the head with his billy club, knocking him out and ending the escape attempt.[131]

The warden was immediately taken to the prison hospital where doctors treated stab wounds on his neck, face, legs, and torso. Hayes and Rock were also taken to the infirmary to recover from the gunshot wounds Conley had managed to inflict.[132] Rock recovered quickly. Hayes, on the other hand, healed much slower. More than a year later, he would walk to his death with one of the warden's bullets still lodged in his body.[133]

A coroner's jury investigated the deadly battle and found both Rock and Hayes responsible for the death of Robinson. While Stevens and Young were implicated in the conspiracy, both "got cold feet" at the start of the fight and fled the scene, throwing their knives away and reentering their cells without a word.[134] Young, who like Hayes had been serving a ten-year sentence, received a life sentence for his role in the attack. And although the jury found that Stevens had played no real role in the attack, his "good behavior time" was revoked.[135]

On April 9, 1908, George Rock stood before Judge George B. Winston, pled guilty, and calmly requested that he be given a death sentence and a speedy execution. The judge would grant his first request, but not the second. When William Hayes stood trial before the same judge, Conley was the state's key witness. He gave a rousing and emotional description of the attack,[136] and Hayes was later also sentenced to hang.

On December 29, 1908, Hayes appealed, arguing that he had not been given a fair and impartial trial. His lawyers also claimed that Hayes was improperly charged for Robinson's murder, which was not part of the original conspiracy. One month later, the appellate court affirmed the jury's decision. Hayes was set to hang on April 1, 1909.[137]

Rock and Hayes would be the first and only men to hang in the Powell County jail yard. And the coconspirators would meet their fates in similar fashion.

On the morning of June 15, 1908, Rock prepared to die in the shadow of the upright jerker. He maintained an apparently unaffected, serious demeanor throughout the morning and afternoon, and rather than accept the "delicacies" and special meals offered to inmates about to be executed, Rock ate normal prison meals and barely touched the fruit basket that was brought to him.[138] As more than two hundred spectators entered the prison yard to witness the execution, Rock met with Father McCormick, a local priest, to receive a final Holy Communion and the sacrament of penance.[139]

At 12:30 A.M. reporters were allowed to enter Rock's cell for a final interview with the condemned. Rock said very little, explaining that he was grateful that he had survived the attack that had led to his death sentence. "I have since made my peace with God," he told his interviewers, "and I am ready to go, knowing full well that I deserve my fate."[140]

Minutes before the execution's scheduled 1:30 start time, the procession to the gallows began. Father McCormick and Father Moran, the two priests who had spent the morning and early afternoon comforting and counseling Rock, walked solemnly at his side chanting the Penitential Psalms. Earlier in the week, the gallows had been brought from Butte, Montana, thirty miles away, and set up in the northeastern edge of the prison yard.[141] To the right of the gallows stood the executioner, cloaked in a canvas shield.

Rock never looked up, even as he walked across the wooden platform to the noose.[142] Once on the platform, Sheriff Fifer asked if Rock had any final words. "Nothing," he said, his voice shaking and his body trembling.[143] The sheriff placed the black cap over Rock's head and stepped back. Within seconds the three-hundred-pound weight was released and Rock's body flew up into the air.[144]

The noose, however, failed to tighten and his neck was not broken. For many minutes witnesses could see the man breathing and his body convulsing. Doctors checked Rock's pulse and found that his heart was still beating steadily.[145] Sometime later, when they checked again, they found no pulse. George Rock was declared dead.

On April 1, 1909, just a little over a year after George Rock's botched hanging, his accomplice, William Hayes, underwent a similar experience. A little before eight in the morning, Hayes walked out into the prison yard towards the gallows without the support of a single guard or priest.[146] Hayes, it was said, met his end bravely,[147] slowly walking up the steps of the platform and to his place beneath the rope. He showed no fear until the rope was tightened around his neck, when he grew pale. Like Rock, when asked if he had any final words, Hayes merely shook his head no.[148]

A large crowd watched as the hangman bungled the execution. When the weight was dropped and as his body jerked into the air, Hayes's neck was not broken. He hung, suspended, before hundreds of people, for several minutes. His body twitched, and at one point Hayes reached futilely above his head for the rope as he strangled. Like Rock, Hayes died a slow, agonizing death. He strangled helplessly, twisting his body, grabbing at his neck, and gasping for air.

Eva Dugan

Decades later, Eva Dugan's hanging was botched in yet another way. Once again, the length of her fall was estimated incorrectly with disastrous results. Dugan, a fifty-two-year-old mother of two, became the first woman executed by the state of Arizona when she was dropped to her death in the execution chamber of the state prison in Florence.[149]

Dugan was charged with murdering A. J. Mathis, an aged Tucson rancher for whom she had worked as a housekeeper. According to Mathis's stepson, she had been asked to leave the ranch several times but had stubbornly refused to accept her dismissal.[150] Shortly after the rancher disappeared, suspicions focused on Dugan. Neighbors told Sheriff Jim McDonald that they had seen her washing out the inside of her employer's car. A local doctor reported that only days before he went missing, Mathis tried yet again to discharge Dugan—accusing her of attempting to poison him. As *Time* magazine reported, Dugan murdered the rancher in hopes of obtaining his property, buried his body in a shallow grave, and fled in the stolen automobile.[151]

When the search for Dugan began, she was described as a heavy-set woman with dark bobbed hair habitually combed back from the forehead. She was said to "have the appearance of being rather good looking when younger."[152] She was apprehended in White Plains, New York, for car theft several months after her former employer disappeared. Dugan was returned to Arizona only after Mathis's body was discovered—nearly a year after his disappearance—in a shoddy grave dug near his house.

Dugan consistently claimed that Mathis was killed by a young man known to her only as "Jack," and that all she had done was to run away with him. This mysterious youth—some reports listed his age as just sixteen—was never located. "'Jack' is just a name as far as the accumulated record of three years is concerned," the *Prescott Evening Courier* reported on the day of Dugan's execution. "He appeared at the Mathis ranch a day or two before Mathis's disappearance and has not been seen since. Following Mathis's disappearance Mrs. Dugan, after attempting to sell a cow and some chickens on the ranch, left in a coupe owned by Mathis, in company with 'Jack.' It is believed that this young man was employed by Mrs. Dugan to drive the car."[153]

Although Jack was never captured, he sent two letters to Eva while she was in prison. Mrs. Eva Dugan, Care of the Warden, State Prison:

Dear Friend:

Sorry you had such a bad break and have decided to come out and explain how I had to hit old man Mathis. He was coming at me with a knife and would have killed me if I had not struck him. You ought to have killed him because he was trying to run off without paying you for what you had done for him, just because he was stuck on that woman in Tucson and wanted to bring her out to take your place. But you had nothing to do with it—you just ran away with me. I want to get some more evidence and some more money.

Yours truly,

Jack[154]

Jack was not heard from again until just a few days before the hanging. He wrote, prophetically, "Well, that was some little failure, wasn't it? Lovingly, Jack."[155]

Following her conviction for first-degree murder, Dugan was sentenced to hang on June 1, 1928. But she obtained a temporary stay of execution from the Arizona Supreme Court. The court eventually affirmed her sentence and rescheduled her execution for February 21, 1930—exactly two years from the date that her trial first began.[156]

One week before she was to be executed, Dr. R. W. Brown, a former physician at the state prison, signed an affidavit claiming that Dugan was insane. After examining the condemned woman in her cell, the former prison doctor allegedly found her symptoms to be even "more pronounced" than they had been the year before.[157] In an "eleventh hour attempt to save her from the gallows," Stanley Samuelson, Dugan's attorney, used the doctor's testimony to secure a hearing on her sanity. Dr. Brown testified that Dugan "has been insane for a long time through gradual development of a disease she contracted more than thirty years ago. This disease has caused both the brain and the spinal cord to degenerate." However, this testimony was to no avail, as Dugan was declared sane.

Commenting on the hearing after the decision was announced, Dugan said:

> You know, before I left here yesterday, I rumpled up my hair and I must have looked like a wild woman—I don't know how they could find their verdict against me in the face of the testimony. And if I had been a flapper dressed in a keen dress, with plenty of powder and rouge on, silk stockings and classy red slippers, the jury never would have found me guilty in the first place. They would have said, "We'll let her out. Maybe we'll meet her on the street someday." But instead they said, "Oh she's just an old, broken down woman and we can't be bothered."[158]

On Thursday, February 20, Dugan was "resigned" and "cheerful."[159] "I am going to die as I lived," she said in one interview. "I have had two years to prepare for this. I am ready."[160] She spent time carefully sewing her burial clothes—a shroud of white silk, embellished with clusters of beads and artificial flowers[161]—played cards with three other women until after midnight, talking only occasionally. Throughout the game, she caressed a telegram, a farewell message from her daughter, Cecil Loveless, of South Bend, Indiana. Dugan never disclosed the name or whereabouts of her son.

During the card game, Dugan asked if her "guests" could be served orangeade. After several minutes had passed with her request unfulfilled, she called to a guard. "Please bring on the orangeade," she said. "Tomorrow will be too late."[162] Later, refusing offers of aid from prison officials, she prepared her own last meal: an oyster stew.[163]

Dugan received another telegram in her cell that night, revealing a "hitherto unknown chapter in her early life." The message read, "I sympathize with you and have the greatest admiration for your bravery and grit." It was signed, "Ada Hostapple, Seattle, Washington." Ada was an old friend, Dugan told reporters, from her "Yukon Days" following the gold rush.[164]

At 1:00 A.M., Lorenzo Wright, warden of the Florence, Arizona, state prison moved Dugan to a holding cell. According to reports, Wright "created a sensation" only a few minutes before she was set to hang when he revealed the existence of "a plot by Mrs. Dugan to cheat the gallows." After she was transferred to the holding cell, a search of her previous cell uncovered, under the mattress of her cot, a two-ounce bottle of a "deadly poison" bearing the label of a Florence drugstore. A subsequent search of her person turned up three razor blades.[165]

Nonetheless, throughout all of this, Dugan appeared unaffected. On the day of her hanging Eva posed happily for photographers, dressed only in her nightgown and slippers. She told assembled reporters, "Shoot your questions boys, there ain't much time left," and then added, "I'm not guilty, that's all I have to say."[166] She announced, "I am going to meet my Maker with a clear conscience, I am innocent of any murder, and God knows I am."[167] "I won't cheat," she told them. "I'll go to the gallows like a man."

She kissed one reporter and, before the group left, collected one dollar from each of them to aid in the purchase of a "better coffin."[168]

Watching all this, the warden seemed "more upset by the hanging than Mrs. Dugan." "She was the best prisoner we ever had here," he said. "We'll hang her although God knows we hate to do it."[169]

As the time for Dugan's execution approached, light rain spattered gently on the roof of the prison and dampened the graveled pathway leading to the death chamber. A group of hushed witnesses huddled outside in the high-walled yard. Her sister and eighty-two-year-old father, William McDaniels, were unable to attend. McDaniels reportedly spent most of his daughter's execution day keeping a lonely vigil in his cabin in Ceres, California.

Dugan wore only a "cheap wrapper" to her execution, deciding at the last moment that the silk shroud she had made "might get mussed" as she fell through the trap.[170] As she walked through the "darkness of the prison yard," Dugan smoked a cigarette and laughed and joked with the guards on either side of her. As the first gate opened, she "gave a little jump through the aperture" and sang out, "I don't know where I'm going but I'm on my way."[171]

The floor of Florence's death house was effectively a raised platform with a trapdoor through which the bodies of the hanged fell into the room below. Death sentences had been carried out there since 1910.[172] As Dugan entered the place where she would die, she said to the guards, "I love everyone connected with the prison. You have all been good to me, and I can't blame you for what the law is going to do to me." As they parted ways at the foot of the platform, Dugan kissed two of them goodbye.[173]

She then calmly took her place beneath the noose. She looked at the warden, as the hangman placed the rope around her neck. "God bless you Eva," he said. A "grim smile flitted across her broad face" and Dugan replied, "Good-bye, Daddy Wright," as her hands were bound and the black hood was adjusted.[174] Still "unshaken in her resolve," Dugan surveyed the crowd of spectators and prison witnesses. And then, only "[a] few seconds later, at [5]:11 a.m., the trap was sprung."[175]

The hanging, however, did not go as planned. The *Prescott Evening Courier* reported that, "As the trap clanged and she dropped more than six feet, the noose tightened, severing her head, and the body catapulted to the floor."[176] The *Mount Airy News* told its readers that "She fell through a hole in the floor of the execution chamber to a room below. Death was instantaneous for the rope, when it snapped at the end of the drop, severed her head from her body."[177] Another paper described the scene with a bit more drama: "when Mrs. Dugan plunged through the trap door and hit the end of the rope with a bounding jolt, her head snapped off and rolled into a corner."[178]

While some reports said that Warden Wright "cleared the gallows room immediately," others recounted a short statement made by the prison chaplain, the Reverend Walter Hofmann, following Dugan's gruesome death.[179] "Now," he addressed the witnesses, "please take a good look and see what capital punishment does." Later, the Reverend would remember Eva's hanging as one of the most "unspeakably horrible" moments of his life.[180]

In the room where Eva Dugan died, sixteen pictures hung on the wall. Before her execution, each photograph showed a man who was hanged on the same gallows that would be the site of her decapitation. Each photograph was encircled by the noose that caused his death. Dugan's picture and noose were placed among the "grim collection" on the morning following her burial.[181] Today eight of the mug shots and nooses remain on display in a corner of the Pinal County Historical Museum. From her noose, Eva Dugan "looks out with a grandmotherly expression."[182]

Along another of the museum's walls stands Arizona's old "hanging board," about five feet high, for the public to see. Under it, a caption reads:

> Used at the Arizona State Prison during legal executions by hanging. The condemned were tied to this board to prevent possible slumping. The length of the drop through the trap door was regulated by the slack in the hangman's rope. The slack in turn was calculated according to the weight of the condemned. There was a miscalculation when Eva Dugan was hanged on the morning of February 21, 1930. Her head was jerked off. Hanging then went out of fashion.[183]

The Disappearance of the Noose

By the end of the nineteenth and start of the twentieth century, hanging was under attack as a method of execution and botched hangings were the particular focus of critique. Bourgeois audiences "might tolerate the ghastliness of death itself, but not incompetence and mismanagement."[184] In an age of rapid scientific advancement, therefore, the state began its search for a "clean, clinical, undisturbing method of execution."[185]

New execution technologies were expected to be both painless for the condemned prisoner and, more importantly, less visually assaulting for spectators. And yet despite the mounting anxieties of government officials and the general public, the gallows survived well into that new century. The history of hanging's evolving technologies, and their frequent mishaps, foretold the fruitless search for other humane and foolproof technologies beyond the scaffold for carrying out the business of state killing.

CHAPTER 3

When Science Fails

Electrocution

In August 1881 a thirty-year-old dockworker, George Lemeul Smith, known to his associates as a drunk, slipped past workers at the Brush Electric Light Company's Ganson Street plant in Buffalo, New York. The Brush Plant, which housed the generators for Buffalo's arc lights, was a local attraction as Buffalo was one of the first cities in the world to install these lights. The city's residents, still wary and curious about the "magic" of electricity, often visited one of the facility's largest generators, which sat just inside the door of the plant. As Smith entered the building that summer night, most likely inebriated, a worker heard him yell that he was going to "stop the generator." He placed both of his hands on the machine, was electrocuted, and died immediately.[1]

Dr. Joseph Fowler, the county coroner, and Dr. Hoffmeyer, another physician, conducted an autopsy the next day. They were surprised to find that Smith had died so quickly, that his skin was neither charred nor burned, and that his body was not disfigured. Fowler found that Smith's lungs were filled with blood. Initially he was unable to decisively identify the cause of death.

Unsatisfied with the first examination, Fowler conducted a second autopsy. He "[peeled back the skin from Smith's arms and chest . . . [discovering] the path of the current: a line stretching from shoulder to shoulder, about two or three inches in width, where the flesh was a little darker than the tissue on either side. A force potent enough to fell a man in seconds left only a delicate tracing upon the flesh."[2] Even more surprising, Smith seemed to have died painlessly. G. W. Chaffee, the plant manager, and doctors Fowler and Hoffmeyer confirmed that fact to the local newspapers.[3]

Buffalo's medical community and in particular a local dentist, Dr. Alfred Porter Southwick, were fascinated by the electrically induced death. Though Southwick never attended medical school, he helped form the State Dental Society and the Dental Department of the University of Buffalo.[4] He focused on oral surgery and, in the course of his career, developed a groundbreaking procedure for treating cleft palates.[5] Though local legend has it that Southwick witnessed Smith's accidental death, in all likelihood he merely read about it in the local newspaper and, interested in learning more, attended a conference where Fowler presented his autopsy findings.[6]

Soon Southwick became obsessed with electricity. When he learned that Smith had died painlessly, he wondered about electricity's potential to reduce pain in more traditional medical practices. That, however, was not the limit of his curiosity. Southwick teamed up with Dr. George Fell, another Buffalo doctor, and with the backing of the Buffalo Society for the Prevention to Animal Cruelty, began experimenting on a humane way of eliminating the city's many stray animals by the use of an electric current.[7]

The results of the experiments were nonetheless brutal. Many of the animals were not killed outright or simply burned to death. After months of experimenting with various voltages, currents, and procedures, Southwick and Fell settled on a method that worked consistently. "They kept careful notes of their experiments and published them in scientific journals. Southwick's articles [called] electrocution 'the safest and kindest method of killing' [and they] drew widespread attention, not just from the SPCA and advocates of kindness to animals, but from a wide cross section of the scientific community, that was interested in anything that had to do with electricity."[8]

Southwick now started promoting electrocution in scientific journals as an alternative to hangings for the execution of humans. His efforts culminated a decade-long crusade against hanging and search for a humane alternative. In the 1870s, the New York Medico-Legal Society began considering lethal injection and lethal gas as acceptable substitutes for hanging. Working with a number of European scientists, the society—a group meant to bring together lawyers, doctors, and scientists interested in "medical jurisprudence"⁹—researched the implications of using gas or injection with poison to induce death. As with Southwick's experiments with electricity, the scientists conducted lethal injection trials on dogs.¹⁰

In the late 1870s and early 1880s, criticism of hanging was coming to a head. Newspapers published increasingly vivid, gruesome, and sensationalist stories about executions. "*The New York Times,*" Craig Brandon argues, "which was far from the worst exploiter of this trend, published fifty long and graphic descriptions of hangings in 1882 and another forty-one in 1883."¹¹ These stories related the sights and the sounds of hangings in such a way as to bring their readers to the very foot of the scaffold. In all of their melodrama, the articles underscored one central, unavoidable truth about hangings: a huge percentage of them were botched.¹²

In 1885, the newly elected governor of New York, David Bennett-Hill, decided to take a stance in the increasingly poignant capital punishment debate. In his annual message to the legislature, Hill declared, "The present mode of executing criminals by hanging has come down to us from the dark ages." "[I]t may well be questioned," he added, "whether the science of the present day cannot provide a means for taking the life of such as condemned to die in a less barbarous manner."¹³ In this, Hill reflected the beliefs of many citizens: the noose was outdated and gruesome, and in the new age of science and invention there must be a better alternative. He went on to call for the creation of a commission to explore more modern instrumentalities of execution.

The following year, New York State senator Daniel MacMillan, with Southwick's support, introduced a bill to create "A Commission to Investigate and Report the Most Humane and Practical Method of Carrying into Effect the Sentence of Death in Capital Cases."¹⁴ The Senate passed MacMillan's bill on May 13, 1886, and the commission was created immediately.¹⁵ MacMillan chaired it and selected its three other members: Dr. Southwick, the legal scholar Matthew Hale, and humanitarian Elbridge T. Gerry. The body later came to be known as the Gerry Commission.

The Gerry Commission posed this question: "Should not the contemporary state seek to discover a way of killing that does not so closely resemble the revolting act which the criminal expiates?"[16] Its first task was to consider all of the possible alternatives to hanging. After reviewing nearly a thousand books, scientific articles, legal reports, and medical journals, the commission released a ninety-five-page report surveying the history of the death penalty. The report described more than forty mechanisms that had been used in executions and listed specific objections to each method. However, the commission devoted most of its attention to hanging.[17] Three years later, the members of that commission said that the gallows "is the only piece of machinery that has stood stock still in this era of progress. There it stands, the same clumsy, inefficient, inhuman thing it was when it first lifted its ghastly framework into the air of the dark ages."

The commission also reported on the results of a survey that had been sent to a number of the state's lawyers, legal officials, doctors, and scientists. The survey asked for opinions about hanging and whether the respondent had ever attended an execution. In addition, respondents were asked to share their opinions about the four alternatives to hanging that the commission had suggested to the legislature: electricity, poison, guillotine, and garrote.[18] In response, almost equal numbers preferred electrocution to hanging, eighty-seven respondents to eighty.[19]

The commission also quoted scientists who swore to electricity's ability to paralyze the brain:

> The velocity of the electric current is so great that the brain is paralyzed; is indeed dead before the nerves can communicate a sense of shock. Prof. Helmholtz estimates the interval necessary for nerve communication with the brain at one-tenth of a second. Professor Tyndal estimates that the electric discharge occurs in one hundred thousandth of a second, or ten thousand times more rapidly than nerve transmission.[20]

The report also detailed Dr. Fell's series of experiments in July 1887, in which dogs at a Buffalo pound were electrocuted. Based on these experiments, the commission concluded that electricity was the most "sufficient," "powerful," "rapid," and "humane" procedure; when electricity is used, death is final and "resuscitation . . . is impossible."[21] As it noted, "Perhaps the most potent agent known for the destruction of human life is electricity. Death, as a result, is instantaneous upon its application. The application may be made without the slightest injury to the officers charged therewith; the place for its infliction may be strictly private, and at the same time its certainty is beyond doubt."

With the support and endorsement of the revered inventor Thomas Edison,[22] the commission recommended:

> First, that the present method of execution, hanging, be "abolished" and that electricity be used instead;
>
> Second, that after death the body of the condemned immediately be given to scientists for experimental use after which time burial be in the prison cemetery;
>
> Third, that the date and time of executions be kept secret;
>
> Fourth, that the press should be barred from attending electrocutions; and
>
> Last, that executions take place only in State prisons "designated by the court in its judgment and death warrant."[23]

Why, one might wonder, would Thomas Edison, a man whose fame and fortune depended on the success of electricity, join in recommending that New York replace the noose with the electric chair? Why would the "Wizard of Menlo Park" risk linking electricity to death when he wanted to put electricity into the homes and onto the streets of every family and neighborhood in America? As Craig Brandon notes, Edison's endorsement was the result of "one of the greatest rivalries in the history of American technology between Thomas A. Edison and George Westinghouse Jr."[24]

In 1879 Thomas Edison had invented the first useable incandescent light bulb, which ran on a system called "direct current," or DC. In this system, electrons flow in one direction, from the positive side of the generator, through the light bulb to the negative side. Though revolutionary, direct current had some flaws: light bulbs closer to a generator faced the weakest resistance and burned brightly. Light bulbs farther away from the generator station faced greater resistance and as a result burned much less brightly. Indeed, as the resistance changed, so too did the voltage. Direct current was also very expensive. The system required thick wires made of copper.[25]

There was, however, another kind of electricity. "Alternating current," or AC, was a system in which generators switched the polarity of the two generator terminals so that electrons moved back and forth across the wire allowing for consistent resistance and voltage at every point.[26] This meant that no matter where the light bulb sat in the circuit, it burned as bright as the next bulb. Transformers of alternating current could regulate the voltage in the circuit, which in turn allowed electricity to be sent safely over long distances.[27]

Though Edison could have used this cheaper and more effective system—he was the first American inventor to own the rights to the European AC system—he stuck with his original plan and by the late 1800s had already produced and sold equipment for the direct current system to a number of major cities. When George Westinghouse, the famous engineer, bought the rights to the AC patent, which Edison had previously rejected, and started his own electrical lighting company, Edison launched a publicity campaign against alternating current. At first Edison was unthreatened by Westinghouse's success. But in 1887, when Edison's own employees began to complain about the difficulties of the direct current system and rising customer preference for alternating current, Edison sent out "A Warning from the Edison Electric Light Company."[28]

The document, based on research done in Edison's Menlo Park laboratory on cats and dogs, detailed many examples of "mishaps with high voltage lights and transmission lines" that used alternating current.[29] In the section captioned "Caution 4. Danger," it explained that "Human life is endangered by electricity only when the electric pressure employed is sufficient to overcome the resistance offered by the body."[30] In direct current's "low-tension system" no one had lost their life. Alternating current, on the other hand, which ran at a higher frequency, would inevitably lead to injury or death. The president of Edison's company, Edward H. Johnson, cited six newspaper articles that detailed the dangers of Westinghouse's system and recounted instances in which human and animal interaction with alternating current had already resulted in serious injury or death.

But Edison and his company did not end their campaign with this warning. Edison had his engineers continue to run and publicize animal experiments to show the dangers of alternating current. In addition, he lobbied state legislatures to limit the voltage level of power lines to 300 volts—enough for the direct current system, but not sufficient for Westinghouse's system.[31] But it was his attempts to persuade New York to use alternating current in its new electric chair that did the greatest damage to Westinghouse and truly launched the "Battle of the Currents."[32]

Edison was aided in this effort by Southwick and Harold P. Brown—a former worker at the Brush electric company and a consultant.[33] On June 5, 1888, just one day after the New York electric chair bill (proposed by the Gerry Commission) was passed and signed into law, Brown published a letter in the *New York Evening Post* calling on the New York Board of Electrical Control to "forbid the use of the 'damnable' alternating current in the city because it was too dangerous."[34] In addition, Brown worked with the department of prisons to design and build the electric chair, which would be used for the first time in the execution of William Kemmler. The chair would run on alternating current.

From Kemmler's 1890 execution to 2010 more than eighty of America's botched executions have involved electrocution. In some of these executions, the condemned had to be shocked more times than the three-shock limit designated in most state protocols.[35] Some electrocutions were plagued by mechanical breakdowns; others resulted in fire, smoke, the smells of burning flesh, and a prolonged period from the start to the completion of the execution. Still other electrocutions were marred by a prisoner's fighting with the execution team. And two men, Willie Francis and F. G. Bullen, had to be executed twice.

What follow are the stories of how the "science" of electrocution strayed from its governing protocols and betrayed the promises of "humanity" and "painlessness" made by proponents of the electric chair.

William Kemmler

At five o'clock in the morning on August 6, 1890, Warden Charles Durston woke William Kemmler in his Auburn Prison cell. Just over sixty minutes later, Kemmler would become the first man put to death in the electric chair.[36] In his final hour, he ate a small breakfast, spoke with the prison chaplain, and participated in a religious service.[37] At 6:38 A.M., just thirty minutes after the witnesses arrived at the prison, Kemmler, wearing a new grey and yellow suit and looking serene, entered the death chamber behind Durston.[38] "The coolest man in the party"[39] was about to be killed in what would forever be known as a "horrible,"[40] "ghastly,"[41] and "bungling"[42] job.

Before his execution, Kemmler gave a short speech in which he wished everyone good luck. Then "Kemmler easily settled back into the chair . . . turned calmly to the Warden and in such tones as one might speak to a barber who was shaving him, said calmly: 'Now take your time and do it all right, Warden. There is no rush. I don't want to take any chances on this thing, you know?'"[43]Believing that a strap was loose, he asked Durston to tighten it.

When all eleven straps around Kemmler's body, face, arms, and legs were properly in place, Durston ordered the electric current turned on.[44] A moment later, Kemmler's body convulsed, then became perfectly rigid as electricity streamed through him. The current was turned off and the attending physician, Dr. Balch, checked Kemmler. He was not dead.

Sometime after the first shock Kemmler began to drool; his chest heaved, and he made strange noises. The warden again ordered the current turned on. But this time, as the electricity pulsed through Kemmler's body, white smoke appeared and a "pungent and sickening odor" filled the death chamber.[45] After seventy-three seconds the current was finally turned off. The execution lasted a total of eight minutes, during which time Kemmler received electric shocks of up to 2,000 volts. Kemmler's death was anything but painless and anything but humane. It would be the first in a long line of electrocution's gruesome spectacles.

Kemmler, one of eleven children, was born in May 1860 in Philadelphia to German immigrants.[46] He dropped out of school at age eleven and began to work, first at his father's butcher shop, then later selling newspapers and shining shoes.[47] His parents died when he was a teenager—his father from an infection and his mother from alcoholism. After their deaths, Kemmler took a job at a brickyard,[48] saved enough money to buy a horse and a cart, and became a vegetable peddler in New York City. When he was not working, Kemmler acquired a reputation for his love of alcohol and his hot temper.

In 1888, he eloped with Matilda "Tillie" Ziegler just days after getting tricked into marrying another woman when he was drunk. Kemmler soon moved to Buffalo[49] and changed his name to John Hort in an attempt to evade his "first wife." There he started a successful peddling business.[50] But his domestic life was anything but successful. Kemmler and Ziegler fought constantly,[51] and when drunk he got jealous and violent.

On the morning of March 29, one of William and Tillie's domestic disputes took a lethal turn. Kemmler, after a long night of drinking, accused her of planning to run away with another man. Neighbors heard screaming, and at the peak of their argument Kemmler attacked Tillie with a hatchet,[52] striking her twenty-six times.[53] As Tillie's four-year-old daughter, Emma, told authorities, "Pappa hit mamma with the hatchet when she was lying on the floor."[54]

Kemmler himself confessed to a neighbor, "I've killed her. I had to do it. There was no help for it. I'll hang for the deed. Either one of us had to die."[55] After a day of questioning by the police, Kemmler repeated his confession and admitted killing Tillie in a jealous rage. She had, he explained, owned up to having an affair with his friend and coworker John DeBella.[56]

Kemmler's trial lasted only a few days. On May 14, 1889, he was convicted of murder in the first degree and was sentenced to death by Judge Henry Childs. Childs told him:

> The sentence of the court is that for the crime of murder in the first degree, whereof you stand convicted, within the week commencing on Monday, the 24th of June, 1889, and within the walls of Auburn State Prison, or within the yard or enclosure adjoining thereto, you suffer the penalty of death, to be inflicted by the application of electricity as provided by the Code of Criminal Procedure of the State of New York, and that in the meantime you be removed to, and until the infliction of such punishment, be kept in solitary confinement at said Auburn State Prison.[57]

This sentence would make Kemmler the first human guinea pig for New York's new execution method.

Indeed Kemmler became a living, breathing advertisement for the pro-electrocution cause. There was nothing sympathetic about him or his case, and his guilt was undisputed. It would not be hard, death penalty advocates believed, to garner public support to execute this terrible man in the new electric chair. Nonetheless some opposed electrocution, even for Kemmler. They believed that it would be more gruesome and torturous than even the rope. George Westinghouse opposed the execution for fear that the new electric chair would discredit his alternating current system,[58] and he secretly hired W. Bourke Cockran, a famous New York attorney, to aid Kemmler on appeal. If his conviction could be overturned or the electric chair found to be unconstitutional, Westinghouse would win the "battle of the currents."

On May 20, Charles Hatch, Kemmler's trial lawyer, filed the first postconviction action, a writ of habeas corpus. In fact, Hatch did not argue that Kemmler's conviction was faulty.[59] Instead, he contended that his client "was entitled to be released because the death penalty imposed under the statute constituted cruel and unusual punishment."[60]

While considering the habeas corpus petition, Judge S. Edwin Day granted a stay of execution and, in an unconventional move, appointed Tracy C. Becker, a well-known lawyer and law professor in Buffalo, to act as an "administrative referee" in a sequence of hearings.[61] In these hearings a number of experts testified about the efficacy of electrocution as a mechanism of death.[62]

On July 30, the legal face-off over alternating current and direct current began. Cockran first questioned Harold Brown, who was secretly working for Edison. Brown said that "the alternating or Westinghouse current [was] the deadliest current and the one which should be used for killing criminals."[63] He described experiments he had conducted at Menlo Park on animals to determine the exact amount of electricity needed to successfully and painlessly kill.[64] He detailed the different voltages and lengths of time tested on each subject,[65] and explained how the experiments proved that Westinghouse's "high-tension alternating current was dangerous," while Edison's "arc-light currents could be rendered comparatively harmless."[66] Brown concluded that alternating current was the only means of instantaneously and painlessly killing a human being with electricity.[67]

But Cockran, a skilled litigator, "induced [Brown] to admit that from experiments made with electricity upon animals only an inferential knowledge was gained as to its effect upon a man, similarly applied, and that not even from fatal accidents which had occurred could it be determined absolutely just how quickly or painlessly death had followed the coming in contact with the current."[68] Nonetheless, Brown continued to defend the use of alternating current. Cockran called a number of other witnesses, among them Elbridge T. Gerry, electricians working for Westinghouse, Daniel Gibbons, and a member of the New York Board of Electrical Control who had witnessed some of Brown's experiments and testified that some of the animals in the studies had not died instantaneously. Most of these witnesses admitted that death by electricity was anything but painless.[69]

Though Cockran's case seemed convincing, when Deputy Attorney General William A. Poste, representing the state, questioned Edison, the tide changed. Maintaining an air of impartiality, Edison proceeded carefully and began by simply describing the differences between the two types of currents. When asked if electricity could be fatal, Edison acknowledged that either alternating current or continuous (direct) current could be used to produce death. On the basis of his experiments, however, he contended that alternating current had a greater ability to kill than direct current: "The perfectly continuous current [didn't] seem to have much effect upon the nerves; for instance . . . you take eight volts and you could not feel it, whereas by taking an alternating current of three volts it [is] about as much as you can stand."[70] Death by alternating current would be easier, instantaneous, and painless. Newspapers published Edison's testimony as quickly as they could. "The Wizard's" word was taken as gospel,[71] and his testimony fundamentally altered the trajectory of the hearing.

On September 17, Judge Day received Becker's report on the hearings and heard oral arguments. At this point, Cockran claimed that the electric chair constituted "cruel and unusual punishment." With tests on animals only, and no certainty around executing human beings, the likelihood of error, Cockran said, was unacceptably high.[72] Attorney General Tabor replied that the evidence presented to Becker established that electrocution was a painless method.

Judge Day handed down his decision on October 9, 1889. He found that electrocution caused painless and immediate death, and as a result, death by electrocution was not cruel and unusual punishment. He held that the electric chair bill, New York Criminal Procedure Law 505, did not violate the Eighth Amendment.[73]

In time, Kemmler's case would be the first Eighth Amendment challenge to capital punishment to reach the United States Supreme Court. In their petition to the Court, Kemmler's attorneys stated:

The petitioner is under sentence of death in the Northern District of New York, under a statute of New York, which imposes the punishment of death by the passing through his body of a current of electricity sufficient, in the opinion of the warden of the State Prison, to cause his death, which current is to be continued until it kills him; the statute also leaves it to the warden to fix the day and hour of his death, and contains other features which he here asserts are in violation of the Fourteenth Amendment. These features abridge his privileges and immunities as a citizen of the United States and deprive him of his life without due process of law.

Chief Justice Melville Fuller wrote the Court's majority opinion stating, as noted in Chapter 1, that "Punishments are cruel because they involve torture or a lingering death, but the punishment of death is not cruel within the meaning of that word as used in the Constitution. It implies something inhuman and barbarous, something more than the mere causing of dissolution."[74] New York's electrocution bill, he said, was designed to provide "the most humane and practical method known to modern science of carrying into effect the sentence of death in capital cases."[75] Though some methods of execution could be deemed "cruel and unusual punishment," electrocution was not one of them.

Kemmler's fate was sealed. Though Kemmler's electrocution was supposed to be the beginning of a new humane age of capital punishment, unfortunately it became the first in a long line of cases in which an electrocution was botched.

Philip Jackson

Forty years after Kemmler's execution, on the morning of May 28, 1928, two guards and the prison chaplain arrived at Philip Jackson's cell to accompany him to the death house.[76] The condemned was then housed in the south wing of the District of Columbia jail in a corner cell,[77] a long walk to his final destination. Jackson, a thirty-year-old black man, made his way along hallways, around the rotunda of the jail, and down thirteen iron steps with the guards on either side of him, pulling at his arms.[78] The guards led the way, while he walked stoically and "stolidly."

Before Jackson, the last man to have made the walk to his death in the District had been hanged three years earlier for killing three policemen.[79] On this grim morning, the electric chair had replaced the noose and the gallows. As Jackson arrived at his destination, he "fixed his eyes on the clergyman, ignoring the guards strapping his arms and legs."[80] The clergyman recited a psalm. When Jackson was securely strapped in, a mask was placed over his face, stifling his words. Just as the psalm was finished, the guards and the clergyman stepped away from the chair, and Captain George Ratherdale, a prison guard of thirty years' experience, threw the switch.[81]

When the current reached Jackson, he "lunged forward against the straps . . . [then he] slumped in the chair, his head hanging down."[82] When the current was turned off, "his chest rose and fell once as if he were breathing a sigh of relief. Dr. Adcock [the physician in attendance] placed a stethoscope over his heart, listened a moment, then stepped back and shook his head."[83] Again, Ratherdale threw the switch, and again Jackson's body lurched forward and strained against the straps. He went limp in the chair but continued to breathe. Four more shocks and seventeen minutes later, Jackson was finally pronounced dead.[84]

The Capitol grounds were a common shortcut for Daisy Welling to take at night on her way home from work at a local hotel. On the evening of February 18, 1927, as Mrs. Welling, a thirty-five-year-old telephone operator, made her way through the trees in the darkness, she was struck on the back of the head with a brick and crumbled in a heap on the ground. Philip Jackson, her assailant, then dragged her behind nearby bushes to rob and rape her.[85] Hours later, the woman would be found in "a dying condition."[86] Though she had a fractured skull, Welling was able to describe the suspect to the police: her "assailant . . . [was] a negro of light complexion."[87]

During that week in February, two other assaults on white women by black men occurred in D.C. The city went on high alert. Congress passed a resolution "proposing rewards for the capture of the man who assaulted" the telephone operator.[88] Four days later, police took Jackson into custody for the assault on Mrs. Welling and a number of other crimes in the area.

After his arrest, Jackson was taken to the scene of the crime, where he reenacted it for investigators; later he signed a confession.[89] At Jackson's trial his attorney, Mr. John H. Williams, mounted a two-pronged defense. First, he argued that the confession was "obtained . . . by use of 'third degree' methods."[90] Second, he claimed that Jackson had an alibi. His landlady testified that he "came home between 8 and 9 o'clock . . . [that] he went to 231 Third Street Northeast where he had his meals and returned shortly. A little after 9 o'clock, she [said] he passed her going upstairs to his room."[91]

Jackson's trial lasted three days. His attorney's attempt to put him on the stand during the trial turned out to be futile since Jackson did not seem to understand what was going on in the courtroom.[92] On the twenty-seventh of April, "a jury of [all] white men returned a verdict of guilty and added the words 'with the death penalty.'"[93] The execution was set for July 1, 1927. Contending that his client was insane, Jackson's lawyer asked the trial judge for a stay of execution.[94]

Newspapers described the convicted criminal as a "moron" and "stupid."[95] Indeed Jackson, who was illiterate and barely capable of signing his name, certainly seemed to be someone of "[low] intelligence."[96] Justice Hoehling rejected the insanity plea and the stay.[97]

It was not until a few newspapermen discovered that Jackson was "the offspring of an incestuous relationship between a brother and a sister"[98] that a thirty-day stay was granted.[99] Yet the trial judge remained unconvinced of the insanity claim. As a last resort, Jackson's lawyer prepared a petition for executive clemency based upon the "possible insanity of Jackson."[100] President Coolidge, however, declined to grant Jackson clemency.

Though he went to his death calmly, Jackson was taken from this world violently. Needing twice the maximum number of prescribed electric shocks and taking seventeen minutes to die, he suffered a prolonged and painful death. Yet again, the use of the latest technology of state killing had turned into a gruesome spectacle of suffering.

Clay Daniels

On December 3, 1955, South Carolina was set to execute two men, Willie Marion Daniels Jr. and his older brother Clay. Willie was executed first, and he died without a fuss as he murmured in a nervous, hushed tone: "I hope I'm saved."[101] Clay would, however, meet his maker in a different manner.

As Clay, a twenty-six-year-old black male, made his way to the death chamber in the South Carolina Penitentiary, he walked "meekly" and quietly to the place where his brother had been executed just minutes before. Captain Fuller Goodman, who was in charge of the execution, escorted the condemned to the electric chair with the help of two lieutenants, a chaplain, and the prison doctor, Dr. M. Whitfield Chatham.[102] However, before the 165-pound Daniels could be strapped into the chair, he jumped up.[103] For twenty minutes he battled the lieutenants and prison officials, punching, kicking, biting, and scratching them as twenty witnesses watched.[104] Only when Daniels was sufficiently exhausted could the prison guards and personnel who responded to his aggression get the prisoner back into the chair.[105] Goodman, so perturbed by the struggle, forgot to ask Clay if he had any final words before the current was turned on.[106]

But the disruption in the execution process was not over. After two shocks and the usual time it takes for electrocution to do its work, Daniels's heart was still beating. Three more shocks and several minutes later Dr. Chatham declared Clay dead.[107] Captain Goodman said Clay's execution was the longest on record, and Dr. Chatham surmised that "the strenuous resistance"[108] and exertion by the inmate "stimulated the heart."[109]

Born in Charleston County, South Carolina, in 1929, Clay Daniels had a wife and two children by the time he was twenty.[110] He worked for three years as an itinerant farmer and day laborer for Conyers Brown, in

South Carolina, between 1952 and 1955. Just two weeks before the crime for which they would be sentenced to die, Clay's younger brother Willie came to live with him in his small house on Highway 15, near the line between Sumter and Lee counties.[111]

On August 12, 1955, a girl from Salem, N.Y., who was in South Carolina visiting her grandparents, went with Danny Smith to a "lover's lane" near the "Swimming Pen."[112] Danny and the girl had only been there a short time when someone hit him over the head with a steel bar.[113] Before the couple could do anything, Danny was hit a second time from behind.

During the fray the girl escaped out the passenger side of the car. Once outside, the young girl watched helplessly as a black man beat Danny until he was unconscious.[114] Danny's assailant then dragged the girl into a nearby wooded area,[115] where he called out to someone else, "Junior come here," and a second black man soon appeared.[116]

The man who had attacked Danny raped her first, then he held her down while "Junior" assaulted her. After the attack, the men led her toward a road, but when a car approached the two men ran.[117] Authorities were soon notified and started looking for two young black men, one who went by the name of "Junior."[118] Using a brown cloth cap found at the scene of the crime, the officers attempted to track the pair with bloodhounds.[119]

At approximately 5 A.M. the search party approached Daniels's home on Highway 15.[120] There they found shoes that matched tracks left at the crime scene, as well as wallets and watches belonging to the victims.[121] Not long after, they arrested Clay and Willie.[122]

Their trial lasted only five and a half hours. The eighteen-year-old victim was the first witness.[123] Though she remained collected and calm throughout her testimony, she quietly sobbed when other witnesses recounted details of the crime. Dr. Ragsdale Hewitt, the physician who had treated the young girl, confirmed that there was no question that she had been raped. At the conclusion of the trial, the all-white, male jury returned its verdict after deliberating for twelve minutes.[124]

Just after the jury's verdict was announced, and before the sentence was handed down, Clay Daniels, who had remained placid throughout the trial, raised his hand and said, "Mercy, judge of the court, Lord have mercy on me, I'm sorry for what I did." But the judge had no mercy on Clay or his brother, both of whom were sentenced to death.

Clay Daniels's execution was an uncommon one because it was botched in two ways, first in the struggle that occurred, and second in the multiple jolts of electricity that had to be administered. In the history of botched executions in the twentieth century, seven other electrocutions involved such a struggle between the condemned and those who were trying to put them to death.

Jesse Joseph Tafero

The evening before his execution, Jesse Joseph Tafero's mother, Kathleen, and a priest visited his cell. Though the last meal he requested was prepared for him, the forty-three-year-old man did not eat most of the scrambled eggs, pepperoni, Italian bread, tomatoes, steamed broccoli, and strawberry shortcake he had requested.[125] Then, at 7:01 on Friday morning, Tafero was brought to the place where he would be electrocuted.[126]

Tafero was strapped into the electric chair just like the twenty-one death row inmates before him whom Florida had executed since the Supreme Court lifted its ban on capital punishment in 1976. He was gagged and a black leather mask was put over his face.[127] At 7:07 A.M., when he received the first jolt of electricity, a shower of sparks and flames surged from his head. But the shock did not kill him.

Tafero continued to move and breathe.[128] Two minutes later another 2,000 volts was sent through his body. Again, flames engulfed his headpiece and a cloud of smoke floated above the electric chair. Tafero's heart continued to beat. He was then given a third and final shock. Seven-inch flames rose from his head, and the smell of burning flesh filled the room.[129] Through each shock, Tafero "clenched his fists . . . [and] convulsed" as if he were in extreme pain, and he continued to breath.[130] At 7:13, he was pronounced dead.[131]

Tafero was a wanderer with a lengthy record of robbery, assault, and attempted rape.[132] By 1976 he was on parole after serving only seven years of a thirty-five-year sentence. When he met Sonia "Sunny" Jacobs, she was a self-proclaimed "peace and love vegetarian."[133] To her, Jesse seemed quiet and kind—he liked to paint—and Sunny thought she had found her soul mate. In February 1976, Jacobs, who considered herself Tafero's "common law wife," moved to Fort Lauderdale, Florida, to live with Tafero, who was the father of her youngest child. Later that month, Jesse, Sunny, and her two children hitched a ride with one of Tafero's prison friends, Walter Rhodes, who was also on parole, and headed to West Palm Beach to get some money from Sunny's parents.

In the early hours of February 20, a Florida Highway Patrol cruiser pulled into the rest area just off Interstate 95 near the Forty-Eighth Street overpass to do a "routine check of the vehicles parked there."[134] Rhodes, Tafero, Jacobs, and her two children were all asleep inside a green Chevrolet Camaro.[135] Trooper Phillip Black, in plainclothes, and his friend Donald Irwin, a Canadian constable on vacation with his family in Florida, approached the vehicle. Black noticed a gun on the driver's side floorboard. Rapping on the window, he woke up Rhodes and ordered him out of the car.

Eyewitnesses' descriptions of the events that followed differ. One truck driver heard shots as both Tafero and Rhodes got out of the car.[136] Another eyewitness said that Officer Black pulled a gun on them. He heard several shots but could not say where they came from.[137] Meanwhile, according to Rhodes, who would later plead guilty and testify against Tafero and Jacobs, as Officer Black asked him to step outside the vehicle Tafero took the gun from the floorboard of the driver's seat and passed another gun to his girlfriend in the backseat.

Rhodes stated that he was standing outside the car as the state trooper attempted to get Tafero out of the vehicle. At this point Rhodes heard a shot and saw Jacobs holding a gun, which Tafero then grabbed from her and used to shoot the two officers again.[138] Rhodes, Tafero, Jacobs, and her children fled the scene in Black's patrol car, leaving the trooper and his friend for dead.[139] The group later ditched the patrol car and hijacked another one, kidnapping the owner, but they were soon detained at a police roadblock further down the highway.[140]

Tafero and Jacobs told a very different story. In their version, they were catching up on some sleep in a rest stop when they were awoken by the state trooper, who asked them to get out of the car. Tafero was "arm-locked" by the officer when shots were fired. Jacobs instinctively ducked into the car to cover her children. The next thing she knew, two officers were lying on the ground covered in blood, and Rhodes was screaming at Tafero and Jacobs to get into the police car. After driving north on I-95, they pulled into a housing complex in Deerfield Beach, where they forced Leonard Levinson, a sixty-three-year-old resident, into his Cadillac at gunpoint.[141] They were, however, soon apprehended.

Sunny and Jesse were tried separately on two counts of first-degree murder and one count each of robbery and kidnapping. Walter Rhodes was the state's primary witness in both trials. In Tafero's first trial, the eyewitness testimony of the two truck drivers, Pierce Hyman and Robert McKenzie, was very damaging. The jury also heard from a jailhouse snitch, Ellis Marlow Haskew, who claimed that Tafero had told him he would never let himself be sent back to prison, even though he was violating his parole.[142] Ballistics proved that the gun in Tafero's possession at the time of the arrest was the gun that had killed both of the police officers.

The prosecution failed to mention that tests performed on Rhodes, Tafero, and Jacobs immediately following their arrest showed that Rhodes, not Tafero or Jacobs, had gunpowder residue on his person consistent with "having discharged a weapon."[143] The residue found on Tafero and Jacobs was consistent with "handling an unclean or recently discharged weapon, or *possibly* discharging a weapon."[144]

In spite of the fact that the prosecution's star witness was himself a suspect, the eyewitness testimony was contradictory, the jailhouse snitch was receiving compensation for his testimony, and the forensic evidence was inconclusive, Tafero was found guilty of first-degree murder. Judge Daniel Futch, known as "Maximum Dan," a former highway patrolman who wore his police hat in the courtroom, imposed the death penalty.[145]

In the years between his sentence and execution Tafero would compile a long record of unsuccessful appeals. The Circuit Court of Broward County affirmed his conviction on his first appeal,[146] a decision which was affirmed by the Florida Supreme Court. That court noted that

> Tafero challenges the sufficiency of the evidence to convict him of murder, but the evidence against him is overwhelming. . . . Similarly, we conclude from our review of the record that the state presented sufficient evidence to support Tafero's kidnapping and robbery convictions. We next consider alleged trial procedure violations. . . . Neither the voir dire of the prospective jurors nor any other portion of the trial reflects that those selected to try this case were not impartial or unable to lay aside any impressions or opinions which may have resulted from pretrial publicity. The jurors vowed that they could and would decide the case on the merits from the evidence presented in open court. We are unable to discern that they violated this oath in any way. . . . Tafero also feels that the trial judge, an ex-highway patrolman, should have recused himself. . . . [However] No personal bias or prejudice had been demonstrated in this case. The mere fact that Judge Futch was, in the distant past, a highway patrol officer does not support a claim of bias or prejudice on the judge's part. . . . We now turn to the death sentence. . . . Tafero claims the penalty assessed him was disproportionate to the offense. We believe otherwise. Further, we reiterate that the death statute provides a sufficient standard for weighing the aggravating and mitigating circumstances.

Tafero again unsuccessfully appealed to the Supreme Court of Florida in November 1983 and 1984, March 1988, and May 1990. The Eleventh Circuit Court of Appeals reviewed Tafero's case twice, in 1986 and 1989, and Tafero appealed his case to the United States Supreme Court in June 1987, April 1990, and May 1990. By then, he had exhausted all of his appeals.

On the morning of May 4, 1990, the world learned about one of the most gruesome botched executions in American history. "In Florida executions, electricity passes from a wire into a sponge filled with saline solution that is placed directly on the head," Bob Macmaster, the former Florida State Prison spokesman, explained after the execution. "The old sponge had been used in 21 executions before it was replaced for the Tafero execution."[147] Indeed, in the previous executions a "natural ocean sponge" was used to help convey the electric chair's voltage to the skull. The morning of Tafero's execution, "with the sponge wearing thin, prison officials replaced it with a synthetic sponge," which in turn caused the problems with his electrocution.[148]

Newspapers all over the country published Florida State Prison officials' responses to the botching:

> After the first two jolts, Tafero's chest moved, and he appeared to continue breathing. But Macmaster said that prison physician, Frank Kilgo, believes that Tafero, 43, was dead within seconds of the first jolt and said there was no indication he felt pain. "It was not (human) tissue that was burning. It was the headpiece," Macmaster said. "There was some arcing in the headpiece itself. We believe he was dead after the first few seconds. I believe he was unconscious from the moment (electricity) hit him."[149]

But those who witnessed the execution, who saw Tafero's clenched fists and his body convulse with each shock, those who saw the flames and the smoke and the ashes, those who smelled the burning flesh, confirmed that he was in fact alive until the last shock and that pain was likely unavoidable as he was burned to death. Following Tafero's botched execution, approximately one hundred protesters marched from the Florida State Prison to Atlanta to express their opposition to the death penalty.[150] But botched electrocutions were not merely the concern of anti–death penalty activists. As electrocutions proved to be increasingly gruesome and painful, prison officials, politicians, and society at large began to question the state's "humane" method of execution.

Pedro Luis Medina

On Monday, March 23, 1997, Pedro Medina, in the company of his attorneys and his pastor, the Reverend Glenn Dickson, learned that his last legal appeal had failed.[151] At the time, Medina told his spiritual advisor that "[He was] not afraid of dying because [he had] Jesus in [his] heart."[152] At 4:30 A.M. Medina had his last meal, a Delmonico steak, well done, French fries, black beans and rice, a yucca salad, a block of American cheese, some coconut pie, a quart of butter pecan ice cream, and a Pepsi.[153]

Medina left his cell at 7 A.M. wearing a "crisp white dress shirt,"[154] and he entered, calmly and deliberately, the six-by-nine-foot room which housed Florida's electric chair.[155] As the guards strapped him into "Old Sparky," Medina squeezed his lips and looked up.[156] Never shifting his focus, he uttered his final words, "I am innocent," before the guards tightened a strap across his chin and mouth and placed a black mask over his head and face.[157]

At 7:06 A.M. an executioner in a black hood threw the switch.[158] For two minutes, 2,000 volts of electricity pulsed through Medina's body.[159] As we noted in Chapter 1, within moments of the current being turned on, flames shot out of the right side of his face mask.[160] The orange and blue flames rose a foot in the air, filling the execution chamber with a thick smoke and the offensive scent of burning flesh.[161]

Medina's body twitched and strained against the straps, and his hands curled into tight fists as the electricity surged through him.[162] Witnesses said they saw him take a deep breath when the first current was shut off, and then again thirty seconds later.[163] "They're burning him alive," one of the witnesses said aloud.[164]

Pedro Luis Medina was a Cuban émigré who had spent much of his teenage years in and out of mental hospitals in his home country. In May 1980 he arrived in the United States to live with his sponsor and half-sister in Orlando.[165] While there, Medina was befriended by his neighbor, Dorothy James, an elementary school gym teacher. By late 1981 he had moved to Tampa.

Sometime between the night of April 3 and the early morning hours of April 4, 1982, Dorothy James was gagged, stabbed repeatedly, and left for dead in the bedroom of her apartment.[166] Her Cadillac was also missing from her apartment. Four days later, Florida highway patrol-man R. A. Wilson spotted a Cadillac, its motor running, parked in a rest stop off Interstate 10. He also noticed that gas was leaking from the car. Before taking a closer look, Wilson checked on the license plate and learned that the car might be connected to a homicide in Orlando.[167] He called for backup and officers searched the vehicle, finding "a silver colored, wood-handled knife with a four inch blade . . . beneath a hub-cap lying on the rear floorboard of the car."[168] Medina was arrested and charged with first-degree murder.[169] His trial began on March 15, 1983.

Throughout the trial Medina was so unstable that he spent most of it shackled and handcuffed.[170] The prosecution called twenty-six wit-nesses; the defense would call just one, the defendant himself.[171] The guilt phase of the trial lasted for three days and the penalty phase began on the first day of April. Medina, the state argued, murdered Dorothy James for money in a cruel manner.[172] On April 11, 1983, the jury, find-ing that the aggravating circumstances outweighed mitigating circum-stances, voted to recommend the death penalty for the murder convic-tion and five years in jail for the auto theft.[173]

Medina appealed his case twelve times in the fourteen years between his conviction and his execution, and his lawyers raised thirteen claims in their appeals. The Eleventh Circuit Court, in his fifth appeal, held that "none of his claims [warranted] relief . . . [and that] the district court did not err in denying his petition for a writ of habeas corpus."[174] Every one of his subsequent appeals also failed, though in one instance the Supreme Court of Florida ordered an evidentiary hearing to deter-mine whether Medina was psychologically competent to be executed.[175] Justice Overton, writing the majority opinion, explained:

> If the circuit judge, upon review of the motion and submissions, has reasonable grounds to believe that the prisoner is insane . . . , the judge shall grant a stay of execution and may order further proceedings which

may include a hearing pursuant to rule 3.812. Medina points to the reports of two psychologists and one psychiatrist which his counsel submitted pursuant to rule 3.811(d)(4). In those reports, the psychologists and psychiatrist state that in their expert opinions, Medina is insane . . . as defined in rule 3.811(b). We agree with Medina that an evidentiary hearing . . . should be held in this case. We conclude that . . . it was an abuse of discretion not to have an evidentiary hearing pursuant to rule 3.812 in view of the conflicting opinions of the experts. For this reason, we have stayed Medina's execution. We reverse the circuit court's order denying the motion . . . , and we remand to the circuit court for a hearing pursuant to 3.811(e) within twenty-one days of the date this opinion is filed. . . . If, at the conclusion of the hearing, the court shall find, by clear and convincing evidence, that the prisoner is insane . . . , the court shall enter its order continuing the stay of the death warrant; otherwise, the court shall deny the motion and enter its order dissolving the stay of execution.[176]

As instructed by the Supreme Court of Florida, the circuit court had two mental health experts examine Medina, both of whom concluded that he was mentally and psychologically able to understand the execution and the reason for it.[177] Three days later the court "held a de novo evidentiary hearing."[178] Testimony on behalf of Medina was given by seven attorneys, three mental health experts, and six death row inmates. The court was also shown videotaped interviews with Medina, corrections officers, and other mental health experts who found him to be competent. They also heard from a sheriff's deputy, thirteen corrections officers, and a prison chaplain. In the end, the circuit court concluded that

It is uncontroverted that Defendant has displayed bizarre behavior over the past few weeks, months, and even years. It is important to remember, though, that some of his behavior is not unusual behavior for inmates to engage in. Additionally, it can probably be said that Defendant suffers from some form of mental pathology or mental illness. However, this Court is not charged with the duty of determining precisely what, if any, mental pathologies or infirmities the Defendant suffers from. Rather, the issue is whether counsel for Defendant has established by clear and convincing evidence that Defendant lacks the mental capacity to understand the fact of the pending execution and the reason for it.[179]

The court found that on the basis of "the totality of *all* the evidence and testimony," Medina was capable of understanding both *that* he was going to be executed and *why* he was going to be executed.

By late March, Medina's final appeals to the Florida Supreme Court and the U.S. Supreme Court had failed. Moreover, Florida governor Lawton Chiles refused to grant clemency, despite numerous letters he and the Florida Board of Clemency had received from Pope John Paul II and members of different churches around the country.[180] Medina would soon have to face the chair. Little did he know that just as it had done seven years earlier in Tafero's execution, Old Sparky would once again live up to its name.

The medical examiner's report released in the week after the execution argued that problems were caused by a piece of corroded copper screen in the chair's headpiece, which is typically used to conduct electricity.[181] In contrast, Michael S. Morse, an electrical engineer, contended that the fire was the result of a dry sponge being placed between the wet sponge and the conductive screen.[182] Regardless of the actual catalyst, "four pathologists present at the autopsy said the jolts from Florida's electric chair killed Medina 'instantly.'" Medical Examiner Stephen J. Nelson wrote that Medina "was not alive" to feel the blue and orange flames nor did he "feel a subsequent burn."[183] Most other witnesses weren't so sure that Medina's execution had been painless.

The Demise of Old Sparky

Starting with William Kemmler's death in 1890, electrocutions regularly failed to be the "humane" and "painless" executions the New York Medico-Legal Society and the state legislature promised they would be.

Just as the gruesomeness and images of pain associated with botched hangings led, at least in part, to the gallows' demise, the blood and gore attached to botched electrocutions—first of Jesse Tafero in 1990, then Pedro Medina in 1997, and finally Allen Lee Davis in 1999—led to the phasing out of the electric chair in the early 2000s.

After Tafero's botched execution in 1990, several Florida death row inmates—Thomas Provenzano, Judias Buenoano, William Squires, Kenneth Stewart, Leo Alexander Jones, and James William Hamblen—saw a chance to avoid their own impending executions and abolish the electric chair in one fell swoop. They filed for stays of their executions on the basis of newspaper reports about the malfunctioning chair.[184] The United States District Court ordered a hearing regarding Florida's electric chair. In July 1990 Professor Mike Morse tested the electric chair.[185] The test was a "success" and the district court was satisfied. When Provenzano appealed to the Florida Supreme Court, it too found "Old Sparky" to be constitutional and allowed executions to resume.

By 1999, however, there was increasing pressure on Florida to do something about its malfunctioning electric chair, as highlighted in Chapter 1. Four months after Davis's botched electrocution, "The United States Supreme Court rewrote a part of death penalty history" when it agreed, for the first time,[186] to consider whether Florida's electric chair violated the Eighth Amendment.[187] In response, Governor Jeb Bush called a special session of the Florida State Legislature to draft a lethal injection bill.[188]

Almost immediately, Florida death penalty proponents denounced electrocution as an out-of-date, unreliable technology and called for its replacement by lethal injection.[189] "Under lethal injection," a Florida newspaper explained, "the condemned is first sedated, then injected with deadly chemicals that painlessly and quickly paralyze the lungs and stop the heart."[190] As one judge observed, commenting on the continuing use of electrocution in Florida, "other less cruel methods of execution are available; lethal injection is readily available . . . and is generally considered more humane."[191] In a similar vein, the Florida Corrections

Commission recommended switching from electrocution to lethal injection. They noted that "Florida has an obligation to ensure that modern technologies keep pace with the level of competence in this area, and, just as changes have occurred in Florida's past in carrying out the death penalty, changes should again occur."[192] Several months after the Medina execution, Florida enacted legislation providing that if "electrocution is held to be unconstitutional . . . all persons sentenced to death for a capital crime shall be executed by lethal injection."[193]

At the turn of the twenty-first century, only Alabama, Nebraska, and Georgia retained electrocution as the sole method of execution.[194] In 1999, Alabama authorized lethal injection for those executed after July 1, 2002.[195] On October 25, 2001, the Georgia Supreme Court ruled death by electrocution unconstitutional, becoming the first state appellate court in the country to do so. Six years later, Nebraska, the final state retaining electrocution as the sole method of execution, abolished the chair.

In *State v. Mata*, the Nebraska Supreme Court found that the determination in *Kemmler*, that the electric chair was constitutional because "death was instantaneous," was based upon bad science and false assumptions.[196] "Our review of these early cases," the court said,

> illustrates that the U.S. Supreme Court's case law on electrocution relies on unexamined factual assumptions about an electric current's physiological effects on a human. This obvious omission in the court's jurisprudence results from three factors: (1) the Court's limited knowledge about an electrocution's effect on the human body (2) the states' desire to find a more humane method of execution than hanging, and (3) the Court's view, when electrocution was first introduced, that the Eighth Amendment was not intended as a restraint on state legislatures' determinations of punishment. *But that view has changed.* The Supreme Court has specifically held that the Eighth Amendment is a restraint on legislative power to impose punishment, and it has held the Eighth Amendment applies to the states through the Fourteenth Amendment.[197]

The Nebraska Supreme Court cited stories of horrifically "botched" electrocutions and concluded that electrocution "has proven itself a dinosaur more befitting the laboratory of Baron Frankenstein than the death chamber."[198] One hundred and eighteen years after the first execution by electricity, the electric chair became essentially extinct, and botched executions were, in part, the reason why.

CHAPTER 4

A Short and Unhappy History

The Gas Chamber

On March 8, 1921, the attention of the Nevada State Assembly was momentarily diverted from the mundane business of legislating when it was presented with a proposal to change that state's method of execution from hanging to lethal gas. Former Arizona district attorney Frank Curran, a staunch critic of the gallows, persuaded two Nevada assemblymen, J. J. Hart and Harry Bartlett, to introduce the so-called Humane Execution Bill, which would make Nevada the first state in the country to use lethal gas. As with every method employed before it, and every one to follow, proponents of the gas chamber claimed that it would be more humane than existing methods of execution, especially death by hanging.[1]

The Hart-Bartlett bill passed the State Assembly almost unanimously[2] before being sent on to the Senate where it was approved the very same day. Less than two weeks later, Governor Emmett Boyle, a longtime opponent of capital punishment, signed the bill into law.[3] Section 431 of the law stated:

> The judgment of death shall be inflicted by the administration of lethal gas. The execution shall take place within the limits of the state prison, wherein a suitable and efficient enclosure and proper means for the administration of such gas for that purpose shall be provided by the board of prison commissioners. The warden of the state prison must be present, and must invite a competent physician, and not less than six reputable citizens, over the age of twenty-one years, to be present at the execution; but no other persons shall be present at the execution.[4]

The Nevada law—in line with the most advanced thinking of the time—called for executions to take place while the condemned was asleep. Death row inmates were to be housed in air-tight, leak-proof cells, separate from other prisoners. On the day of execution, valves would be opened that would fill the chamber with gas, killing the prisoner painlessly.[5] The legislation, however, gave no details as to how the cell should be built or which form of gas should be used. As it turned out, the actual practice of execution by lethal gas diverged substantially from the statutory language.

With no inmates on death row, the governor and prison warden seemed to be in no hurry. But by December 1921, Nevada had sentenced its first person to be executed by lethal gas.

Though no gas chamber had been built in the United States prior to Nevada's death house at the Carson City penitentiary, death by lethal gas was not, at the start of the twentieth century, a new concept. The earliest documented use of lethal gas for the execution of prisoners was in the Dominican Republic after the slave revolt of 1791, when one of Napoleon Bonaparte's commanders filled a ship full of rebel slaves with sulfur dioxide gas, killing them all.[6] Almost a hundred years later, politicians and activists in the United States began to consider lethal gas as a potential improvement in death penalty practices.

In Pennsylvania, for example, the Medical Society reviewing the state's execution methods focused its attention on lethal gas. Many of its members thought that gassing was the most humane way to extinguish life.[7] Eventually a Medical Society committee recommended that carbonic acid be used as the lethal agent in all Pennsylvania executions.[8] As Dr. J. Chris Lange wrote in the *Pennsylvania Medical Journal*,

> The lethal agent selected is carbon dioxide. It is to be admitted into the cell in which the prisoner is confined through the influent pipe of the ventilator at the bottom of the cell. Death will happen in from three to eight minutes after the gas ascends to a level with the mouth and nose of the prisoner. To insure the absence of all punishment but death itself it is a necessity that the action of the heart be stilled during natural sleep. . . .

Experiments on animals, cats and dogs, have convinced the committee that these animals, though much more vigilant during sleep, and much more easily aroused from sleep than man, almost invariably succumb to this gas when asleep without stirring. The gas does not act as a poison in the usual sense of the word; it merely deprives the animal of oxygen by displacement of the air, the consequent death being the result of an auto-intoxication, at least in large part. . . . It is a species of starvation which is fatal in from 3 to 8 minutes.[9]

The doctor concluded by claiming that such a death—"without preliminaries" and "without the possibility of accidents"—would "leave the criminal little more to dread of the future than the common lot of all mankind." He promised, yet again, the technological revolution death penalty proponents had dreamed of.

While Pennsylvania did not adopt the gas chamber, lethal gas continued to be a topic of interest among those who sought an alternative to the gallows. Indeed, throughout the late 1800s and the first two decades of the 1900s, lethal gas was employed in a variety of other contexts. Starting in the 1870s and 1880s, the Society for the Prevention of Cruelty to Animals opened pounds throughout the United States which used gas to put down unwanted animals. The first such pound was opened in 1872.[10] Twenty years later, the president of the New York branch of the SPCA recommended that gas be used in animal euthanasia.[11] By 1910, the number of animal gassings had increased dramatically. In Baltimore, the SPCA used carbonic acid to kill 109 "worthless" dogs, "marauders," in just one day.[12] And in the year 1915 alone, the New York SPCA reported using gas to kill 276,683 animals.[13]

As the world went to war in 1914, lethal gas soon garnered attention as the newest and most cutting-edge weapon. At the start of the war, Germany had the world's most well-developed chemical industry. It came as no surprise then that it was the first to move forward aggressively with chemical warfare. At the battle of Ypres, in April 1915, German troops shot six thousand cylinders of liquid chlorine into French trenches.[14] Following their success at Ypres, the Germans continued their gas attacks throughout the war.

After many deadly German attacks that summer, the Allies tried to counter, selecting scientists and other high army officials to run labs and chemical factories.[15] The British chose Major Charles Howard Foulkes to head their program.[16] Assembling at Porton Down, the British War Department's testing site, Foulkes and his colleagues worked with a variety of lethal gasses, including chlorine, mustard, phosgene, and cyanide gas.[17]

The British and French first used tear gas in battle in January 1915.[18] This attack failed miserably when the gas cylinders they fired did not discharge in the field.[19] In response, the Germans deployed phosgene gas, a chemical approximately eighteen times as strong as chlorine.[20] At the Battle of the Somme, the British followed the German's lead and unleashed phosgene gas upon their enemies for the first time.[21] By 1917, both the British and the Germans had moved on to mustard gas, an even more lethal poison.[22]

By the time the United States entered the war, it had, with the efforts of its best scientists and the funds of the Rockefeller and Mellon fortunes,[23] started to work on producing new and improved poisons and protective gas masks. Led by Amos A. Fries, the U.S. military accomplished in a single month—in terms of the growth and production of a well-developed chemical industry—what the Germans had only managed to accomplish in four years.[24] By the end of the war, "100,000 tons of gas had been used by the various nations involved."[25] Some time would have to pass from the horrors of the war before lethal gas could be considered an acceptable execution method.

The postwar road to the first use of the gas chamber began on August 28, 1921, at eight in the morning, some 175 miles from Reno, Nevada, when Tom Quong Kee was found dead from a single gunshot at his cabin's front door.[26] Two days before, Hughie Sing and a companion, Gee Jon, took a taxi from Reno to the outskirts of a small town called Mina. They asked the driver, a man named Pappas, to wait there until they returned, but soon he got hungry and drove into town looking for food. Along the way, he caught up with Sing and Jon who were on foot. Dropping them off outside of a cabin, Pappas went to get beer.[27]

Returning thirty minutes later, he joined Sing and Jon as they drank, leaning against the taxi. Soon they started back to Reno.

In the meantime, Mina's deputy sheriff, J. W. Hamill, received a tip about two strangers who had been seen walking around the small town. The tip alleged that they were members of a Chinese gang who had been sent to Mina to carry out a hit.[28] Hamill immediately started a search for the two men and apprehended them without a fight on the highway as they were heading for Reno.[29]

Assuming that he would be freed if he cooperated, Sing confessed during his first night in jail.[30] On the basis of this confession and evidence from the crime scene, both men were tried and ultimately convicted of first-degree murder. The trial judge, J. Emmitt Walsh, sentenced them to death under Nevada's new death penalty law.[31]

James Frame, Sing and Jon's attorney, initiated the postconviction process by filing a motion for a new trial[32] and appealing his clients' convictions to the State Supreme Court. He contended that execution by lethal gas would constitute "cruel and unusual punishment" under Nevada's constitution.[33] In January 1923, the Nevada Supreme Court affirmed the district court judge's sentence and upheld Nevada's new death penalty law.[34] Frame's two subsequent efforts to get the State Supreme Court to intervene failed, as did his appeal to the United States Supreme Court.[35]

With all avenues of appeal exhausted and an execution date set for February 8, 1924, Sing and Jon's attorneys petitioned the state's Board of Pardons in a typical last-ditch effort to save their clients from the gas chamber. On January 25, 1924, the board turned down Jon's petition but commuted Sing's sentence, citing his youth and the fact that he was only an accomplice in Kee's murder. Gee Jon would face the gas chamber alone.[36]

By this time, the original idea of gassing an inmate in his cell while he slept had been abandoned. Instead, an old stone and concrete building in the prison yard—previously the prison barbershop—was converted into a specially designed gas chamber.[37] It was fitted with pipes, an exhaust fan, and glass windows on the front and back walls for witness viewing.[38] Perhaps most importantly, the room where the gas would be used was insulated in order to be "leak-proof."[39]

Nevada's food and drug commissioner, Sanford C. Dinsmore, advised the state as to the specific chemicals and apparatus that should be employed. He selected hydrocyanic acid (HCN), traditionally used for fumigating citrus trees, claiming that it was the deadliest and fastest-acting known poison.[40] Unfortunately, "The closest available commercial source for HCN was in Los Angeles, and no railroad would agree to transport the hazardous substance to Nevada."[41] Tom Pickett, an aide to the prison warden, was charged with traveling to Los Angeles and returning with a sufficient amount of the volatile liquid. Using his own truck, and accompanied by his wife, Pickett drove to a Los Angeles laboratory and returned with a substance allegedly powerful enough to kill a prisoner in a single breath.[42]

On the morning of February 8, 1924, Gee Jon nervously ate a traditional breakfast of ham, eggs, toast, and coffee. After finishing his last meal, the twenty-nine-year-old man had to be dragged, sobbing, to the gas chamber across the prison yard.[43] Once inside the chamber, Jon was strapped into a wooden chair that resembled the electric chairs used in other states. A second, nearby chair remained empty.[44] Alone in the converted concrete barbershop, Gee Jon, a man who spoke barely any English, met his fate as he inhaled deeply while the rest of the world held its breath and waited.

Thirty witnesses, newspapermen, physicians, prison officials, and politicians all crowded together in the prison yard to watch Jon's execution from behind the thick glass.[45] Many of them were concerned about their own safety.[46] But at 9:40 A.M., when the gas began pumping with a sickening hissing sound, even the faint smell of gas leaking from small holes in the death chamber could not divert their attention.[47]

Unbeknownst to them, the chemical properties of HCN—most crucially the fact that it only becomes gaseous and deadly at approximately seventy-nine degrees Fahrenheit[48]—would complicate the execution unfolding before them. The plan was to pump the HCN, which had been brought to the prison in its more stable liquid form, into the chamber, where a heating device was to warm the liquid as it left the pipes, and in so doing, turn it into poison gas.[49] However, February 8 was a particularly cold winter morning, and the heater inside of the chamber malfunctioned. The HCN left the pipes in both liquid and gaseous forms, pooling on the floor even as it also wafted into the air.[50]

In spite of this malfunction and the brief panic it caused prison officials, moments after the poison entered the chamber Jon's head fell forward.[51] Several minutes later he was still breathing, and his head rolled back and fell forward a number of times as he continued inhaling the gas. The witnesses watched in nervous amazement.[52] Six minutes later, Gee Jon, the first man to be executed in the gas chamber, was dead.[53] Newspapers quoted witnesses who said that gas was "swift and painless . . . less gruesome than hanging, entailing less suffering than shooting or beheading, or any of the other traditional ways of executions."[54] The press labeled Jon's execution a success and lauded the gas chamber for providing the "progressive" death penalty mechanism Nevada had hoped for.

Yet the execution had not gone as smoothly as the newspapers suggested. Jon did not die immediately. Indeed, because the heater was broken, it took a significant amount of time to fill the chamber with the lethal gas.[55] Moreover, cracks in the walls of the death house created a dangerous situation for witnesses and prison officials alike as the hydrocyanic acid seeped through holes in the walls.

Responding to the problems encountered during the execution, some reformers urged repeal of the lethal gas law while others called for a complete redesign and reconstruction of the gas chamber.[56] After a second execution in a semi-redesigned death house—the chamber was equipped with a steam heat radiator to keep the temperature at a constant eighty degrees Fahrenheit—Nevada's first death chamber was torn down.[57]

In 1929, the state prison built a "new and improved" gas chamber,[58] which included even more insulation, making it "air-tight."[59]

Six by eight feet with two rooms—one a working death chamber, the other a room for the prison's execution team—the building was outfitted with the most up-to-date equipment.[60] Perhaps most importantly, Nevada chose to use another kind of cyanide gas for its new chamber. Instead of pumping in liquid hydrocyanic acid, the gas chamber was equipped with a system that dropped pellets of potassium cyanide into a pot of sulfuric acid.[61] The resulting chemical reaction released deadly gas quickly and thus, scientists concluded, would lead to instantaneous death for the condemned.[62]

Though Nevada's early uses of lethal gas continued to run into problems,[63] favorable news coverage along with concerted efforts by opponents of hanging, led ten other states to adopt lethal gas over the next two decades. After the gruesome beheading of Eva Dugan in 1930, Arizona became the first state to follow Nevada's lead by replacing the gallows with the gas chamber. Colorado soon did the same. In 1935, North Carolina and Wyoming constructed their own gas chambers. The year 1937 saw three more states—California, Missouri, and Oregon—adopt lethal gas as their sole method of execution. During the 1950s, Mississippi, Maryland, and New Mexico all began using lethal gas.[64]

The gruesome spectacles of the gas chamber, however, once again confounded high hopes. Far from solving the problems associated with botched executions, the gas chamber introduced its own set of horrors to the institution of capital punishment. The examples that follow expand upon the history of failures we've been following thus far.

Allen Foster

Between March 1910 and December 1935, North Carolina executed 160 condemned men, all by electrocution. On May 2, 1935, the North Carolina *News and Observer* applauded the decision of the General Assembly to replace the electric chair with the gas chamber. Local historian Trina Seitz explains her state's switch to lethal gas as an attempt by legislators to reaffirm North Carolina's at once "reformist" and "retributivist" image.[65]

At the time of the shift, North Carolina boasted the first gas chamber east of the Mississippi River. Under the new statute, "Cyanide gas, believed by scientists to be the world's most deadly gas, is used in administering the death penalty." During an execution by lethal gas, "The prisoner is strapped in a chair in the death cell, cyanide gas eggs are dropped in a sulfuric acid solution in a jar suspended above him, the heavy gas falls and one deep inhalation is sufficient to cause death. The gas is odorless and so swift in its action that there can be no suffering."[66] However, on January 24, 1936, when Allen Foster became the first person to die in North Carolina's gas chamber, this cheery optimism was abruptly undone.

On that January morning, it took eleven minutes for the state to kill Foster. Afterwards, many witnesses changed their minds about the gas chamber and were "quick to advance the opinion that the electric chair was more humane."[67] Foster—a "youthful Alabama negro" and the convicted rapist of a local white woman—once the epitome of Southern fears, suddenly became a sympathetic victim of the state.[68]

During the summer of 1935, nineteen-year-old Allen Foster had traveled from his home in Alabama to the Hoke County Civilian Conservation Corps (CCC) camp at North Carolina's Fort Bragg Reservation, in search of a new start. He was attempting to leave his troubled teenage years behind him. Foster's juvenile criminal history included multiple charges of burglary and larceny—his first infraction involved sneaking aboard a boxcar and stealing eggs. At the age of thirteen, Foster escaped from a juvenile treatment facility.

In North Carolina, Foster's unhappy past seemed to overtake him almost immediately. On the morning of September 28, 1935, he strayed from his work assignment to the farmhouse of a young Hoke County couple and for some time watched Mrs. Ernest Capps as she worked in the potato garden, finally assuring himself that she was alone.[69] Foster then followed her into the house, with the admitted intention to rob her. A struggle ensued. Foster struck the young woman over the head with a bottle he had found in the yard. He demanded money and Mrs. Capps, already bleeding from a gash in the back of her head, led him to the bedroom where she nervously retrieved five dollars from a dresser drawer. The exact nature of the sexual assault that followed is unclear. While the young woman claimed that she was raped at knifepoint, Foster maintained that he never "completed" the act. The medical examiner, however, corroborated Capps's story.[70]

Armed with a description and following footprints left in the yard as Foster fled the scene, the police had little trouble locating him. He was later transported from the Raeford jail to Laurinburg and then finally to Central Prison, where he stayed until his trial in Hoke County. In November 1935, Foster was convicted of capital rape and sentenced to die in North Carolina's new lethal gas chamber.

Foster's mother immediately began pleading for her son's life. She wrote a number of distressed letters to Governor Ehringhaus, begging him to spare her boy. Her first letter, dated November 20, 1935, read:

> Dear Governor, I am asking you as I am his mother and know him he was rais without a father with no schooling. And therefor he is half crazey. . . . By him being boy 19. . . . Please Governor I am asking you for god sake as my son is sentence to die in December. Give me time to try to get him life in prison . . . I am collared woman this my only son . . . Governor please give my son a chance. Respectfully your, Maggie Olds. Allen Foster's mother.[71]

The governor briefly stayed Foster's execution until "the clemency office might have an opportunity to give [the case] a routine examination." This outraged many in Hoke County who erroneously believed that Foster had been granted clemency. One man wrote Edwin Gill, the commissioner of paroles, accusing him of failing justice: "If Foster had been lynched without trial, you would have put up a howl about 'mob law.' What do you expect *mob law* if you are going to stay the execution of a confessed first-degree criminal?" In the end, neither Gill nor the governor thought that Foster merited leniency and his execution was set for January 24, 1936.[72]

The night before he was scheduled to die, Foster was "openly terrified." All night, inmates sang Southern hymns and prayers echoed throughout the long halls of Central Prison. Before he left his holding cell, Foster addressed his fellow prisoners. "You all shore bin good to me," he began, "I certainly does appreciate everything you all's done for me. You've been tellin' me to find God. I've found God, and I'll always keep him in my heart."[73]

Dressed only in undershorts, with a large blanket draped over his shoulders, Foster was led to the entryway of the execution chamber. He halted only for a moment at the door of the "gleaming white" room and called back to death row, only a few steps away. "Sing for me, preacher," he shouted somberly to one of the doomed men he had just left. "Sing 'On That Shore, On That Beautiful Shore,'" he implored.[74]

Foster was quickly strapped into the high-backed oak chair at the center of the room. As he examined the thick leather restraints, some thirty witnesses stared in at him from the opposite side of several thick panes of glass.[75] Witnesses included a number of physicians and other medical professionals interested in North Carolina's newest technology of death. Among those present were Dr. Charles Peterson, who had sponsored his state's lethal gas bill, Dr. George S. Coleman, the prison physician, and W. T. Bost, a well-known Raleigh reporter who had witnessed electrocutions, hangings, and lynchings throughout his career.

Although he declined to make an official final statement, Foster maintained his innocence to the last. A newspaperman who followed the boy to the entrance of the chamber reportedly overheard him remark, "I fought Joe Louis . . . tell my mother good-bye."

R. A. Bridges pulled the lever releasing the cyanide pellets into a bath of sulfuric acid. Grayish fumes rose from beneath the chair. As the fumes surrounded him, Foster watched them intently, wide-eyed, until they reached about nostril-high. Then he took a deep breath—meant to be his last—and "exhaled the greyish vapor as if it had been cigarette smoke."[76] One newspaper account read: "'Good-bye.' The Negro's lips framed the words so clearly that no man in the witness room could doubt what he had said. As he said it, he winked and then forced a smile at the witnesses peering in at him. Then he began to suffer. No man could look squarely into his eyes and fail to perceive that they were registering pain."[77]

As the gas continued to rise, Foster seemed to "fight against breathing. He threw his head back, inhaling desperately and deeply. He coughed and twisted. His chest heaved."[78] Foster's "small but powerfully built torso" began to "retch and jerk, throwing his head forward where witnesses could see his eyes slowly glaze." The "torturous, convulsive retching continued spasmodically for several minutes."[79] Several more minutes passed until Foster finally lost consciousness and the prison physician signaled that his heart had stopped. It was another twenty-four minutes before the chamber and observation room could be cleared. Witnesses sat in silence as undertakers removed Foster's body from the high-backed chair.

Everyone present was shocked. Witnesses unanimously described the execution of Allen Foster as a "slow and horrible death."[80] W. T. Bost commented, "I think it was an awful butchery . . . I am opposed to capital punishment, but if we've got to have it, there are ways and ways of killing a man, and almost any way is better than this."[81] Letters of protest streamed into the governor's office, and citizens decried the gas chamber as "disgusting," "revolting," and thoroughly "despicable."

Roy M. Brown, a professor of social work at the University of North Carolina, offered Governor Ehringhaus a particularly eloquent response to execution by lethal gas. In his letter, Brown called North Carolina's lethal gas bill "a pitiably brutal failure in the search for a more humane way of killing those condemned to death." He adamantly refused to "remain a silent unwilling accomplice in the deliberate, cold-blooded, and brutal killing of [his] fellow-men," and he felt "defiled and brutalized by being forced to participate in such a killing."[82]

The "storm of indignation" that arose from the time of North Carolina's adoption of lethal gas continued to ebb and flow well into the 1940s.[83] On numerous occasions, bills attempting to revive electrocution were introduced and then defeated in the General Assembly. Finally, on August 2, 2000, the gas chamber chair was removed from Central Prison, loaded in a large wooden crate, and transported to a local museum.[84]

Aaron Mitchell

On the morning of April 12, 1967, Aaron Mitchell took a final drag of a cigarette and let out an audible groan as he was escorted from his holding cell to the gas chamber.[85] Then, without warning, he went limp, forcing two guards to carry him into the chamber and lift him into the chair inside. "I'm Jesus Christ," he shouted as he was strapped down and then left alone in the chamber. "I'm Jesus Christ."

Mitchell closed his eyes and leaned his head back as he inhaled the lethal gas. Soon his head nodded forward and his body jerked violently. His head then went backwards as the rest of his body slumped forward and continued to twitch and convulse. Dr. Phillip McNamara, San Quentin's chief medical officer, listened to Mitchell's heartbeat through a stethoscope taped to Mitchell's chest. At 10:10 A.M., the doctor pronounced Mitchell dead, twelve minutes after the gassing had begun.[86]

Aaron Mitchell's journey to the death house began on February 15, 1963. That night Mitchell, who was out on bail and heavily in debt after being arrested for holding up a Laundromat, went to the Stadium Club, a tavern in Sacramento. Once inside, he fired a sawed-off shotgun toward the tavern ceiling and ordered the thirty people who were inside to stand against the wall. While Mitchell was busy stealing what would total $321, an employee crawled undetected to a phone and called the police. When an officer showed up, Mitchell quickly disarmed him and used him as a shield.

Mitchell insisted that what happened next was an accident. As he attempted to leave the tavern, a gun battle erupted during which Mitchell himself was shot seven times.[87] Officer Arnold Gamble, a forty-three-year-old veteran of the Sacramento police department, was hit in the chest and later died from the wound. Witnesses at Mitchell's trial insisted that he had fired the shot that killed Gamble. The defendant, however, continued to claim that the shooting was accidental and occurred only after another policeman attempted to subdue him: "It was an accident. The first officer grabbed my hand and we were wrestling. It was during this wrestling that the gun went off."[88]

By the time he was arrested for Gamble's murder, Mitchell already had compiled a long criminal record. He had been in and out of jail since the age of fourteen.[89] He believed that all these problems were as much a product of racism as they were caused by his own criminal transgressions. Just being born an African American, Mitchell said, put "two strikes against [him]."[90] "A colored man goes to prison for the same crime that a white man walks away from, a free man," he once said.[91]

Mitchell's conviction and death sentence were reviewed and reaffirmed on appeal twice by both the California Supreme Court and the Supreme Court of the United States.[92] All appeals having been denied, Mitchell's lawyers asked California governor Ronald Reagan to grant clemency. They had some reason to be hopeful since it had been four years since anyone had been executed in the California gas chamber. California's executions had been halted by Reagan's predecessor's generous use of his clemency power.[93]

Nevertheless, unlike the governors before him, Reagan chose not to attend Mitchell's clemency hearing. He said that since he was not a lawyer the process was better left to his clemency secretary, Edwin Meese, a former prosecutor.[94] Reagan's absence moved Mitchell's mother Virgie to tears. When she learned that her son's petition had been denied, she screamed, "Lord, Lord, why can't you give us a chance like the rest? Why, Jesus, why?"

The day before her son's execution, Virgie went to the chambers of a federal district judge in San Francisco and said to him, "All I beg of you is that you save my son's life." The judge, Alfonso Zirpoli, had stayed her son's execution the previous year, just thirty-four hours before he was to be executed. This time, however, Zirpoli did not intervene. "There is no relief that can be accorded by the courts," he said.[95]

After Reagan turned down his plea for executive clemency, Mitchell attempted to take his own life.[96] Every morning inmates were allowed to shave using a razor supplied for that purpose. He removed the locked blade from his razor and used it to cut deeply into his flesh just below his left elbow. But his wound was discovered quickly,[97] and the suicide attempt did not derail the execution plan.

At 5 P.M. on the day before his execution, Mitchell was moved from death row to the holding cell just outside the gas chamber.[98] Demonstrators picketed at the governor's office in Sacramento, hoping to convince Reagan to issue a last-minute stay; but Reagan was unmoved. "The law is the law and must be upheld," the governor said, explaining his refusal.[99]

Others tried different methods to stop the execution. California state senator George Moscone sent a telegram to Supreme Court justice William O. Douglas imploring him to stay the execution until the California State Senate could decide on a bill Moscone had introduced, which would allow the people of California to vote on a proposed repeal of the death penalty.[100] An hour before the execution, San Quentin warden Lawrence E. Wilson informed Mitchell that Douglas would not issue a stay of execution. When he was told that his execution would be the first in the nation in more than a year, as well as the first in California since 1963, Mitchell observed, "I kind of hate having that distinction."[101]

The night before the execution, protestors pressed against a prison gate that they had decorated with flowers, and sang "We Shall Overcome." At 10:00 A.M., the hour set for Mitchell's execution, they held a moment of silence, and forty-five minutes after the execution, the all-night vigil came to an end—but not before one of the death penalty opponents got in a tussle with the chief of the American Nazi party, who was carrying a sign that read, "Gas, the only cure for black crime and Red treason."[102]

In Sacramento, clergymen stood on the capitol steps during Mitchell's execution and read aloud from the New Testament. The passage they chose told the story of Pilate and his refusal to stop the crucifixion of Christ, no doubt a direct reference to Reagan's failure to grant clemency. Some demonstrators lowered the capitol's flag to half-mast before a policeman rushed to raise it again.[103]

California's Episcopal bishop urged all Episcopal churches in the San Francisco Bay Area to toll their bells at the hour of Mitchell's execution. The tolling, he said, was in "penitence for our part in this judicial and legalized murder."[104] When she heard of this plan, Nancy Reagan, the governor's wife, said, "I think it would be nice, too, if they rang church bells every time a man is murdered."[105]

Heavily bearded and dressed in a white shirt and the same kind of denim trousers given to all prisoners,[106] Mitchell could not make it to the gas chamber on his own. Two guards half carried him as he wiped tears from his eyes.[107] He moaned loudly, resisting as guards led him to the green, octagonal structure.

Two state legislators, three policemen from Sacramento, and fifty-eight newsmen all watched Mitchell die through the gas chamber's five windows. For a few moments, before the execution began, Mitchell lowered his head; then he looked at the crowd gathered outside the chamber and nodded at the Reverend Samuel Callier, whom he had asked to be present.

Witnesses soon heard the first clicks of the cyanide pellets as they dropped into a tank of sulfuric acid. Mitchell writhed and twisted for twelve minutes as spectators looked on.[108] About two hours after Mitchell's death, a State Senate committee rejected Moscone's bill.[109] As a result, the other fifty-nine inmates on California's death row would remain there, awaiting their moment in the gas chamber.[110]

On the day of the execution, Mitchell's mother awoke at 6:00 A.M. to begin her own private vigil. She waited quietly at her Sacramento home for word of his death, but grew hysterical after his passing was confirmed. Mitchell's sister, bitter at the governor's failure to intervene, said, "I can tell you one thing, I didn't vote for [Reagan]—and I wouldn't vote for him again. That's for sure." When she received word of her brother's death, she cried, "I hope they are satisfied, Jesus. I hope they are satisfied that by taking his life they have brought back another man."[111] Reagan had no comment on Mitchell's death.[112]

Following his execution, three hundred people came to pay their respects and mourn Aaron Mitchell. Most were African American. The Reverend Callier, presiding at the funeral service, remembered him as someone who had changed dramatically from the time he was convicted of murder to the time of his death. Mitchell, he said, had become a "new man" on death row.[113] Virgie Mitchell sobbed as she proclaimed, "Lord, I've done all I can. Now you don't have to worry anymore, Aaron."[114]

Jimmy Lee Gray

On September 2, 1983, Jimmy Lee Gray died violently in Mississippi's gas chamber. Shortly after midnight, T. Berry Bruce, who was paid $250 for his work, dropped cyanide pellets into a solution of water and sulfuric acid under the metal chair where Gray sat. Bruce, a sixty-four-year-old grandfather and school custodian, had been Mississippi's executioner since 1955, when the gas chamber itself was first constructed.[115]

Cyanide gas filled the grey metal chamber where Gray sat strapped to the metal chair. Officials, monitoring his heart via remote stethoscope, claimed that it had soon stopped beating after the fumes of cyanide gas began to swell up around the condemned. However, the exact time of his death is disputed. Corrections commissioner Morris Thigpen said Gray died at 12:18 A.M., eight minutes after the pellets were dropped. Bruce stated that it took less than three minutes after the poison gas began to rise for Gray to die.[116] But in the official report, Gray was not pronounced dead until 12:47 A.M., nearly forty minutes after he entered the death chamber.[117]

According to most witnesses, including four journalists, Gray suffered a violent end. Gray, they explained, was gasping for breath, wheezing, and convulsing as the lethal gas took longer than usual to render him unconscious.[118] They reported that Gray moaned and shook eleven times before succumbing in a series of "wrenching spasms,"[119] and that "three times over the next eight minutes, Gray's head snapped back—

his chest, arms and legs heaving at the restraints—and he emitted a series of groans clearly audible to the witnesses two feet away, outside the chamber."[120] His whole body jerked and twisted against the leather straps which bound his arms, chest, and legs. Indeed, the gas did not kill Gray quickly, and his body's violent reaction to the cyanide appeared to cause him severe pain. Gray writhed for many minutes after the gas was supposed to have ended his life. As one witness put it, "Jimmy Lee Gray died a gasping, choking death in Mississippi's gas chamber."[121] Then, suddenly, the curtains were pulled closed and the witnesses were escorted out. At least one of the reporters was convinced that Gray was still alive at the time officials ushered everyone out of the witness box.

Gray's lawyers also contended that the execution did not go according to plan. Dennis Balske of the Southern Poverty Law Center in Montgomery, Alabama, said: "That man was breathing when I was told to leave. . . . He had been suffering and strangling and trying to breathe the entire time I was in there. That was five or six minutes. I asked to stay because I saw him still breathing, but I was told I could not stay any longer."[122] Witnesses were not present to observe the minutes between 12:18 A.M. and 12:47 A.M., when he was officially pronounced death.[123] Exactly what happened during that time remains unknown.

Gray was executed for the rape and murder of three-year-old Deressa Jean Scales, of Pascagoula, Mississippi, whom he suffocated in a muddy ditch.[124] Scales was not Gray's first victim. As early as 1968 he had murdered his sixteen-year-old fiancée. The girl, Elda Louise Prince, had been his high school sweetheart.[125]

Prince and Gray met in Parker, Arizona, where Prince lived in a mobile home with her parents. At that time, Gray lived with his father and stepmother at the nearby Metropolitan Pumping station. By all accounts, Gray had had a troubled childhood. Former teachers and family members recall Gray's early life as lonely and fatherless. Before his fifth birthday, his father abandoned the family, leaving his mother depressed and suicidal. Sometime later, Verna Smith sent her son to live with his father, but he soon returned to his mother's home. For the next decade,

Gray was shuttled between his mother's and his great-aunt's homes. The latter later testified that Smith was an abusive mother with "the face of the Devil" when she went into a fit of rage.[126]

In school, Gray seemed to mimic his mother's erratic behavior. Although he was also reportedly an extremely intelligent boy with a high IQ, teachers remembered his explosive tantrums when he did not like the work they assigned him. Gray followed his violent outbursts with apologies and weeks of appropriate behavior, but the tantrums always resurfaced.[127] During high school he moved back in with his father.

Because of his troubled home life, Gray spent much of his adolescence with the Prince family. According to Elda Louise's parents, Harold and Opal Prince, Gray first became friends with their son Elvin because the two were in the same grade at school. The Prince family took him fishing and to baseball games, bought him clothes, and helped him with school. They even allowed him to live with them when he and Elda, their daughter, began to date.[128]

On January 8, 1968, the then eighteen-year-old Gray strangled Elda Louise Prince with a wire, cut her throat, and hid her body in a culvert. After he returned to the Princes' home, he accompanied Mrs. Prince to the sheriff's office to search for the missing girl. While aiding in the investigation, he came under suspicion and eventually led the sheriff to the culvert where they found his victim's body.[129] He later claimed that in the time leading up to the murder, Elda Louise had teased him about his sexual prowess.[130]

Gray was convicted of murder in the second degree and received a twenty-year prison sentence. He served only seven years before being released on parole.[131] After his release, he took a job with a Chicago-based computer programming firm in one of their offices at a shipyard in Pascagoula, Mississippi.[132] It was while living in Mississippi that Gray killed his next victim.

At first, Gray would invite little Deressa Scales to his apartment to play with his kittens.[133] Then, fourteen months after moving to Pascagoula, he abducted her from her family's nearby apartment and took her to a remote area on the Mississippi Gulf Coast.[134] In a wooded area, near a creek off of a logging road, he sodomized and raped her, and then suffocated the child by pressing her face into the muddy ground.[135] Trying to cover up this second brutal murder, he threw her body off a bridge.[136]

It did not take the police long to arrest Gray. After Scales's disappearance, police ran a computer search and found that Gray, a convicted murderer, lived in the same apartment complex as the child's family. They brought him in for questioning, and that very day he led them to the creek where Scales's small body was floating near the bridge. He initially claimed that she had accidentally fallen off the bridge, but faced with evidence that the toddler had been raped and sodomized and had mud in her lungs, he admitted his crime.[137]

In December 1976, a jury convicted Gray of rape, kidnapping, and capital murder, and one month later he was sentenced to die in the gas chamber at Mississippi's Parchman Prison.[138] During the next seven years, Gray's lawyers made three unsuccessful appeals to the Supreme Court of the United States. In 1978 his conviction was actually overturned by the Mississippi Supreme Court, and Gray was retried. Once again he was sentenced to death for the murder of Deressa Scales.[139]

On death row, Gray stayed out of trouble. His execution was scheduled for October 31, 1979, but he received a stay of execution because of alleged problems with Mississippi's gas chamber. With this stay and another chance at life, more appeals followed.[140]

During this second phase of the appeals process, Gray began to write poetry and, hauntingly, won a prize in 1981 for a poem that he had written to an eight-year-old girl who sent him a Christmas card. He also corresponded with lawyers representing the Scales family[141] and started meeting with members of nearby churches, eventually becoming a born-again Christian.[142]

The United States Supreme Court refused Gray's appeal for the last time in 1983.[143] In this final appeal, Gray's attorneys had argued that death by cyanide gas constituted cruel and unusual punishment because inmates were subjected to excruciating pain, similar to that of a heart attack. The condemned also suffered muscle contractions, urination, defecation, and vomiting, Gray's lawyers claimed. Lethal gas, they reminded the Court, was no longer used to kill animals due to the pain incurred during oxygen deprivation.

The Supreme Court, however, summarily dismissed these contentions. As Chief Justice Burger wrote:

> For purposes of my vote in this case, I accept the truth of the affidavits submitted by the petitioner, but nevertheless conclude—as did the Court of Appeals that they do not as a matter of law establish an Eighth Amendment violation. I agree with the Court of Appeals that the showing made by petitioner does not justify a court holding that, as a matter of law or fact, the pain and terror resulting from death by cyanide is so different in degree or nature from that resulting from other traditional modes of execution as to implicate the eighth amendment right.[144]

Gray's impending execution inspired a wide range of responses. Though his mother, Verna Smith, initially supported him, during the seven-year period between Scales's death and Gray's execution, she came to believe that he should be executed. She wrote to Scales's parents agreeing that it would be best for them if her son were put to death.[145] Smith stated publically that "This is the second girl my son has killed in less than 10 years. If I had been on that jury, I would have gone the same way they did."[146] For the families of Gray's victims his execution could not come soon enough.[147] Richard Scales, Deressa's father, put it simply: "He took the life of my daughter and therefore I did not think he should live."[148]

Still, the prospect of Gray's execution outraged others. "Ministers, social workers and lawyers who came to know him in his long incarceration, described Mr. Gray as a born-again Christian and used terms like 'sensitive,' 'shy,' 'gentle,' 'bright' and 'troubled.'" They said he had described himself as "an abused child and the product of a broken home," reported the *New York Times*.[149]

In the hours before his death, Gray ate a large last meal of enchiladas, tacos, burritos, refried beans, and salad—the food of his childhood in Southern California and Arizona. He also enjoyed strawberries and pizza brought to him by church members who sat with him during his last night.[150] Gray talked by telephone with his parents and met with the Reverend Joseph B. Ingle, who gave him communion.[151] The clergyman made a direct request to Governor William Winter for clemency, but the governor quickly declined to intervene.[152] "Jimmy is disappointed but also in good spirits," Ingle said. "Is he prepared to die? I can't say that about Jimmy. I can't say that about anyone."[153] Corrections commissioner Thigpen reported that Gray appeared "to be relatively calm." He had "seemingly accepted what [was] going to happen."[154]

At 12:01 on the morning of September 2, 1983, the five-foot-eight-and-a-half-inch, 140-pound Gray walked, head down, to the gas chamber.[155] Once inside the six-sided metal gas chamber, he calmly sat down and the guards strapped him into the chair.[156] In his red jumpsuit and brown shoes, Gray spoke softly for a few moments to the two guards who had brought him in, and then the guards exited and closed the door.[157]Although he had entered calmly, Gray did not die a quiet death.

After his execution, Gray's body was released to Natchez Church members and was carried away from the prison in a gold limousine.[158]

Donald Eugene Harding

On Monday, April 6, 1992, Donald Eugene Harding's team of lawyers made their final appeals to the United States Supreme Court.[159] Their client's criminal activity, they claimed, could be explained by brain damage he had endured during childbirth, which left him with uncontrollable violent impulses.[160] After the Supreme Court rejected this argument, Harding's lawyers petitioned the Arizona Board of Pardons and Paroles, and it also unanimously rejected Harding's appeal.[161] In his last hours, Harding asked the Ninth Circuit Court of Appeals for a stay of execution. There too his pleas went unanswered.[162]

Donald Eugene Harding would be the first man executed at the state prison in Florence, Arizona, in twenty-nine years.[163] At midnight, the curtains were drawn open on the whitewashed room as witnesses watched while Harding, seated in the black steel chair in the center of the airtight room, was restrained by nylon straps. Once Harding was properly secured, the guards exited the chamber, and the "locking wheel" on the door was turned and pulled tightly closed. Next the exhaust fan and mercury gauge were turned on.[164] And finally, a signal was given and the executioner pulled a lever releasing crystals of sodium cyanide into a waiting pail of sulfuric acid.[165] As a cloud of cyanide gas engulfed him, Harding struggled against the straps, turned red, and began convulsing.[166] He gasped, stuttered, and continued to strain against the straps for more than ten minutes.[167]

Witnesses watched in horror. One reporter, visibly shaken by the "ugly event" he had just observed, proclaimed that "animals [are put to] sleep more humanely."[168] An aide to the Arizona governor watched as Harding's heart rate slowly dropped from 140 beats to 30. Though Harding continued to twitch and convulse, he appeared to be unconscious and on the verge of death. The governor's aide was relieved; the execution seemed to have been a success. But then, suddenly, Harding's heart rate rose to sixty beats per minute. As the aide put it, "I was awfully nervous. I thought maybe the guy wasn't going to die. You hate the thought of a botched execution."[169] At 12:18, Harding's heart rate dropped to zero and the prison doctor pronounced him dead.

Donald Eugene Harding grew up in an unstable and abusive home.[170] When he was barely six months old, his father abandoned the family. Because his mother did not feel she could support him, Harding was sent to live with his grandparents.[171] In 1954 his mother remarried. However, in his new home, in addition to being abused both physically and mentally himself, Harding was also forced to watch the extreme violence between his mother and stepfather.[172]

From a very early age, Harding was "hyperactive, aggressive, depressed" and exhibited many signs of mental illness.[173] At the age of nine he threatened to commit suicide. Though doctors recognized Harding's distress early, he received no treatment. Instead, Harding spent much of his life in juvenile reform schools and adult prisons, where the physical, mental, emotional, and sexual abuse of his childhood continued.[174]

On September 17, 1979, Harding, who was awaiting trial for murder in the Pulaski County Jail, escaped with five other prisoners.[175] Over the eleven months between his escape and recapture, Harding committed a string of serious crimes—twelve robberies, two kidnappings, four murders, and numerous assaults in seven different states.

On January 24, 1980, Harding bound, gagged, and robbed Allan Gage in his motel room in Phoenix, Arizona, and left him there to die.[176] The next day, posing as a security guard at La Quinta Motel in Tucson, he entered the motel room of two businessmen, Robert Wise and Martin Concannon.[177] Harding then bound them, beat Wise with a lamp, stuffed a sock into Concannon's mouth, and shot the men at close range in the head and the chest.

After rearranging the room slightly, Harding fled in Concannon's car. Around 8:40 P.M., Harding, wearing "a rust colored jacket and a burgundy shirt,"[178] showed up at Robert Wise's home. When his wife, Jeri, answered the door with her child and large dog in tow, Harding nervously asked if "Bob" was home, holding out one of Wise's business cards. Ms. Wise said no, and Harding soon left.[179]

The next day, the Tucson Police Department was called to La Quinta Motel where officers found two bodies. Concannon, tightly bound and covered with a bed sheet, was lying dead on the bathroom floor.[180] Wise was on the bed with his head bound to the headboard and his feet and arms tied together with sheets and belts.[181] Blood was splattered all over the wall behind the bed, and a bloody lamp was found near Wise's body. The police obtained prints on a number of surfaces in the motel room, positively identifying Harding as the killer.[182]

The following day, at Northern Arizona University in Flagstaff, almost three hundred miles north of La Quinta Motel, a university police officer stationed in a parking lot near the school's athletic center noticed an Oldsmobile with Ohio plates pull into the lot.[183] Not recognizing the car or the driver, the officer told the man that he could not park there.

Because the driver appeared anxious and spoke with a Southern accent even though his car had Ohio license plates,[184] the officer ran warrant checks on the car and quickly determined that it had been stolen in Tucson. When backup units arrived, the driver, later identified as Harding, was arrested.[185]

On March 23, 1982, during a pretrial hearing for the murders of Wise and Concannon, Harding asked to represent himself.[186] Judge Harry Gin of the Superior Court in Pima County, Arizona, strongly suggested that Harding consider retaining a defense attorney.[187]

Nonetheless, after a day of questioning, the judge granted Harding's request. His trial began a week later and lasted six days.[188] Harding's guilt was undeniable, and his crimes were gruesome and violent. The jury saw over 150 pictures taken at the crime scene and during the autopsies.[189] Pathologists detailed the ways in which the two businessmen were killed.[190] Jeri Wise identified Harding as the man who had come to her door on the night of the crime.[191] The Northern Arizona University police guard also identified Harding.[192]

The prosecution introduced a statement Harding made as he was being transported from Flagstaff to Tucson. A Tucson police detective testified that it was a cold day and Harding was wearing only a short-sleeved shirt. As the detective offered Harding a jacket to protect him from the wind, Harding looked at him and said, "You don't need to do that, I deserve whatever I get."[193]

On April 27, 1982, Harding was found guilty of two counts of first-degree murder, two counts of armed robbery, two counts of kidnapping, and one count of theft. A month later, he was sentenced to die in the gas chamber.

Over the ten years between his sentence and his execution, Harding and his lawyers filed many appeals arguing, among other things, that the trial court erred in allowing him to waive his right to counsel, that the court also erred in admitting certain evidence into the trial, and that the death penalty violated the Eighth Amendment.[194] None of these arguments were persuasive.

In the period leading up to Harding's execution, Arizona cleaned and tested its gas chamber, which had sat idle since the execution of Manuel Silvas in 1963. In May 1991, the Arizona Department of Corrections applied for the permit that would allow it to release cyanide gas.[195] The week before Harding's execution date, prison officials conducted final tests and prepared for Arizona's first execution in almost three decades.

During his execution Harding fought for his last breaths violently, convulsed, and struggled for over ten minutes. His botched execution soon sparked a debate that would eventually lead the state of Arizona to abandon the gas chamber in favor of lethal injection.

The Last Gasp of the Gas Chamber

The year 1945 marked the end of an era. The aftermath of World War II, and the recognition of the role played by lethal gas in the Holocaust led many nations to reconsider the death penalty and the gas chamber. But in the United States, not only did gassings continue but three states, Maryland, Mississippi, and New Mexico, adopted the gas chamber.

Nonetheless, executions by gas continued to encounter problems. After the war, California's gas chamber became known worldwide because of a series of botched executions and highly publicized legal battles. In 1953, Leandress Riley's execution garnered a great deal of attention when he went to his death fighting. After attempting suicide, he was finally subdued, handcuffed, and dragged into the gas chamber. Riley somehow managed to get free from the chair's straps. When the gas finally entered the chamber, Riley held his breath for many minutes before allowing himself to begin to die.[196] Only a few years later, Caryl Chessman garnered public and celebrity support in his efforts to escape California's gas chamber. Chessman wrote a best-selling memoir about his time on death row and managed his own legal proceedings from prison. When his 1960 execution was botched, anti–death penalty campaigns around the world erupted in anger.[197]

As the twentieth century came to a close, five out of every one hundred executions by lethal gas had been botched. The eventual demise of the gas chamber came as death penalty proponents, propelled in part by gruesome spectacles of the kind we have described, sought new alternatives. Although lethal gas had once been touted as a progressive, humane, and painless method of execution, the gas chamber had a relatively short life. It was used as the sole method of execution in several states, from 1924 to 1977, and was last used in 1999.[198] By then, the gas chamber had become a relic of the past, in large part because of its inability to deliver on its promise to be "swift and painless . . . less gruesome than hanging, entailing less suffering than shooting or beheading, or any of the other traditional ways of executions."

CHAPTER 5

"How Enviable a Quiet Death"

Lethal Injection

On May 10, 1977, one year after the Supreme Court's *Gregg v. Georgia* decision, Oklahoma became the first state to authorize the use of lethal injection. The next day, Texas passed a very similar law.[1] Other states quickly followed suit, without serious investigation into the efficacy or humaneness of the method.[2]

Oklahoma's adoption of lethal injection resulted from the particular efforts of state representative Bill Wiseman and state senator Bill Dawson to find an alternative to the "inhumanity, visceral brutality, and cost" of the electric chair.[3] They fought hard to enlist the help of the medical community, but in the end the Oklahoma Medical Association refused to assist them. They did, however, manage to win the support of the state's chief medical examiner, A. Jay Chapman, "despite his admitted dearth of relevant experience."[4] They also consulted with the head of the Oklahoma Medical School's Anesthesiology Department, Dr. Stanley Deutsch, who suggested specific drugs that could be used to induce death.[5]

In spite of Deutsch's suggestions, Wiseman and Dawson decided to leave the statutory language vague in order to accommodate the development of new and better drug technologies in the future. Their legislation contained no specific instructions regarding the types or amounts of drugs that should be used in executions and no specifications regarding record-keeping or reporting. In other words, the legislation provided for "no oversight of any kind."[6] The result was to delegate "to Oklahoma prison officials all critical decisions regarding the implementation of lethal injection."[7]

Across the country, supporters of lethal injection applauded its ease of administration and claimed, in addition, that it *"appears* more humane and *visually* palatable relative to other methods."[8] As other states adopted lethal injection, they "mirrored Oklahoma's vague legislative approach and drug combination choices." Most, like Oklahoma, did little to verify lethal injection scientifically or to seek professional guidance from the medical community.[9] It was enough that lethal injection seemed a quicker, more humane and sterile method of state killing.[10] In a typical lethal injection procedure, the anticipated time of death is between two and ten minutes from the time the deadly chemicals enter the body.[11]

The history of lethal injection in the United States dates back to the late nineteenth century. At that time, reformers, public officials and ordinary citizens alike, were offended by the gruesome spectacle of the gallows and began to look for alternatives to hanging. As detailed in Chapter 3, New York's Gerry Commission considered lethal injection as a possible means of "humane" execution.[12] However, it was ultimately rejected "based on the procedures available at the time and as a result of objections from the medical community."[13] Similarly, in Great Britain, members of the medical community resisted efforts to introduce lethal injection there, concluding that "based on medical and scientific input concerning the feasibility of lethal injection and its administration at the time, that there was a lack of 'reasonable certainty' that lethal injection executions could be carried out 'quickly, painlessly and decently.'"[14]

Almost a century later, lethal injection made a comeback in the United States prompted in part by a series of horrifically botched electrocutions of the kind discussed in Chapter 3. These events "led to broad concerns as to whether the electric chair . . . was the humane method of execution that originally it was thought to be." Similar concerns were raised about death by lethal gas. In California, for example, where the gas chamber was the prescribed method of execution, legal challenges "prompted a search for a less controversial alternative."[15]

Death penalty scholar Deborah Denno notes that with the advent of lethal injection the modern death chamber has come to resemble a hospital room, and executioners to resemble medical professionals.[16] Lethal injection "simulates a medical procedure—the intravenous induction of general anesthesia."[17] One doctor recently remarked that the procedures of lethal injection "would have looked familiar to a surgeon (or any doctor who performs procedures under sedation)."[18]

As in a hospital, the insertion of intravenous needles and the proper administration of drugs require that executioners have a basic level of medical knowledge.[19] Especially when inmates are obese or heavy drug users, "the advanced skills of doctors are sometimes needed."[20] In some death penalty states, including Georgia and Nevada, state law requires a physician to be present at each execution.[21]

Yet professional medical organizations have rallied against the involvement of health care professionals in lethal injection procedures.[22] The American Medical Association denounces doctor participation in these procedures, or any other type of execution for that matter, and the American Nursing Association is likewise "strongly opposed" to nurses' participation. In the early 1990s, the latter joined forces with the American Medical Association, the American College of Physicians, and the American Public Health Association to take a clear stand. In a joint statement they said that "When the healthcare professional serves in an execution under circumstances that mimic care, the healing purposes of health services and technology becomes distorted."[23]

Individual doctors have also spoken out against physician participation in lethal injection. In a 2002 article published in the *British Medical Journal,* Jonathan Groner, an Ohio doctor, called lethal injection "a stain on the face of medicine."[24] He went so far as to link America's death penalty with Nazism and claimed that the system of capital punishment in the United States today relies on a "medical *charade.*"[25] This "charade" makes lethal injection out to be something that it is not—a sterile, medicalized, painless procedure. In his view, because lethal injections resemble medical procedures, "[e]ven without doctors' participation, lethal injection—with its intravenous lines, electrocardiograph monitors, and anesthetic drugs—has a deeply corrupting influence on medicine as a whole."[26]

Until recently, in almost all states, execution by lethal injection followed a three-drug protocol, which kills the condemned in stages.[27] The first drug in the typical protocol, sodium thiopental, anesthetizes inmates and puts them to sleep before the lethal drugs are administered. The second drug, pancuronium bromide, is a paralytic which renders the inmate unable to show pain. The condemned thus look peaceful before they die, and the spectacles of the severed head in a botched hanging or the smoke-filled death chamber after an electrocution gone wrong have all but disappeared. However, both the pancuronium bromide and the third drug, potassium chloride, which causes cardiac arrest and death, have the potential to cause severe pain that would be masked by the sodium thiopental and/or the pancuronium bromide.

Despite the effort to medicalize executions, the history of lethal injection has been anything but smooth, sterile, and predictable. In fact, of the approximately one thousand executions carried out from 1980 to 2010 by lethal injection, more than 7 percent were botched.[28] Although less gruesome and dramatic perhaps than botched hangings, gassings, or electrocutions, lethal injection has had its own distinctive mishaps. It is not uncommon for executioners to have trouble finding a vein into which they can insert a line to deliver the lethal drugs, especially in overweight inmates, or inmates with a history of drug abuse.

Despite this undeniable history of botching over the decades, courts have been consistently unsympathetic to challenges to lethal injection. Some of these challenges have focused on "the dosing and procedures used in lethal injection and whether the drug combinations and measures for administering the drugs truly produce a timely, pain-free, and fail-safe death."[29] Other suits have raised "issues regarding the 'medicalization' of execution and the ethics of health care professionals' participation in any part of the lethal injection process."[30] These legal challenges culminated in the Supreme Court case, *Baze v. Rees*.[31] In that case, the plaintiffs neither argued that lethal injection was categorically unconstitutional nor challenged capital punishment itself. Instead, they focused on the narrower question of whether or not Kentucky's three-drug lethal injection protocol constituted cruel and unusual punishment under the Eighth Amendment.[32]

On April 16, 2008, the Court held, in a 7–2 decision, that Kentucky's three-drug protocol did not violate the Eighth Amendment since it did not pose a "substantial risk of serious harm" to the condemned. The Court also ruled that a risk of "improper administration" did not render execution by lethal injection cruel and unusual. Chief Justice Roberts stated in an opinion, joined by Justices Kennedy and Alito, that "a State with a lethal injection protocol substantially similar to the protocol we uphold today would not create a risk that meets this standard."[33]

To successfully challenge lethal injection post-*Baze*, an inmate must show that the lethal injection protocol in his or her state poses a "substantial risk of serious harm" or an "objectively intolerable risk of harm."[34] In addition, the inmate must identify a feasible alternative that could be readily implemented and would "significantly reduce a substantial risk of severe pain."[35] These factors make litigation against lethal injection substantially more difficult.

Moreover, following *Baze*, states wishing to avoid challenges to their lethal injection protocols could simply bring their methods in line with Kentucky's. As Harvey Gee put it, "the *Baze* decision . . . created a safe harbor for states."[36] Thus, the Sixth Circuit held in *Harbison v. Little* that Tennessee's lethal injection protocol was similar enough to Kentucky's that it could not be considered unconstitutional.[37] In *Raby v. Livingston*, the Fifth Circuit "held that the potential problems associated with intravenous insertions did not render Texas's lethal injection protocol in violation of the Eighth Amendment."[38]

Nonetheless, *Baze* did not end all debate about lethal injection. The decision left open a number of major questions surrounding its constitutionality. It remains unclear when a risk is sufficiently "substantial" or which elements of lethal injection protocols might generate this substantial risk of serious harm.[39] Thus, challenges to lethal injection have continued. *Baze* also left the legality of single-drug lethal injection protocols open to question. Ohio became the first state to use such a procedure in December 2010.[40] Other states, including Florida, Kentucky, South Carolina, Texas, and Virginia, are considering adopting a similar single-drug protocol. In addition, states recently have had to modify their lethal injection protocols due to the unavailability of sodium thiopental.[41]

Some states, such as Georgia, have used pentobarbital or phenobarbital even though these drugs were initially considered in Oklahoma in the 1970s and were rejected because they are normally used only for animal euthanasia.[42] Attorneys for Georgia death row inmate Gregory Walker recently claimed that Georgia's lethal injection protocol does not adequately sedate the condemned before the other two drugs are administered, and thus causes an unnecessary risk of pain. "Pentobarbital is a wholly untested drug that is not used to administer anesthesia to healthy human subjects, so it basically amounts to Russian roulette," stated Walker's attorney Brian Kramer.[43] Kramer claimed that in the June 23, 2011, execution of Roy Blankenship, the pentobarbital did not sufficiently sedate Blankenship before the administration of the pancuronium bromide and the potassium chloride. Blankenship apparently moved his head around, looked at the injection site, and muttered several times.

To provide "the best evidence possible" for their case, Walker's attorneys requested that the Georgia execution of Andrew DeYoung be videotaped so that the alleged inadequacies of pentobarbital might be fully documented.[44] Prosecutors opposed filming DeYoung's execution, and state officials argued that safeguards such as a consciousness check were already in place to prevent unnecessary suffering.[45] When he was executed, DeYoung appeared to die a quiet death.[46] But Georgia's decision to videotape his execution may lead to similar requests across the nation as abolitionists continue to challenge lethal injection.[47]

As these challenges continue, so too do botched lethal injections. Indeed the rate of botched executions where lethal injection is the method used is considerably *higher* than it has been when other, supposedly less humane, methods have been employed. This is in part a function of the elaboration of more precise and detailed execution protocols. Yet botched lethal injections may also occur because of negative physical reactions to the drugs used, such as choking, convulsing, and sputtering.

Moreover, inmates who are extremely heavy or have a history of drug abuse often have veins which are difficult or impossible to find. In such cases, prison staff often engage in prolonged efforts to insert intravenous lines or are forced to use a "cut-down procedure," in which the top layers of the condemned person's skin are scraped off to locate a usable vein. Intravenous lines collapse, drugs leak into soft tissue, and inmates have to be poked dozens of times by inexperienced personnel before usable veins can be located. In some instances, inmates have even been known to help executioners locate veins, and veins in the legs, groin, or neck have all had to be used in executions.

From Velma Barfield, in 1984, who attempted to speak after lethal drugs were injected into her veins and who died fourteen minutes later, to Ricky Ray Rector, for whom it took executioners almost an hour to find a suitable vein, to the 2009 unsuccessful execution of Romell Broom, to Emmitt Foster, during whose execution the drugs stopped circulating through the intravenous line attached to his body, leaving him convulsing and gasping for air, condemned Americans have died hard by the needle.

The remainder of this chapter takes up the cases of Barfield, Rector, Broom, and Foster and offers them as examples of the ways lethal injections go wrong. Although these four cases represent only a small sample of botched lethal injections, they epitomize the most common ways that these procedures go awry: execution teams often have trouble finding a vein or struggle with the lethal injection equipment, and inmates sometimes have an atypical negative reaction to the lethal drugs or, for a variety of reasons, simply take an abnormally long time to die.

All of these problems represent potential sources of pain for the inmate and suggest that lethal injection has not guaranteed the sterile, quiet deaths that proponents promised.

Velma Barfield

At the time Velma Barfield was led to her death in November 1984, thirty-nine prisoners awaited execution on North Carolina's death row. As she passed by them, they banged rhythmically on the Plexiglas windows of their cells in a solemn ceremony of farewell to their fellow inmate.[48] Once inside the death chamber, Barfield would not die quickly.

A signal instructed the executioners to begin the saline drip. For twenty minutes, Barfield lay on a steel gurney with a stethoscope and heart monitor affixed to her chest while saline solution drifted into her veins to open them. Then, at 2 A.M., the saline was replaced, first with a drug designed to induce sleep and then with a lethal dose of a chemical "commonly used to kill animals at a dog pound."

According to witnesses, Barfield's neck muscles eventually relaxed and she appeared to stop breathing,[49] but this was only after those gathered to watch the execution had waited for fourteen more minutes. During those minutes, they saw her lips moving as if in prayer and she appeared to try to speak. Her breathing came quickly, and her body moved under the green sheet that covered her. Then, finally, she grew still.[50]

Margie Velma Barfield, the second of nine children,[51] was born to a cotton mill worker[52] and his wife on October 29, 1932. She was raised in rural North Carolina where she left school in the tenth grade and eloped with a local boy when she was only seventeen. The pair, together for nearly fifteen years, had two children, a boy and a girl. Barfield's husband drove a Pepsi truck and made enough money for a down payment on a family home.

All was apparently well in Barfield's life. However, after her husband suffered head injuries in a car accident, which changed his personality, he turned into an abusive alcoholic. Around this time Barfield herself became addicted to tranquilizers and painkillers. She would hide the pills around the house so that her children could not throw them away,[53] and they later recalled seeing their mother passed out after taking pills. When she was awake her moods would change quickly, alternating between extremes, some of which were violent.

When Barfield's husband passed away in 1969, the cause of death was listed initially as smoke inhalation, but his sister maintained that Barfield had murdered him. Barfield quickly remarried, but her second husband also died, in 1971, just six months after their wedding. His death was originally thought to be from natural causes; however, it was later determined that he died from a lethal dose of arsenic, an ingredient in roach killer.[54]

Soon after the death of her second husband, Barfield began dating again and soon got engaged to Stuart Taylor,[55] a tobacco farmer.[56] Not long after the engagement, however, Taylor became violently ill while he and Barfield were at an evangelist's speech in a nearby town. For three days she "nursed" her ailing fiancé before finally taking him to the hospital, where he died.[57]

Doctors attributed Taylor's death to gastroenteritis—inflammation of the stomach and intestines—but his family was not satisfied with their conclusion and demanded a more thorough investigation. Additional testing revealed that Taylor had died of arsenic poisoning. Soon thereafter, Barfield was arrested and charged with murder.[58]

After being questioned by the police, she confessed to poisoning Taylor,[59] and also to murdering her mother in 1974,[60] and an elderly couple for whom she worked as a live-in caretaker and housekeeper in 1977.[61] She explained that she killed her victims by slipping arsenic into their food.[62] Despite her confessions to these other crimes, Barfield would stand trial only for Taylor's murder.[63]

During her 1978 trial, Barfield insisted that she could not remember much of what she had done while on pills: "I didn't have a clear day for 10 years," she said. Barfield testified that she had suffered from a decade-long addiction to prescription drugs. During that time, she claimed, she would visit different doctors to get her fix, often taking double and triple dosages of drugs like Valium, Tylenol, and codeine.

Barfield claimed that due to her addiction she was nothing more than "a zombie" when she put ant poison into her fiancé's tea and beer.[64] Her court-appointed attorney, who had never before tried a capital case, advised her to enter a plea of guilty by reason of insanity. Using evidence of her long-term drug habit, including four hospitalizations for overdoses, he hoped to convince the jury that his client was not in her right mind when she murdered Taylor.[65]

Joe Britt, the district attorney who prosecuted Barfield, was listed in the 1980 *Guinness Book of World Records* as the "world's deadliest prosecutor" for the large number of death verdicts he had won.[66] Although she was only on trial for the murder of her fiancé, Britt managed to introduce a great deal of evidence about her other crimes.[67] Barfield, he said, would forge checks in order to fund her drug habit and then poison her victims with odorless and tasteless poisons, Singletary Rat Killer and Terro Ant and Roach Killer.

Britt's "antagonizing style" bothered Barfield so much that she openly argued with him. As a result she appeared sarcastic and belligerent instead of remorseful during cross-examination. This frustrated her lawyer, who had urged Barfield to be tearful and subdued when she took the stand. The jury found Barfield guilty of first-degree murder in less than an hour,[68] and she was sentenced to death.[69]

One year later the United States Supreme Court upheld Barfield's conviction. At this point her court-appointed lawyer left the case.[70] While on death row Barfield appealed to eight different courts and twenty-one different judges. The Supreme Court reviewed her case three times.

Barfield's will to live was rekindled in prison. She hoped "to contribute something to the other ladies that are here [in prison], in helping them to better understand how to cope with their own situations." She knew "what it [was] to hurt."[71] In December 1979 Barfield met with Richard Burr, an attorney from the Southern Prisoners' Defense Committee, and the two agreed that he would represent her in further appeals.[72] As her appeals wound down, Burr arranged several psychiatric evaluations in preparation for a clemency presentation before North Carolina governor Hunt.[73]

In late September 1984, Burr and James Little—a local lawyer recruited to assist with the case—met privately with the governor.[74] In addition, the warden at the Women's Prison made a tearful plea on Barfield's behalf, praising her positive impact at the prison; and fellow inmates spoke out in support of her. Governor Hunt, who was in the final days of a closely contested Senate race, was unmoved by their pleas. He denied Barfield clemency on September 27.[75]

Governor Hunt reiterated his support for capital punishment, which was also widely supported by North Carolina voters. Discussing Barfield's impending execution, Hunt said that he hoped "the first execution of a woman in this country for 22 years would help deter premeditated killings."[76] He cleared his campaign schedule for the execution day, which fell four days before the November 6 general election.[77]

Barfield filed her final appeal on October 29.[78] Her attorneys argued, in the Robeson County Court, that Barfield had been incompetent to stand trial in 1978 by reason of withdrawal from drugs. In an interview on ABC's *Good Morning America*, Barfield claimed that the "real her" could never have committed the murders. She told her interviewers that she had not realized the full impact of her actions until three months after she entered prison, where she shook her addiction.[79]

Nevertheless, when this last appeal was ultimately denied, Barfield resigned herself to her fate and her defense attorney said Barfield's decision not to carry her case to the Supreme Court for the fourth time was a "clear-headed" one.[80] He also explained prior to the execution that Barfield chose lethal injection over the gas chamber because of "the dignity factor." She would not be able to see the witnesses while lying on the gurney. In the gas chamber, she would have been forced to sit facing witnesses in the next room.[81]

On the morning of her execution, Barfield awoke at 6:00, rolled her hair, and ate a bowl of frosted flakes and a piece of cake. She drank a few cups of coffee and read the newspaper before receiving visitors. Friends and family who visited with Barfield in the final hours of her life reported that she displayed a deep "religious fervor" and remained in good spirits. A friend later recalled that Barfield had said she believed that execution was her "gateway to heaven,"[82] but her son remembered tearfully that "she wanted to live very badly."

As visiting hours ended, Barfield asked her children to remain at the prison during her execution even though they would not be allowed to witness it.[83] After all her visitors left, a clergyperson played her tapes of religious music and they sang hymns together. The prison chaplain sent her a bouquet of flowers,[84] and James Little gave her two additional red roses.[85] For her last meal Barfield made no special requests, but neither did she eat the usual prison fare of macaroni with chicken livers, beans, bread, and cake. Instead she had a Coke and Cheeze Doodles—a snack from the prison canteen.[86]

Barfield's execution by lethal injection drew a large crowd of newspaper reporters, television crews, photographers, and death penalty supporters and opponents. This strange mix of spectators gathered in order to be part of Barfield's sensational story—a grandmother executed for murder.[87] One hundred demonstrators joined in worship at the state capitol before marching to the prison in protest,[88] while death penalty supporters chanted "Bye-bye, Velma" in front of the prison and told her to go to hell and burn.[89]

While many gathered outside, only sixteen witnesses were present at the execution itself. This small group included eight law enforcement officers as well as two corrections department officers, James Little, who stood behind the officers, and Anne Lotz, the daughter of evangelist Billy Graham. The eyewitnesses stared through a heavy glass window into a trapezoid-shaped death chamber.[90] The only sound was the "whirr of a ventilation system and the occasional scrape of a chair as one of the witnesses changed position."[91]

Barfield's windowless holding cell, meagerly equipped with a metal bunk, sink, and toilet, was only eighteen steps from the death chamber.[92] Before leaving her quarters for the last time, Barfield changed out of her brown prison dress and into pink cotton pajamas. Wearing these pajamas along with blue slippers[93] and her signature glasses,[94] she was wheeled down the hall on a gurney.[95] Soon the bolt on the door of the death chamber opened and witnesses could finally see Barfield lying on her hospital gurney in the dark hallway outside,[96] her wrists and ankles bound with straps.[97] As she was covered up to her neck with a green sheet, her pink pajamas were barely visible.

Two officers wheeled her into the chamber, placed the gurney against the window, and pulled two tan plastic shower curtains behind it to separate Barfield from the chair used for executions by cyanide gas. Three technicians, hidden from onlookers, busied themselves behind another curtain beside the gurney,[98] attaching intravenous needles to her arm.[99] Offered the chance to say some last words, Barfield expressed regret for "all of the hurt [she had] caused," though she never directly apologized for her crimes.[100] She said, "I know that everybody has gone through a lot of pain, all the families connected, and I am sorry, and I want to thank everybody who has been supporting me all these six years."[101]

The warden gave the order to start the execution, and the tubes in Barfield's arm began to steadily drip three solutions into her veins: first sodium thiopental to put her to sleep, and then muscle relaxants to stop her heart and breathing.[102] As the lethal chemicals flowed, her face gradually relaxed and her coloring turned from rosy to "ashen gray." A doctor moved the gurney away from the window, stepping in front of it to listen to Barfield's heart with a stethoscope. Barfield was pronounced dead at 2:15 A.M.,[103] an excruciating fourteen minutes after the warden's order.[104] One reporter observed that "inside the chamber, a fly buzzed past Mrs. Barfield's lifeless body."[105]

Barfield had offered to be an organ donor just hours before she died. Her defense lawyer, "choked with emotion," said that volunteering to be a donor helped Barfield feel that she had not lived her life in vain.

After her execution, state troopers rushed her body to a local medical school where workers unsuccessfully tried to restart her heart in order to keep blood flowing to her organs. As a result, most could not be donated or used for transplants,[106] although her skin and eyes were removed for transplantations.[107]

Barfield's was the twenty-ninth execution since the death penalty's reinstatement in 1976.[108] At the time, she was the 307th woman legally executed in the United States since 1632. In North Carolina, she was the seventeenth woman executed and the first since 1944. At the time of her death, there were sixteen other women sitting on death rows across the nation.[109]

On the Sunday following her execution, Barfield was buried before a crowd of two hundred friends and relatives, including several of her attorneys and some of the prison officials she had known best. All joined in singing "Amazing Grace" before her flower-covered casket. The minister proclaimed that the religion she found while in prison was a "living demonstration" of the grace of God. Several other religious figures said that Barfield had greatly helped other inmates while incarcerated and that many had relied on her support. The Reverend Phillip Carter, a local chaplain, talked about how she had touched and changed lives. Just before her death, he remembered, "her face glowed" and "her eyes were peaceful and content." Barfield was buried alongside her first husband,[110] near her childhood home in Parkton, North Carolina.[111]

Rickey Ray Rector

If Barfield's execution seemed drawn out, Rickey Ray Rector's death played out in slow motion. By the time he died, Rector had spent almost an hour in Arkansas's execution chamber,[112] during which time medical staff struggled to find a suitable vein in his arm. Witnesses overheard him sporadically crying out from behind the curtain that separated them from the condemned. "Sounds like they're really having trouble," said a sheriff in attendance.[113]

The problem of finding a usable vein is in fact a persistent one for lethal injection. In Texas in 1986, drug addict Randy Woolls had to help struggling technicians locate a suitable place for the injection needle. In April 1992, several months after Rector's execution, Billy Wayne White was strapped to the execution gurney for some forty-seven minutes while executioners searched for a vein in his arms. A longtime heroin user, White also attempted to assist authorities as they fumbled in putting him to death.

Rector's execution came after over a decade of heartache and delays. Born in the black quarter of Conway, a small town in Faulkner County, Arkansas, Rector was the sixth of seven children. His father was a cook at a steakhouse, and his mother worked as a maid at a local college. As a child, Rector liked to play alone, intentionally withdrawn from those around him. His only friend was a local elderly man. Years later he was remembered by classmates and teachers as different, seemingly lost.

Rector's father was a harsh taskmaster and often hit him with a strap for being "too slow." The boy struggled in junior high school and sunk further into his private world, growing ever more fearful of the outside. The abrupt racial integration of his middle school only heightened his fears. Rector once told his sister that the new white students did not want him in their classes, which, although perhaps amplified by his paranoia, was likely true.[114]

Rector started getting into fights, and in tenth grade he was expelled for his aggressive behavior. He lashed out at his parents when they tried to talk to him, and he started disappearing for days at a time. By age sixteen, Rector lived almost entirely in the world he had long ago created for himself.[115] He wandered the streets in the middle of the night. Although he managed to work on and off, Rector could never keep a job for long. Eventually he got married but had several children with other women. He was frequently jailed, or fined and released, by local police for crimes ranging from assault to grand larceny.[116]

One cool weekend evening in the summer of 1980, Rector went out with two friends to a local dance where two hundred people from the local black community gathered in the back room of a family restaurant. Rector, dressed all in leather, got into an argument over the entrance fee. He insisted that he and his friends should not have to pay. In the midst of the dispute he pulled a pistol from the waistband of his pants and fired, wounding two men and killing another whom he had shot in the throat and forehead.

After the shooting, Rector demanded that his friends take him home, and once there, he paced nervously before announcing to his wife that he was leaving. For two days he lingered around Conway before calling one of his sisters to say that he was in trouble and feared he would be killed. When the call ended he walked to another sister's house on the outskirts of town where she advised him to turn himself in to the police. Rector followed her advice.[117]

He agreed to meet the police at his mother's house. Bob Martin, the officer who came to arrest Rector, had known him since childhood. Even though he had arrested Rector once before, he maintained a good relationship with the family.[118] When he arrived at the house, Rector's mother invited Martin to wait in her parlor, where he talked amicably with her and two of Rector's siblings. Rector entered the parlor quietly, dressed in cotton work pants and a T-shirt.

The two men greeted each other from a short distance, and Martin continued chatting with his mother while Rector wordlessly pulled a pistol from behind his back and shot Martin through the neck and jaw. As the officer fell to the floor, Rector's mother and sister screamed and ran from the house. Rector walked out the door silently and into a neighboring garden, where he stopped at the foot of a pecan tree, lifted the pistol to his left temple, and fired.

Police called to the scene first discovered Rector and then found Martin's body inside the Rector home.[119] After seeing his dead colleague, one officer threatened to shoot the man's killer right on the spot.[120] But Rector did not respond; he lay motionless.[121]

Rector was rushed to Little Rock's University Hospital for emergency brain surgery.[122] Doctors found the bullet lodged just behind his right ear, where it had landed after blasting through the front of his skull. Postoperative reports described extensive and irreparable damage throughout his entire brain. Surgeons said that despite their best efforts Rector would suffer "gross memory loss" and struggle to comprehend the content and meaning of even the simplest events and ideas.[123]

These injuries amounted to a frontal lobotomy: after the surgery Rector could not understand the distinction between past and future, and could not wrap his mind around what had happened to him or what he himself had just done. One of Rector's attorneys later testified that when asked why he was in the hospital, Rector denied that he had had brain surgery at all, ignored any mention of scarring on his scalp, and insisted that it was his leg that had been operated on. More than once, Rector announced that he had not killed anyone but that the police had shot him in the head after killing Martin themselves.[124] His story changed often.[125]

Litigation arising from Rector's case spanned ten years. It centered on two main issues. The first question was whether Rector was capable of meaningfully assisting his counsel in his defense, as required by the Sixth Amendment. The second was whether Rector could comprehend his death sentence and what he had done to deserve his punishment, as required by the Supreme Court's *Ford v. Wainwright* decision.[126] A judge ruled in two separate competency hearings that Rector was in fact competent to stand trial and, if convicted, to be executed.[127]

At those hearings, Rector's attorneys nonetheless claimed that Rector was no longer the man who had murdered a police officer. "The person who shot Officer Martin cannot be executed," one later said. "He no longer lives. If we cannot execute that person, must we, nevertheless, execute his body?"[128]

His lawyers continued to paint Rector as incompetent. They said that their client could not carry on a meaningful conversation and that he had no real understanding of the finality of death. John Jewell, looking back on the process of Rector's defense, recalled that he came to feel great pity for his client. Another lawyer said that "we didn't have a client to defend. Rector was a nonexistent part of the trial."[129] Nonetheless, in

November 1982, an all-white jury, in just fifteen minutes,[130] found Rector guilty of capital murder and sentenced him to death.[131] After hearing his sentence, Rector asked whether he would get a television in his cell.[132]

At the time of Rector's execution, physical and mental disabilities did not exempt an inmate from the death penalty. In fact, several states executed disabled inmates in the years immediately preceding Rector's death.[133] Federal district judge Henry Woods, who denied one of Rector's many appeals, found that no one who had considered the claims about Rector's mental capacity concluded that he was "incompetent to be executed."[134] The Supreme Court twice refused to review Rector's conviction, first in 1984 and again in 1991.[135]

Executive clemency was Rector's only remaining hope, and his lawyers thought that Governor Bill Clinton might be merciful.[136] Because of Rector's severely impaired mental capacity, his execution "would be remembered as a disgrace to the state," a disgrace, his attorneys hoped, Clinton would want to avoid at all costs.[137] "He is, in the vernacular, a zombie," Rector's lawyer Jeff Rosenzweig told reporters before the execution. Even the Arkansas Supreme Court considered the case to be a good candidate for executive clemency.

In 1992 Bill Clinton was running for president. At the time, the presidential nominee had ordered close to seventy-seven execution dates for twenty-six death row inmates. Rector himself had four separate execution dates scheduled by the governor.[138] Thus it came as no surprise when Clinton denied Rector's clemency request in January 1992.[139] By some accounts Clinton wanted to make an example of Rector: "I am tough on crime: Who has Bush ever killed?"[140] Clinton even interrupted his campaign and returned to Arkansas to oversee the execution,[141] which was scheduled a short time before the New Hampshire primary.

In the time leading up to his execution Rector was held at Cummins Prison in southeastern Arkansas[142] in a seven-and-a-half-square-foot, windowless cell.[143] Prison records recount that in the hours before his death Rector was dancing, singing, howling and barking like a dog, laughing strangely, and even claiming that he would vote for Clinton.

The warden and prison medical supervisor attempted to explain the process of lethal injection to him, telling Rector that he would go to sleep "with as little pain as possible."

Despite this explanation Rector told one of his sisters, "I know they're gonna fry me." When asked to sign a form that confirmed he had chosen to die by lethal injection, he said, "I don't want to die, but I'm going to go on and take it because I don't want to get gassed and shocked." That night he ate a dinner of pork and cabbage, watched news about himself, and barked and howled some more before going to sleep.[144]

The morning of his execution Rector awoke for an early breakfast, yelling that he was a "Cold Duck" and that he would not see the guards again. By midday Rector shaved his beard, telling his lawyer, "I want to look good." In the evening, as he changed into an all-white cotton outfit, he nervously asked questions and started howling yet again. Just after 8:30 P.M. the guards took him from his cell and led him to the execution chamber.[145]

At the start of the execution, witnesses heard Rector moaning as technicians tried to find a vein. Originally, only two executioners were assigned to carry out Rector's lethal injection. But as the execution progressed, that number increased to five. Repeatedly unable to find a vein, they hurried to kill Rector by midnight—after which time another execution date would need to be set. After an hour, executioners were forced to use the so-called cut-down method in order to locate a suitable vein. This involved using a scalpel to cut into Rector's arm. During this procedure, Rector cried out eight times. Although the catheter and tube were—finally—correctly placed, blood was seen on the sheet laid across the gurney.

The drugs that would kill him, called the "Texas Mix," sat just above Rector's head as his sentence was read to him.[146] After saying his final words, "I got baptized and saved,"[147] he closed his eyes and shivered slightly.[148] At 10:09 P.M.,[149] a full nineteen minutes after executioners started the flow of lethal drugs, Rector was pronounced dead.[150]

Rector was forty years old at the time of his execution,[151] which came more than a decade after the killing of Officer Martin. By the time Rector's ashes were buried in Conway, Clinton was back on the campaign trail.[152] A group of death penalty opponents put Rector's death warrant up for sale, signed by Governor Clinton and by Rector himself in large, childlike letters. The warrant sold at auction for $1,500.[153]

After the execution Mr. Rosenzweig reiterated his belief that his client "didn't understand that death was permanent." In prison, Rosenzweig continued, "where they had dinner early, he used to save his dessert to eat right before he went to sleep." On the day of his execution, Rector ate his meal—chicken, baked potato. "After he was executed," Rosenzweig said, "they found his pecan pie in his cell."[154]

Romell Broom

In 2009, executioners in Ohio attempted unsuccessfully to insert an intravenous line into the arms and legs of Romell Broom for more than two hours before the execution was finally halted. During the failed procedure, Broom winced and grimaced with pain. At one point, he covered his face with both hands and appeared to be sobbing, his stomach heaving.

After the first hour had passed, Broom tried to help his executioners, turning onto his side, sliding the rubber tubing that served as a tourniquet up his left arm, and alternatively squeezing his fingers together and apart. Even when executioners found what they believed to be a suitable vein, it quickly collapsed as they tried to inject the saline fluid. Broom was once again brought to tears. After a full two hours of executioners sticking Broom's arms and legs with the needle, the prison director decided that the execution team should rest. As they did so, he contacted the governor of Ohio, who issued a reprieve stopping the execution.[155]

Broom had been sentenced to death for the rape and murder of Tryna Middleton, a fourteen-year-old girl, in Cleveland in 1984.[156] He abducted her as she was walking home from a Friday night football game with two friends.[157] According to prosecutors, Broom had a history of molesting young girls, and before Middleton's murder, he served eight and a half years in prison for the rape of a twelve-year-old babysitter.

Three months after Middleton's murder, Broom was arrested when he tried to force an eleven-year-old girl into his car.[158] After the arrest, Middleton's two thirteen-year-old friends picked Broom out of a police lineup.[159] Nonetheless, Broom maintained his innocence.[160]

By the time he found himself on Ohio's death row, Romell Broom had had a difficult life. Born in Michigan, he was five when his family moved to an Ohio neighborhood racked with poverty and violence, where his father and uncles ran a brothel.[161] When Broom was still young, his father made a regular point of explaining to his son that he was named "Romell" after the German field marshal in Hitler's army.[162]

His parents had children together but also with other people, some of whom lived with Broom.[163] They fought almost constantly. Once, his father, high on speed and cough syrup, beat his mother across the back with a coat hanger because she was on the phone with another man. He then dragged her through broken glass, which caused her to bleed so badly that she had to go to the hospital.

Romell was the eldest of ten children,[164] and even as a young child he was left with a tremendous amount of responsibility by his decidedly irresponsible parents. His mother would intentionally overdose on drugs, using admission to the hospital as a way to avoid the obligations of motherhood.[165] She would tell Broom to watch her until she passed out, at which point he was to call an ambulance.[166]

Unsurprisingly, young Broom struggled in school; he could barely read.[167] He stuttered,[168] and his embarrassment over being made to read aloud in class led him to skip school often, and then, after he turned thirteen, to stop going altogether.[169] His troubles with the police began when he was twelve,[170] when he learned from older boys in the neighborhood how to steal.[171] Eventually he was sent to the Ohio State Reformatory for boys.[172]

In a letter to author Clare Nonhebel, written in November following his failed execution, Broom, then fifty-three years old, described how throughout his life no one had ever cared about him.[173] At the time he wrote this letter, Broom had not seen his three half brothers in more than forty years. While he saw two of his brothers and his one surviving sister just before his execution, he had not seen them before this for twenty-five years.[174]

On Monday, the day before what would be his failed execution, Broom was transported from the Ohio State Penitentiary to the Southern Ohio Correctional Facility where officials placed him in a holding cell. Several hours later, prison medical staff inspected his veins and concluded that the veins in his right arm looked passable. After the examination, Broom ate the normal prison fare for dinner, chicken stir-fry with rice and bread.

Although he received no visitors that night, he spoke with his brother on the phone, telling him that he was tired of being in prison and of "having people tell him what to do every day." But he also told his brother that he was not ready to die.[175] Just after midnight, Broom fell asleep while watching television.[176]

He awoke early the next morning at about the time that the thiopental sodium, pancuronium bromide, and potassium chloride, used in Ohio's lethal injections, arrived at the facility. Preparations for the execution were halted, however, while the Sixth U.S. Circuit Court of Appeals decided what to do about Broom's last-minute appeal. His execution, originally scheduled for 10 A.M., was postponed for several hours while he awaited the court ruling.[177]

When the court announced it would not review his case, the execution was rescheduled for 1:30 P.M. After a first round of lethal drugs was destroyed for reasons that were never clearly explained, replacement drugs were delivered to the death house.[178] Broom's execution began at around 2 P.M., four hours after the original start time.[179]

Because the execution team experienced difficulty right from the start, they never moved Broom to the gurney.[180] When they could not find a suitable vein in his arms, they probed his legs. A technician stuck a needle into one leg and Broom grimaced in pain. Another member of the team patted him on the back.[181]

At 2:30, the team asked Broom if he wanted a break.[182] Broom responded that he would rather keep going, but the prison director insisted that the execution stop while he contacted the governor with news of the delays.[183] The team returned to work just over ten minutes later.[184] Every time an apparently usable vein was found, it would collapse as soon as executioners attempted injection.[185] At 3 P.M., more than an hour into the execution, the team speculated that Broom's history of drug use was responsible for their troubles.[186] Around 4 P.M., they told the prison director that they did not think Broom's veins would accept the saline fluid or the lethal drugs. The director again contacted the governor.[187]

At this point, Broom requested that one of his attorneys be brought into the witness area. But when the attorney asked to speak with her client, she was told that she could not since the execution process had already begun.[188] She responded, "I want to know what Romell wants," and was told her client was being cooperative. "He's always cooperative," she retorted. "I want to know what he wants me to do."[189]

Meanwhile, another of Broom's lawyers contacted the chief justice of the Ohio Supreme Court asking him to halt the execution. He claimed that continuation of the execution after such extraordinary delays would violate Ohio's statutory requirement that lethal injection be quick and painless. Sometime later, the ACLU of Ohio, pointing to a series of recent botched executions, asked state officials to halt all executions.[190]

The Middletons—the parents and aunt of Broom's victim—seated alongside four news reporters, watched the botched execution on television monitors. Broom occasionally looked into the camera above him and grimaced in pain.[191] Outside, about twenty protestors had come to show their disapproval of the execution, but according to one reporter, "many left for home by 1:30 p.m. because of the long drive home and the sweltering heat." Those that remained prayed and wept for the condemned and his victims while the empty hearse drove out of the prison gate.[192]

After the governor decided to stop the execution, the prison director thanked Broom for his positive demeanor throughout the whole process.[193] Taken from the death chamber, Broom ate dinner and was brought to a new cell in the prison infirmary,[194] where he remained under close observation.[195] According to his attorneys, Broom had over eighteen different needle sticks in his arms and legs.[196] One insisted that the execution attempt had left her client physically and emotionally traumatized and suggested that because the process had failed the first time, when Broom's veins had not been touched, it would be a disaster to try to execute him a second time.[197]

Broom was the first man since Willie Francis whose execution could not be completed. "This is uncharted territory for us," a prison spokeswoman said, referring to the difficulties of Broom's execution.[198] She confirmed that the execution procedure would not be adjusted for the second attempt.[199] Governor Strickland echoed her resolve. In response to the ACLU's call for a stay of all executions, he reaffirmed his support for the death penalty and said that he believed it "an appropriate measure" when members of society commit the most heinous acts. He rescheduled Broom's execution for September 22, 2009.[200]

On the Friday after the execution attempt, Broom's attorneys filed lawsuits alleging that another execution attempt would violate their client's civil rights. The attorneys also appealed to the Supreme Court,[201] arguing that either the execution should be stayed until Ohio modified its procedures, or Broom should not be executed at all. "Once you try and fail, you do not have the right to try again," one lawyer said.[202]

Their appeals coincided with a federal lawsuit, based on Broom's botched execution, challenging Ohio's lethal injection procedure.[203] The attorneys argued that the protocol was completely inadequate. The federal public defenders who filed the suit in the Federal District Court in Columbus hoped to delay the lethal injection of another inmate, Lawrence Reynolds, who was scheduled for execution the following week.[204]

They argued that their case required that they have the opportunity to interview Broom; a judge ordered Broom deposed on the day before his second scheduled execution.[205] The Ohio attorney general responded to the suit and asserted that difficulties experienced during Broom's execution did not preclude the successful carrying out of subsequent executions. "The relatively minor pain he experienced," did not "rise to the level of extreme pain or torture prohibited by the Eighth Amendment."[206]

In the years since Broom's failed execution, little has been resolved. At the time of this writing, Broom was still on death row and it remained to be seen whether the state of Ohio would in fact attempt to kill him again.[207]

Emmitt Foster

Seven minutes after lethal chemicals began to drip into Emmitt Foster's veins, the drugs stopped flowing. As Foster gasped and convulsed, the execution team tried to figure out what was causing the problem. Twenty minutes later, Washington County, Missouri, coroner William "Mal" Gum entered the death chamber to find out why the inmate was still alive. Noticing that virtually none of the drugs were flowing through the IV drip chamber, he quickly diagnosed what had gone wrong.

The plastic catheter tube that was close to the inmate's wrist and the arm strap that attached Foster to the gurney were cutting off circulation near his elbow. After the coroner suggested loosening it, "things happened quickly." Foster already registered a "dying heartbeat," which fell rapidly after the strap was loosened.[208] He was pronounced dead thirty minutes after the execution began. In an editorial, the *St. Louis Post-Dispatch* called the execution "a particularly sordid chapter in Missouri's capital punishment experience."[209]

On November 20, 1983, in St. Louis County, Missouri, De Ann Keys and her boyfriend, Travis Walker, were reportedly awakened by a phone call at 2:00 A.M. The call was from two of Walker's friends, who later were identified as Michael Phillips and another man known initially only as John Lee. The two men arrived at the couple's residence soon after the call. While Walker went with the men into the living room, Keys stayed in the bedroom. Phillips, however, quickly forced her to join them and instructed her to lie next to her boyfriend on the floor. She could see Lee, later identified as Emmitt Foster, standing over Walker with a pistol in hand. Phillips ransacked the apartment.

The men shot both Keys and Walker before they left. Keys regained consciousness at some point and sought help. Finding none, she returned to the apartment and wrote the names of their attackers— Phillips and "John Lee"—on an envelope. By the time police arrived, Walker was dead on the living room floor, and Keys was lying on the bed. She told police officers that the names she had written on the envelope were those of the perpetrators. Police soon identified John Lee as Emmitt Foster, and they arrested him two days later, charging him with murder.[210]

By this time in his life, Foster had compiled a long history of legal trouble. In August 1968 he was sentenced to eighteen months at the Federal Youth Correctional Center at Inglewood, California, for unlawful possession of U.S. mail. In October 1970 he was found guilty of two counts of first-degree robbery by means of a dangerous and deadly weapon. Five years later, in June 1975, Foster was again imprisoned for robbery.

In April 1984, Foster was indicted in St. Louis County on the charge of capital murder for the shooting death of Travis Walker. Phillips, Foster's accomplice, pled guilty and was sentenced to life in prison without parole.[211] Foster, on the other hand, insisted on having his day in court. In September of that year he was found guilty and sentenced to death. He filed an appeal in December, which was denied.[212] Years of motions, petitions, and denials would follow.[213]

In November 1985, the Missouri Supreme Court affirmed Foster's conviction and sentence. The next year the United States Supreme Court denied certiorari. Foster's motion for state postconviction relief in the Circuit Court of St. Charles County was later denied and the Eastern District of the Missouri Court of Appeals affirmed the decision. In 1992, Foster's habeas petition was turned down by the Federal District Court for the Eastern District of Missouri.[214]

In April 1993, the U.S. Court of Appeals for the Eighth Circuit reversed the district court's order and granted Foster's petition, only to affirm his conviction and sentence in November of that same year. After the U.S. Supreme Court declined to review that decision, Missouri set Foster's execution date for May 3, 1995.[215] Foster would be the eleventh man executed by lethal injection since the state adopted the procedure as a replacement for the gas chamber in 1988.[216]

Before his execution, Foster was housed in the Potosi Correctional Center[217] in Washington County, Missouri.[218] On the evening of his death he was served a last meal of catfish, shrimp, French fries, lemon meringue pie, and a strawberry milkshake.[219] Just before midnight, prison officials strapped Foster to a gurney in the death chamber.[220] Ten witnesses watched him through the glass that separated the death chamber from the viewing room.[221] In his final statement, Foster said, "I do have remorse for the legal system because I did not commit this particular murder."[222]

The lethal chemicals began to flow at 12:03 A.M. Seven minutes later, at 12:10, officials closed the curtains that separated the execution chamber from witnesses. At 12:36, they reopened the curtains and announced that Foster had died three minutes earlier. Attempting to explain the length of time it took to execute Foster, a corrections spokesman merely said, "There are individuals who take a longer time to die than others." He went on to explain that prison officials had drawn the blinds only in order to preserve the anonymity of the workers who examined the lethal injection apparatus, which they believed had malfunctioned.

A spokesman for the Missouri Department of Corrections admitted that Foster's execution "did take a bit longer than they usually do," and assured reporters that the Department of Corrections would investigate to see "if the execution process [needed] fixing,"[223] although he also insisted that prison staff had followed normal procedures and that Foster did not feel any pain. Coroner Gum shrugged off the incident, calling it a "little error." "It's not like the guy suffered," he said.[224]

After Foster's execution, two Kansas City lawyers filed a lawsuit in federal court on behalf of Missouri's ninety-one death row inmates, challenging the constitutionality of lethal injection.[225] They argued that lethal injection constituted "cruel and unusual punishment," citing botched lethal injections in Texas, Oklahoma, Arkansas, and Illinois.[226]

The ultimately unsuccessful lawsuit pointed to the "extraordinary painful death" that inmates suffered during botched lethal injections. It cited the inventor of the machine used on Foster and other inmates executed at Potosi as saying that death was meant to occur within five minutes of the start of the process. The attorneys also claimed that Missouri's execution process was entirely unregulated: no law governed what substances must be injected, who should perform the execution, or the type of training an executioner must have.

A lawyer from the Missouri Capital Punishment Resource Center later said, "It must be pretty painful, I'd imagine," referring to what he believed was the failure of the drugs to knock Foster out, leaving him awake when his organs failed. "That's why he was writhing around," the lawyer explained.[227] Gino Battisti, Foster's own attorney, called his client's prolonged death "totally barbaric and inexcusable."[228]

An Enviable Way to Die?

Lethal injection was once widely thought to be the final step in the evolution of the technology of state killing. Medicalized, bureaucratic, private, quick—it seemed to provide the ultimate answer to the state's commitment to "impose no more pain than is necessary" on those it subjects to the ultimate punishment. As Justice Antonin Scalia wrote in *Callins v. Collins*, responding to Justice Blackmun's call for the state to stop "tinkering with the machinery of death,"

> Justice Blackmun begins his statement by describing with poignancy the death of a convicted murderer by lethal injection. He chooses, as

the case in which to make that statement, one of the less brutal of the murders that regularly come before us, the murder of a man ripped by a bullet suddenly and unexpectedly, with no opportunity to prepare himself and his affairs, and left to bleed to death on the floor of a tavern. *The death-by-injection which Justice Blackmun describes looks pretty desirable next to that.* It looks even better next to some of the other cases currently before us, which Justice Blackmun did not select as the vehicle for his announcement that the death penalty is always unconstitutional, for example, the case of the 11-year-old girl raped by four men and then killed by stuffing her panties down her throat. *How enviable a quiet death by lethal injection compared with that!*[29]

Whether or not we agree with Scalia that death by lethal injection is "enviable" in comparison to other ways of dying, the history of botched lethal injections proves that it is by no means a foolproof method of killing and that its use cannot guarantee that those subjected to it—like Velma Barfield, Ricky Ray Rector, Romell Broom, or Emmit Foster—will die quickly, quietly, and painlessly.

CHAPTER 6

Botched Executions and the Struggle to End Capital Punishment

On October 12, 1906, Joda Hamilton, a twenty-year-old Missouri farm boy, followed Barney Parsons along a dirt road near their neighboring farms. For a long time the two men had not gotten along, having repeatedly fought over money in the past. Their quarrel that day centered on a soured land deal.

The Parsons family, preparing to leave town for their old home in Litchfield, looked on from the side of the road as Hamilton approached. An argument erupted and quickly got out of control. In the heat of the dispute, Hamilton shot and killed Barney Parsons, and then brutally clubbed his wife and three young children to death. After the murders he calmly drove the Parsonses' wagon back to his nearby home.

Two days later, fishermen discovered the bodies in Piney Creek about a mile downstream from where the murders had occurred. The bodies of two of the Parsons children were lodged in a mill dam. Authorities arrested Hamilton soon after, and it was not long before he confessed. Hamilton was ultimately sentenced to death for his crimes.

The day before his execution, the "boy murderer" was reportedly calm and self-possessed.[1] Accompanied by the sheriff, he was even allowed to examine the scaffold for himself. He asked the sheriff to pad the edges of the trapdoor on the gallows so that his body would not be scraped as it fell.

The next day, December 22, 1906, the town of Houston, Missouri, filled with curious visitors, had a "holiday appearance" about it.[2] Hamilton's hanging was to be the first legal execution ever carried out in the county. Vendors sold pictures of the condemned and his victims in the streets. Everything, it seemed, was in full readiness for the execution.

In this case, however, something went very wrong. Joda Hamilton had to be hung twice on that Saturday morning, and his execution was aptly described as an unmistakably "horrible affair."[3] In the midst of the hanging the rope broke, and the crowds watched as Hamilton struggled, alive yet close to death, on the ground beneath the gallows. Still partially conscious, he was lifted and carried back to the scaffold. At 11:10 A.M., the rope was again tied around his neck. The trapdoor was sprung, and Hamilton was pronounced dead.

All over the country, newspapers—from the *Boston Globe* to the *Dubuque Telegraph-Herald* and the *San Francisco Call*—reported Hamilton's execution. Headlines announced, "Hamilton Hangs Twice,"[4] "Hang Boy Twice Before He Dies,"[5] "Strung Up a Second Time,"[6] "Bungle at Houston Hanging,"[7] and "Hanging of Youth a Gruesome Bungle."[8] In most cases, newspapers focused particularly on spectators' horror at the failure of the first hanging. Reading, Pennsylvania's, *Reading Eagle* wrote that "spectators saw Hamilton drop to the ground and lie there writhing" as the rope was mended by supervising officials.[9] The *San Francisco Call* subtitled its article "Agony Racks Body" and reported that "At the first attempt Hamilton shot through the trap with a jerk and the spectators were horrified to see the rope part."[10] Similarly, the *Los Angeles Herald* headlined its article "Rope Parts at First Drop and Youth Writhes on the Ground in Agony While the Break Is Repaired."[11]

Hamilton's execution was universally treated as an "*unusually* gruesome" affair.[12] The *Yellowstone News* called the hanging "badly bungled."[13] Yet newspapers followed up their sensationalistic accounts of the execution scene with careful disclaimers, treating Hamilton's execution as an aberration, an uncharacteristically brutal death on the scaffold. Moreover, their reports minimized his pain and offered reassurance: "The attending physician expressed the belief that Hamilton was fatally injured by the first fall and died before he dropped the second time."[14] Even the *Yellowstone News*, in a segment running only two sentences, reported that "Hamilton was probably fatally hurt by the fall."[15] The *Lawrence Daily World* noted that Hamilton's already "Lifeless Body" was dropped a second time.[16] Despite the unquestionable botching of his execution, newspapers made it appear as if Hamilton had suffered little as a result. The second drop was presented as an almost inconsequential detail.

Some papers went so far as to blame the problems in the execution on Hamilton himself. The *Lawrence Daily World* said that "Hamilton's weight broke the rope."[17] The state, in this instance, was given no agency for its failure to efficiently discharge its power to kill.

The *World's* account is merely a particularly vivid example of a more general pattern. Newspaper reports of Hamilton's death did not treat his botched execution as the failure of the state or the failure of the institution of capital punishment. America's death penalty system remained safely intact and entirely unchallenged. Only one short commentary alluded to the potential shortcomings of hanging as a method of execution, proclaiming offhandedly, "Electrocute, if kill we must!"[18] By and large, newspapers offered Hamilton's botched execution as little more than sensationalized entertainment for their readers: a voyeuristic pleasure without consequence or injured conscience.

As noted in Chapter 1, botched executions seem to reveal the pain, violence, and inhumanity of capital punishment hidden behind today's meticulous execution protocols and modern technology. They can turn organized, state-controlled ritual into torture, solemn spectacles of sovereign power into spectacles of horror. Executions like Hamilton's and the others discussed in this book might have posed a direct challenge to the state's desired presentation of its own killing. This chapter returns to a question with which the book began; namely, what role have botched executions in fact played in the struggle to end capital punishment in the United States?

The answer to this question depends less on abstract, theoretical speculation or the normative commitments articulated by courts than it does on the "cultural reception" of botched executions. The power of botched executions to expose the brutality of capital punishment, and therefore their impact on its continuing legitimation, depends on how they are received, constructed, and construed in popular culture. The remainder of the chapter thus investigates newspaper accounts of botched executions from 1890 to 2010 in order to understand both how the meanings attributed to those events evolved over the course of the twentieth century as well as the consequences of those attributions in the struggle to end capital punishment in the United States.

Media accounts of otherwise silent, virtually invisible executions hold "up a magnifying looking glass to a precarious ritual that the authorities [take pains] to conceal from the general public."[19] We rely on the press to show us what we cannot see. And with regard to botched executions, the press has allowed us to see relatively little.[20]

Like the judicial opinions discussed in Chapter 1, newspapers also assume the legibility of pain and their capacity to represent it accurately. Although at times botched executions have occasioned challenges to particular execution methods, throughout the course of the twentieth century they have contributed little to the effort to end capital punishment itself. The question is why this has been the case.

As the newspaper coverage of Hamilton's execution suggests, part of the answer lies in cultural reception. The failure of newspapers to heighten the abolitionist potential of botched executions is a recurrent trend in their coverage throughout the twentieth century. Newspaper accounts have served as a source of "cultural reinforcement" for capital punishment in the face of the brutality which botched executions expose.[21]

According to political theorist Judith Shklar, injury can only become injustice when *we recognize it as such*. The definition of injustice, then, turns on reception—on how particular injuries are received and read by witnesses. "Injustices" are, by Shklar's account, socially constructed.[22] During the course of the twentieth century, newspapers generally treated botched executions as "misfortunes" rather than injustices and, in so doing, helped neutralize the abolitionist potential of the botched executions they reported. This result is as much a function of journalistic conventions as political convictions. As journalistic style evolved, so did the ways in which newspaper coverage defused the violence and disorder of botched executions.

Sensationalism and Recuperation in Early-Twentieth-Century Coverage of Botched Executions

On May 9, 1883, Joseph Pulitzer purchased the failing *New York World* for a mere $346,000. His onslaught of the dull New York dailies began almost immediately when on May 11 the *World* shocked New York with sensational coverage of a hanging in Pittsburgh, a riot in Haiti, and a devastating storm in New Jersey.[23] Pulitzer was by no means the first publisher to use sensationalism as a business strategy, but he embraced it more fully than any who had come before. "At a time when many newspapers labored under Victorian codes of propriety," Chris Daly explains, "Pulitzer waded into the sordid, the squalid, and the shocking."[24] His writers reported the news in a uniquely narrative style and used vivid, highly suggestive language.

In this context, consider the *World*'s coverage of the botched 1890 electrocution of William Kemmler, whose case was discussed in Chapter 3. The *World*'s report described the reaction of onlookers to Kemmler's surviving the first fifteen-second electrical shock:

> Warden, physicians, everybody lost their wits. There was a startled cry for the current to be turned on again. Signals, only half understood, were given to those in the next room at the switchboard. When they knew what had happened, they were prompt to act, and the switch-handle could be heard as it was pulled back and forth, breaking the deadly current into jets. The rigor of death came on the instant. An odor of burning flesh and singed hair filled the room. For a moment a blue flame played about the base of the victim's spine. One of the witnesses nearly fell to the floor. Another lost control of his stomach. Cold perspiration beaded every face. This time the electricity flowed four minutes. Kemmler was dead. Part of his brain had been baked hard.

Some of the blood in his head had been turned into charcoal. The flesh at the small of his back was black with fire.[25]

Here the newspaper mobilizes the language of "weapons and wounds" to represent Kemmler's pain. And in its coverage, the *World* made no effort to lend dignity to the performance; on the contrary, the reporter sought to bring the sights, sounds, and smells of the death chamber to the masses.

The ultimate goal of sensationalizing the news was, of course, to sell newspapers. The late nineteenth and early twentieth centuries was an era of intense competition for readership, as "the financial stability of the new metropolitan dailies always depended on winning more and more readers in order to attract larger advertising revenues."[26] And sensation worked. In its first year under Pulitzer's leadership, the *World* quadrupled its circulation.[27] Such success inevitably spawned imitators—most notoriously William Randolph Hearst and his *New York Journal*. By the turn of the twentieth century, "yellow journalism" had emerged as a distinctive and increasingly dominant branch of the American newspaper business.[28] Furthermore, "in almost every big city, the yellowest paper was the circulation leader."[29]

While yellow journalism arguably reached its high-water mark during the Spanish-American War, around 1900, it retained significant influence well into the new century. As late as 1915, in its description of Thomas Tarpy's botched electrocution, the *New York Tribune* reported that "five times the current leaped through his mighty body before life was entirely driven out. 'My God!' whispered one of the guards as they carried him away. 'What a man!'"[30] This account deliberately dramatized the execution spectacle. The various participants become caricatures, helping the storyteller sell tales of blood, violence, heroes, and villains.

Nevertheless, the scandalous and bloody stories that thrived on the pages of daily newspapers belied an entirely different trend in American life: an increasingly squeamish middle class. Sensationalism did not entirely rule the day. As noted in Chapter 2, by the turn of the century, "a newly sensitized middle-class wanted to shield itself from the brutalities of violence, whether private or public."[31]

The heyday of sensationalized yellow journalism came just as the American middle classes were beginning to develop the cultural sensibilities that would demand the distancing of state killing from bodily pain and uncontrolled violence. As the nineteenth century progressed, the more affluent members of society increasingly sought to distinguish themselves as refined and polite in contrast to the "boorish" masses. The execution event, as a scene not just of death but of killing, clearly offended such sensibilities.

The "death house" became the site of a new cultural taboo, at once alluring and grotesque. "The new sentiments," Linders writes, "were directed not only at the unpleasantness of the execution itself but also at the uncivilized manner in which the lower-class crowd conducted itself during the public spectacle."[32] The emergent middle classes desired order, especially when it came to the execution spectacle. They disdained and feared uncontrolled mob violence. Disorder was especially inexcusable when the state took a life.

Thus sensational violence might still have had a place in the pages of newspapers, but it no longer belonged in the public square. These two trends pulled newspaper coverage of botched executions in opposite directions.

This tension is evident in the coverage of Washington, D.C.'s, execution of Benjamin Snell on June 29, 1900, in what the *Atlanta Constitution* described as "a spectacle that was most revolting."[33] Snell had been convicted of murdering Lizzie Weisenberger, a thirteen-year-old girl with whom he was infatuated. Around noon on the day of the execution, jail officials marched Snell to the scaffold as he "mumbled incoherent words" at the ground.[34] At 12:07, the warden gave the signal, and the trapdoor opened. The *Constitution* described what followed:

The affair was almost a decapitation. The heavy rope cut through the neck of the murderer and severed the windpipe and blood vessels, and practically pulverized the bones of the neck. The tough muscles at the back of the neck saved the total severance of the head from the body. Blood gushed from the severed arteries almost instantly, and dyed the white linen shirt and collar, and then flowed down the clothing, extending to the shoes.

In this account, the reporter is, at once, painfully precise about the apparent causes of death—Snell's severed windpipe, blood vessels, and pulverized bones—and artful in his description of the scene as a whole. In the end, he confidently assumes the legibility of the body in pain and offers readers the violent image of a man bathed in blood from his shirt collar to his shoes.

Other newspapers carried equally gruesome accounts. The *Washington Times* meticulously listed the severed tissues in Snell's neck.[35] The *Washington Post* reported that "When the rope tightened as the drop fell Snell was almost decapitated. It was probably as gruesome a sight as any beheld at the District Jail."[36] Snell's death was, in short, a "horrible exhibition."[37] Quotations like these exemplify what we term the "sensationalist" narrative.

If judges like Burton and Reed in the *Francis* case elide the suffering of those whose executions are botched, early-twentieth-century newspaper reports of botched executions played up their grisly effects on the body of the condemned, highlighting blood-soaked garments, burned flesh, and slow death. All the same, sensationalist narratives did not typically make any normative claims about the death penalty or even about the particular botched execution they described. For the most part, images of blood and gore did not denote unjustifiable violence—or even unnecessary suffering on the part of the condemned.

In addition, the newspaper coverage of Snell's botched hanging contained a second, entirely different narrative strain. Let's consider the *Constitution's* account once more. From the very first lines, we encounter several important details: the rope, we are told, "cut through the neck of *the murderer*." Snell was, after all, a pedophile and child killer who had been made to pay the price. And yes, the *Times* did list every tissue severed in Snell's neck; however, all this was cited from a medical examination, which was offered to prove that his death had been instantaneous.

The *Post* called the execution scene "gruesome" and "horrible," but first wrote that *"As the crime was horrible,* so was the execution of the big murderer *almost* equally ghastly."[38] Snell's death might have been a hard one, but then again, he probably deserved it. Just a few lines after describing Snell's execution as "as gruesome a sight as any beheld at the district jail," the *Post*, like the *Times*, tempered its account: "It was an *unfortunate* circumstance, for which only Snell's great weight was responsible. . . . As it was, though somewhat revolting, death was instantaneous. There was not even the twitching of a muscle."[39] In the context of botched executions, revulsion does not automatically signal injustice.

Other newspapers similarly underlined the lack of suffering on the part of the condemned. "Snell met death quickly," the *Washington Times* reported.[40] Occasionally they provided explicit justifications for the execution. The *Boston Globe,* for example, titled its article on Snell's execution "Paid 'the Wages of Sin.'"[41] And even more importantly, every report stressed the atypical nature of Snell's execution. His was the "Execution of a Giant."[42] Benjamin Snell stood six and a half feet and weighed somewhere on the order of 240 pounds. He was "the largest man ever executed" at the District jail.[43] If there was any injustice in the execution of Benjamin Snell, it had nothing to do with capital punishment as a system.

Still, Snell's case was not unique on all counts; attenuating claims like those we have just described feature prominently in early-twentieth-century coverage of botched executions. Taken together, they constitute a "recuperative" narrative: a storyline that offers justifications and reasoned explanations for the gruesome spectacles it meticulously describes. If botched executions threaten the legitimacy of state killing by unmasking the violence inherent in its practice, the recuperative narrative aims to mitigate this potential damage. It treats them not as systemic injustices but as misfortunes and reassures readers that capital punishment is both humane and just. In so doing, it veils again the fleetingly exposed brutality of a botched execution.

In the early twentieth century, sensationalist and recuperative narratives coexisted precariously. The first amplified the violence that the second sought to downplay. In this sense, they were always in tension, if not entirely contradictory.

Beyond maintaining the appearance of order, modern execution ritual purportedly ensures that the condemned does not unduly suffer as he is put to death. As argued in earlier chapters, the deployment of new technologies of execution has been rationalized in terms of their success in offering "painless" killing. Like the 1888 New York state commission that recommended the replacement of hanging with electrocution, each new technology has promised "a fast, painless, certain, and clean execution . . . more humane for the condemned person and less troubling for spectators."[44] As we have seen, however, no technology has completely realized this aspiration. And when a bungled job resulted in smoke, fire, appalling smells, and a lingering death, newspapers eagerly reported it—and then helped repair the damage of doing so.

After it took five shocks and eight minutes for the state of New York to kill Antonio Ferraro in the chair at Sing Sing, the *New York Times* noted that "it is not believed, however, that he retained consciousness after the first charge."[45] The *Tribune's* reassurances bordered on the comical: "Ferraro was of a brutish nature, and it has been the experience at Sing Sing that men of that stamp offer more resistance to the electric current than those of more delicate composition."[46] In emphasizing the deviant quality of Ferraro in the context of his execution, the *Tribune* plainly classifies his botched execution as a misfortune—an important hallmark of the recuperative narrative. Misfortunes simply cannot be helped; brutes will inevitably have a different experience in the electric chair than others.

Three years later, Frank White was put to death at Sing Sing in what the *Tacoma Times* called a thoroughly "Frightful Execution."[47] The *Washington Post's* article was headlined "Six Contacts Used to Kill" and subtitled "Painful Scenes at the Execution of Frank White at Auburn."[48] In its short piece, "Six Shocks Necessary to Kill Negro," the *Washington Times* remarked that although White "did not make any demonstration," there was "an unusual happening in the death chamber."[49] The *Atlanta Constitution* headlined its article with true sensationalistic flair: "Buckled in Death Chair, Negro Defied Lightning."[50]

Newspapers described the execution scene in dramatic detail. The *San Francisco Call* reported that

> Six contacts, each of 1,740 volts 7 ½ amperes, were applied before White was pronounced dead. After the fourth contact a strange gurgling in his throat made the physicians step back and horrified spectators. The contact was quickly repeated, but still the stethoscope recorded cardiac action, and two more contacts were given. During the second contact the head of the electrode flashed brilliantly and there was an odor of burning hair.[51]

Nearly every other account included similar details. The *Tacoma Times* noted that at one point the electrode "emitted sparks."[52] Other papers reported that "Just as the sixth shock was being given," Dr. Stein, an attending physician from Buffalo, fainted and "pitched forward from his chair almost into the electric box."[53] The *San Francisco Call* wrote, even more melodramatically, that the doctor "fell to the floor in a swoon."[54]

Still newspapers made determined attempts to soothe any anxieties their sensationalistic reporting might have produced. After noting that the "electrode flashed brilliantly and there was an odor of burning hair," the *San Francisco Call* explained that "The executioner said it was the sponge beneath the electrode" and that he "adjusted it more tightly before the next shock."[55] The sponge, not White's flesh, had caught fire. In addition to this reassurance, almost every article offered a recuperative explanation for the "strange gurgling" which had terrified spectators. Both the *Call* and the *Washington Post*, for example, concluded their description of the execution scene as follows: "State Electrician Davis, in charge of the execution explained the gurgling in White's throat by saying that he held his breath for a few moments after the first contact and it was simply air escaping from his lungs. He declared that White was practically dead after the first contact."[56]

The gurgling sound, then, was not a sign of pain but "simply" a sort of abnormal exhalation. White could not have suffered any pain after the first shock anyway, for the young man was "practically dead" from the very beginning. The *San Francisco Call* titled its report "Negro Suffers Death Penalty." And as newspapers would have had their readers believe, there was little more to it than that. The pairing of sensationalist and recuperative narratives soothed the anxieties of society's fledgling humanitarians by allowing them to enjoy the scandal and then quickly forget the reality.

Robert Blecker summarizes the modern attitude toward pain that began to solidify in the early twentieth century: "At every opportunity we banish pain from our sight; we professionalize and bureaucratize its infliction in private settings. Pain, and with it punishment itself, became an abstraction; its intentional infliction is a sight and act to be avoided, a source of shame."[57]

Joseph Pulitzer, defending his newspapers' sensationalism, offered a very different portrait of American society at the turn of the century: "The complaint of the 'low moral tone of the press' is common but very unjust. A newspaper relates the events of the day. . . . Let those who are startled by it blame the people who are before the mirror, and not the mirror, which only reflects their features and actions."[58]

Read side by side, these two pictures of American life capture the peculiar contradiction that characterizes the cultural reception of botched executions in this period. Just as newspapermen built empires on scandal and carnage, states sought to conceal and control the violence of state killing. Newspapers tried to satisfy both the continuing voyeuristic inclinations and the emerging sense of public decency of their readership. The press unabashedly sold grisly details of executions gone wrong but then reassured readers of capital punishment's continued legitimacy. In the end, the recuperative narrative they offered neutered the abolitionist impact of even the most brutal botched execution.

The Emergence of Journalistic Professionalism and the Cultural Reception of Botched Executions

By 1920 the era of yellow journalism was drawing to a close. Joseph Pulitzer died in 1911, and his brand of journalism did not long outlive him. The University of Missouri had founded the world's first school of journalism in 1908, and in 1912 Columbia University launched its own school with a generous endowment from Pulitzer himself. Walter Williams, the first dean of the Missouri school, published a treatise called "The Journalist's Creed," in which he argued that "the journalist should answer to no one and nothing but the truth and should be absolutely *independent*—independent from the government, independent from partisan loyalties, independent from the advertisers and even the paper's own business office."[59] The truly professional journalist, therefore, would not write sensationalist stories merely to sell newspapers.

By 1924 there were about sixty journalism schools and programs nationwide.[60] With their influence over the profession quickly growing, sensationalism gradually lost its place as metropolitan dailies "toned down from vivid yellows to pastels."[61] In this context, graphic descriptions of botched executions all but disappeared, first from the major urban papers and not long after from the small-town press.

To take one example, on September 15, 1922, the state of Iowa executed Eugene Weeks, who had murdered a grocer in Des Moines. The rope used for the hanging, wet from the morning's rain, stretched so much after the drop that Weeks's feet hit the ground beneath the scaffold. The sheriff was obliged to physically hoist the condemned man up, wrap slack from the rope around a post, and wait while Weeks slowly strangled to death. Though the metropolitan dailies gave fairly detailed accounts of the execution, none emphasized its horror in particularly vivid language.

The *Washington Post* reported, "Sheriff Robb conducted the execution unflinchingly, and when an unfortunate adjustment of the rope permitted Weeks's feet to touch the ground, the former army chaplain seized the rope and helped the prison warden wrap it around a post so that Weeks's suffering would not be prolonged."[62] Instead of focusing on the violence of Weeks's death, the *Post* praised the quick thinking of a well-practiced executioner cum former preacher, whose actions were portrayed as almost noble. Robb's errors went unreported. He had helped make the pain stop: forget the fact that he had neglected to prevent it. He became the hero, carefully ensuring that the murderer's "suffering would not be prolonged," in an unfortunate, unforeseeable mishap.

The *Chicago Tribune* similarly focused its report of Weeks's botched execution on the valiant efforts of the minister-sheriff: "A heavy rain caused a stretching of the rope with which Weeks was hanged, allowing his feet to drag on the ground after he had been dropped through the trap. The preacher-sheriff and Warden T. P. Hollowell caught the rope and tightened it with a piece of timber, permitting Weeks's body to hang free."[63]

Just as in the *Post* article, the reporter here is methodical in his description of the botched execution—so methodical, in fact, that there appears to be virtually no interruption in the intended procedure. Sheriff Robb "performed his duty without a moment of hesitation."[64] Robb's actions, then, allegedly saved Weeks from prolonged suffering and rescued the execution ritual. Both reports do not conceal that something went wrong at the execution, but neither do they highlight the violence that ensued. They exemplify the more subdued style of reporting that became dominant as the era of yellow journalism came to an end. Without sensationalist descriptions of the scene, Weeks's "misfortune" is barely visible at all. The thought of any systemic injustice is never called to mind.

Now consider the version published by the *Telegraph-Herald* in the small town of Dubuque, Iowa: "The rain this morning had stretched the rope and Weeks's toes touched the ground. His body twisted and writhed convulsively as he fought for air. Warden Hollowell and Sheriff Robb, on the platform of the scaffold, caught the rope with Weeks's body at the end and twisted it about a large timber to keep Weeks's full weight on the rope."[65] The second sentence of this quotation communicates vividly the pain that Weeks endured at the hands of the state, in contrast to the more sanitized accounts of the *Post* and the *Tribune*. This example is part of a larger phenomenon: sensationalist coverage persisted in small-town newspapers for at least a decade after it disappeared from the big cities,[66] a difference which gradually eroded as the century progressed.[67]

The demise of sensationalism had important implications for the cultural meanings assigned to botched executions. No longer would gruesome descriptive accounts invite citizens to contemplate the exposed violence of the killing act. Increasingly, newspapers did not signal the significance of botched executions in any way. Previously the press allowed the public to learn of the violence of botched executions through vivid description—albeit without any abolitionist motivation. Though sensationalism on its own does not imply any assertion of injustice, it does put the damaging effects of a botch on display by laying bare the resulting pain and suffering. During the earlier period, the sensationalist narrative muddied an otherwise straightforward recuperative tale of misfortune when executions went wrong. Free of this complication, newspapers after 1920 more clearly treated botched executions as inevitable misfortunes.

For the most part, newspapers in this period wrote nothing that might have undermined the legitimacy of state killing. Frequently, an article would describe a botched execution without even labeling it as such. Consider, for instance, the portrayal of Donald Frohner's 1948 execution in the *Meriden Daily Journal* from the small town of Meriden, Connecticut:

> Suddenly the electrode attached to Frohner's bare right ankle began to smoke violently. It burst into a bright red and purple flame that shot inches away and missed setting fire to the top of Frohner's black sock only by a quarter inch. The current was turned off. Slowly the smoke and flame subsided. The current whined again. In an instant, the electrode flamed anew until at last the current clipped off and he was pronounced dead.[68]

Although this article describes the execution in meticulous detail, nowhere does it explicitly recognize that Frohner's execution was botched. Nowhere does it mention the possibility of pain or suffering. The mishap is entirely separated from the body of the condemned. The *electrode* began to "smoke violently." The *current*, somehow more human than Frohner, "whined." Images of smoke and flame are not once associated directly with images of burning flesh. It is as if readers were being invited to imagine the burning of an empty electric chair.

In the absence of any commentary to the contrary, readers are left to assume that the broken performance was neither typical nor preventable—nor even consequential. By repeatedly using the passive voice, the news report effectively obscures any acting agent and the attendant possibility of injustice: "the current was turned off . . . the current whined again . . . the current clipped off and he was pronounced dead." Without sensationalistic descriptions, gruesome spectacles maintain all the apparent order of the well-practiced execution ritual. Nothing is upset.

To take another example, the *New York Times* headlined its report of the 1923 execution of F. G. Bullen at the state penitentiary in Little Rock, "'Dead' Convict Moves After Death Shock." The description that follows, however, exemplifies the dispassionate accounts of an increasingly professionalized press:

> After a heavy charge of electricity had been sent through his body and he had remained strapped in the chair for five minutes, the discovery was made that F. G. Bullen, 50 years old, one of the four men executed at the Arkansas penitentiary today, still showed signs of life. Another application of the current was necessary before he was pronounced dead. When the undertaker began to prepare Bullen's body for burial he detected a slight movement and notified the death chamber attendants. A second "execution" was carried out.[69]

The *Times* gives more attention to the fact that four men were "successfully" executed in a single day than to the fact that one of them was sent to the chair more than once. The article reads like a summary of the official procedure for "executing a man twice." While the headline signals abnormality, the remainder of the article portrays the undoubtedly strange execution scene as controlled and rather uninteresting.

The *Chicago Daily Tribune* ran a very similar three-paragraph article in which Bullen was reportedly "placed into a wooden box and preparations started for burial," until physicians "found he was still alive." The report continues almost nonchalantly: "He was then taken from the coffin and again placed in the electric chair. He was pronounced dead three minutes later."[70] It concludes by briefly listing the names and crimes of the other three men killed that same day.

The sensationalist writers of an earlier era would have pounced on a story as thoroughly extraordinary as this. Bullen would have been the man "buried alive," his half-lifeless body dragged from its coffin, haphazardly slumped over the armrests, and reshocked in the chair. Instead, he was simply represented as one of four men routinely put to death, barely noteworthy on the pages of the midcentury press.

Even as grisly accounts of botches vanished, recuperative elements continued to appear in coverage of botched executions well into the middle of the century. Alongside articles that downplayed the damage of botched executions were reports that, as before, insistently stressed the aberrational, unfortunate nature of the botch, and which tended to blame anyone but the state for executions gone wrong. Thus, Chester Novack, like Hamilton and Snell earlier in the century, somehow caused his own botched execution. And Novack, like Bullen, paid with a "double penalty."[71] The *St. Joseph News-Press* in Missouri reported without the slightest sensationalist intonation: "After the typical three charges of electricity were administered Novack was removed from the death chair. An examination by the jail physician revealed signs of life, and again he was strapped in the chair. Two more charges were shot through his body and at 12:12 a.m. he was formally pronounced dead."[72]

The coverage of Novack's botched execution was both objective and highly recuperative. The *News-Press* went on to say that before his execution Novack had boasted he was "the toughest guy that ever got the hot seat." The article reassured readers that "Officials said his resistance to the powerful electric current was extremely unusual."[73] New London, Connecticut's *The Day* similarly wrote that Novack, known for his toughness, had said "he could take it." And then, *The Day* states, "Sheriff Toman said it was his opinion that Novack . . . probably resisted the current because the continuous drinking of coffee had stimulated his heart action."[74] If not the state, blame it on the coffee habit.

Now consider the 1939 double execution of Wallace Green and Walter St. Sauveuer. For this occasion, the state of Massachusetts was obliged to call in a substitute executioner because Robert Elliott, the veteran New Englander, had fallen ill. The *Pittsburgh Post* titled its report "Novice Drags Out Deaths of Killers to 42 Minutes."[75] Indeed, it took three shocks to kill St. Sauveuer and five shocks to finally put Green to death.

Newspapers provided readers with two explanatory accounts of this execution. First, they pointed to Green's sturdy constitution: "doctors said Green's heart was unusually strong."[76] Second, as the *Post* headline implies, they blamed the inexperience of the electrician who acted as the executioner: "[the substitute] took 42 minutes to do the job the regular one would have done in 15."[77]

At first glance, this claim seems to mark the botched execution as an injustice; there is a culpable actor who caused the victims' suffering. But keeping the institution of capital punishment as a whole in mind, Green's suffering is portrayed mostly as a misfortune, as the unlucky result of a last-minute substitution of executioners. The torture that Green endured was entirely the fault of one man: the novice executioner. In telling this story, the article exonerates the jailers, the judges, the politicians, and ultimately the practice of state killing itself.

The *Victoria Advocate* in Texas furnishes an even more extreme example of the recuperative narrative's continued presence. The first sentence of its two-sentence article on the botched execution of Wallace Green reads as follows: "Two youthful convicted murderers died in the Massachusetts electric chair today as a substitute executioner performed a precise, workmanlike job in place of Robert Elliott, official death's handy-man now ailing at his Long Island home."[78]

In this account, the recuperative impulse culminated in actual misreporting. Having received from its wire service the story of a mishap, the *Victoria Advocate* told the story of a flawless execution.

From the 1940s to the early 1970s, the death penalty was in decline in the United States. The number of executions reached an all-time high in 1935, when 197 Americans were put to death. Thereafter, the figure began a slow but steady decline. During the 1940s, state governments executed an average of just under 130 people a year. In the 1950s that figure declined to a little over seventy, with only fifty executions taking place in 1958. Only twenty people a year on average were killed during the 1960s, with no executions in either 1968 or 1969.[79]

As the number of executions dropped precipitously, botched executions of course became less frequent. There were only seven botches between 1955 and the start of the de facto moratorium in 1967: four electrocutions and three lethal gassings. In a departure from past trends, however, newspaper reports of these incidents did not offer assurances of painless death in the rhetoric of misfortune.

On May 12, 1960, the state of New York executed Pablo Vargas, a man apparently intent on living. Upon entering the execution chamber at Sing Sing, he cried out, "Please don't," and tried to escape the guards escorting him. His fight did not last long; eight guards quickly subdued him and strapped him into the chair. Though not typical, executions in which the condemned fights back also disrupt the carefully constructed serenity of the execution ceremony. There is no dignified way to forcibly restrain a man before he is killed. Prison guards must resort to naked force in order to carry out the execution. Even after the condemned is successfully bound to the chair or gurney, the preceding battle gives the lie to what follows, reminding the audience that force and state killing are inextricable.

The newspapers covering Vargas's execution, however, did not include any such commentary in their stories. All limited themselves to a straightforward recounting of the events: "He fought with eight guards until they overpowered him."[80] "[A] doomed man physically fought at the last moment to prevent his execution."[81] The *New York Times* noted the presence of student picketers outside the prison gates, even reporting that "One of the signs they carried said, 'They Shall Not Kill.'" Nonetheless, the article did not connect this protest to the grisly details of Vargas's execution. Although the *Times* did note that "it was the first time in Sing Sing's history that a condemned prisoner had put up such desperate resistance," it made no effort to explain or excuse the violent aberration.[82]

Such accounts belie the great contention that embroiled the death penalty during this period. Botched executions might have represented particularly charged moments in a questioning America. Nonetheless, as in the past, the press did not treat them as particularly important in ongoing arguments about capital punishment. These executions were not newsworthy because they exposed the flaws in a controversial system; in fact, it seems they were barely newsworthy at all. Journalists were assigned to cover executions, so they did. Some men simply went harder than others. An execution, it seems, was somehow always just another execution.

By the late 1960s, the American press was changing again in important ways. Detached, disinterested reporting became even more the norm and set the highest standard of journalistic quality. Journalism became even more attached to "the belief that one can and should separate facts from values." As Schudson explains:

> Facts, in this view, are assertions about the world open to independent validation. They stand beyond the distorting influences of any individual's personal preferences. Values, in this view, are an individual's conscious or unconscious preferences for what the world should be; they are seen as ultimately subjective and so without legitimate claim on other people. The belief in objectivity is a faith in "facts," a distrust of "values," and a commitment to their segregation.[83]

In Schudson's view, few journalists gave any thought to the idea of objective reporting before 1920. By the mid-1930s, the "term 'objectivity,' unknown to journalism before World War I, appears to have become common parlance."[84] And by 1960, commentators across the political spectrum saw objectivity as "the emblem of American journalism."[85] This new hallmark may explain the straightforward accounts of botched executions we observe from the mid-1950s to *Furman v. Georgia*, the 1972 Supreme Court decision which temporarily halted all executions in the United States.

Consider the 1956 execution of Robert Pierce at San Quentin, which the prison warden labeled "the most difficult, the most violent execution we have ever had."[86] As a priest was leading Pierce in prayer immediately before the execution, the condemned drew out a "three inch sliver of broken mirror" and sliced at his neck. In the scene that followed, "blood spurting from the gash splattered on guards who dragged him to the gas chamber. Pierce's white shirt was stained crimson."[87] Eventually the guards managed to strap Pierce into the chair in the gas chamber, and the execution proceeded. Here, as in Pablo Vargas's case, prison officials failed to maintain the decorum and dignity of a "painless" death. What was supposed to be a quiet, clinical procedure turned into a bloody death struggle.

Even a decade or two earlier, newspaper accounts might have attributed more agency to Pierce, holding the condemned solely responsible for the violence of his own death. As a matter of fact, when Walter Holmes fought back before his 1932 execution, the *Spokane Daily Chronicle* observed, "Walter Holmes, 31, Chicago negro, temporarily delayed his execution in the electric chair here last night."[88] The reporters who wrote about Robert Pierce's battle for his life, in contrast, largely ignored the question of responsibility, and at the *Hartford Courant* reporters somehow managed to ignore the violence altogether. Their piece, "Two Executed for Murder," was only one sentence long: "Robert O. Pierce, 27, went to his death in San Quentin's gas chamber today for the murder of an Oakland cab driver. Smith B. Jordan, 28, his companion in crime, died with him." Instead of an article about violence and blood in the state's death chamber, the *Courant* published what amounted to an obituary.

The years leading up to the national moratorium in the late 1960s were a time of transition and uncertainty for America's death penalty. Botched executions, however, remained in the background. Given the increasingly professional and objective American press, botched executions were made out to be unfortunate errors. In the late 1950s and 1960s, when Vargas and Pierce were put to death, capital punishment itself seemed to be slowly dying. By this time, there was little left of capital punishment to recuperate—little left to explain or justify. Death seemed to be disappearing from the front lines of punishment and its cultural life in the United States.

Botched Executions from Gregg v. Georgia to 2010: Balanced Reporting in an Age of Debate

As is well known, in the 1970s the death penalty staged an unprecedented and unparalleled comeback. The Supreme Court's 1976 decision in *Gregg v. Georgia* reinstated America's death penalty, and on January 17, 1977, the state of Utah executed Gary Gilmore by firing squad, ending the nearly decade-long moratorium on state killing. As the pace of executions accelerated, botches inevitably followed. Newspapers once again began to take notice.

Though softened by certain conventions of modern journalism, accounts of botched electrocutions in this period acknowledged the threat posed by gruesome mishaps to a particular method of execution. In the 1970s and 1980s news reports of botched electrocutions increasingly underlined electrocution's controversial status. In the end, this attention served mostly to emphasize the comparative "humanity" of lethal injection.

While David Garland describes the *Gregg* decision as "the single most important affirmation that capital punishment had received anywhere in the Western world in recent times,"[89] in the post-*Gregg* period methods of execution nonetheless were highly contested, perhaps more so than ever before. Electrocution, rarely a subject of contention before the moratorium, became, as we saw in Chapter 3, quite controversial almost immediately after the death penalty was reinstated. The newspaper coverage of John Evans's botched execution in 1983 reflects—and participates in—this controversy.

On April 22, 1983, sparks and fire attended the electrocution of Evans in Alabama. The electrode attached to Evans's leg burst into flame and broke free from its strap. With Evans still alive, technicians had to replace the electrode and administer two more shocks, which were accompanied by more smoke and charred flesh.

After Evans's execution, the headline in the *Washington Post* read "Attorney Charges Evans Was Tortured by Alabama in Botched Electrocution." The piece described the repeated shocks, the flames, and the attorney's horrified reaction. It noted, "Authorities had insisted [the first charge] would kill Evans instantly."[90] This remark seems to assign blame, not to a specific executioner but to a general set of "authorities" who failed to carry out a humane, dignified procedure. The *Philadelphia Inquirer* reported that "Prison officials could not explain yesterday why it took 10 minutes and three jolts of electricity to execute murderer John Louis Evans in what his attorney called 'a barbaric ritual.'"[91] Newspaper accounts of botched executions from the first half of the century rarely used such accusatory language.

In 1989, again in Alabama, technicians misconnected the cables to the electric chair so that the first surge of electricity failed to kill Horace Dunkins. The *Gadsden Times* described the incident as "the third [botched execution in Alabama] since 1983." Dunkins's execution was thus treated as part of a troubling pattern of electrocutions gone wrong. The article went on to note how, during the procedure, one prison guard spoke up and told the other, "I believe you've got the jacks on wrong."[92]

The *Rome-News Tribune* in Georgia headlined its article on Dunkins's botched execution "Crossed Wires Bungle Killer's Electrocution." The first line read, "The electric chair rigged wrong," and the report called Dunkins's execution a "19-minute ordeal" and, citing his lawyer, "a grisly scene." Instead of offering reassurance in the last lines, the *Rome-News Tribune* article highlighted the possibility that Dunkins had suffered. The police chief is quoted as saying, "I just hope he wasn't conscious and didn't suffer." Looking on, his attorney told other official witnesses, "They're torturing him."[93] Newspaper coverage of Dunkins's botched execution highlighted more general problems with electrocution, though not with capital punishment itself.

Still this new willingness to talk about particular botched executions as part of a larger story about a problematic technology was tempered by another new aspect of journalistic style. "Balanced" reporting, the convention of quoting two opposing sources side by side, was fast becoming the trademark of quality journalism. One consequence of this new development was the effort to suppress the journalist's voice. As we have seen in the coverage of Evans's and Dunkins's executions, instead of framing reports in terms of their own individual witnessing, writers began to use a series of quotations from opposing sides to tell the story.

In 1984, the state of Georgia took nineteen minutes to kill Alpha Otis Stephens in the electric chair. After the first two-minute surge, executioners waited eight minutes before administering a second shock as Stephens gasped for breath and rolled his head from side to side. The *Miami Herald* reported:

> Officials said he was "brain dead" after the first surge, although he was still breathing. "Everything was right down the line," said prison spokesman John Siler. "He [Stephens] was just not a conductor [of electricity]. It's apparent that he did not have the conductivity in his system that the other two [recently executed prisoners] did." . . .
>
> The fact that it took two jolts of electricity eight minutes apart to carry out Wednesday's execution brought an outcry from opponents of capital punishment. "It's just another example of how barbaric this practice is," said the Rev. Currie Burris of Amnesty International. "It should horrify any decent and sensitive human being."[94]

Prison officials asserted, and death penalty opponents countered. In the 1980s, this framing became the new normal in reports of botched executions.

The coverage of William Vandiver's execution furnishes another case in point. On October 16, 1985, the state of Indiana took seventeen minutes and four jolts of electricity to kill Vandiver. The attending physician conceded that the execution "did not go according to plan."[95] The *Times-Union* of Warsaw, Indiana, led its article with the following two sentences: "A defense attorney who witnessed the execution of William E. Vandiver says the state could choose a more humane method of execution. A prison official, meanwhile, defended procedures used to test the electric chair that took five jolts of voltage and 17 minutes to complete the execution."[96]

David Mindich, a professor of journalism, describes this style as the "seesaw" model of objectivity. "The idea here," he explains, "is that journalists can find truth by offering two competing truth claims."[97] When covering a controversial subject like botched executions, the journalist is obliged to gather quotations from two sides of the issue to satisfy the demand of objectivity.

In constructing the seesaw, reporters must include the position of the state, which almost always portrays the botch as a regrettable misfortune. Thus by the 1980s, the recuperative narrative made its return in the form of quotations from prison and government officials, politicians, and other state authority figures. Examples are not difficult to find. In 1988 the state of Texas executed Raymond Landry by lethal injection. Unfortunately, the catheter popped out of the vein during the procedure and had to be reinserted. The *Houston Chronicle* passed on the statement of a corrections officer that "it was the first time such an incident occurred since Texas pioneered the use of lethal injections for executions in 1982."[98]

The coverage of Landry's botched lethal injection, however, differed from the coverage of Vandiver's electrocution. Accounts of botched lethal injections in the 1980s were markedly less disparaging than analogous reports of botched electrocutions. At the 1985 execution of Stephen Morin in Texas, technicians took forty-five minutes in repeated attempts before they were able to place a needle in Morin's arm. The *New York Times* did not report the mishap at all.[99] The *Dallas Morn-*

ing News mentioned the incident but in a decidedly subdued manner: "After initial attempts to place the needle in both Morin's arms failed, officials examined his legs to determine if veins there could be used, prison officials said. The veins in his legs were determined to be unacceptable, and the needle was finally placed in Morin's right arm."[100] The reporter prefaced this brief description with an explanation from a prison spokesman: "He said he (Morin) had been a heavy drug user and dealt drugs in the past."

This claim—that past drug use hindered technicians' efforts to find a vein—once again shifts blame for the botch from the state to the condemned. The drug abuse explanation soon became a cliché in newspaper coverage of similarly botched lethal injections. Thus the 1986 execution of Randy Woolls was said to be botched due to the fact that "prominent veins in his arms had collapsed long ago from drug use."[101] Elliot Rod Johnson spent an hour on the gurney in 1987 because "years of drug abuse made it difficult to get the lethal injection into a vein."[102] Billy Wayne White was obliged to help executioners find a suitable vein for his injection because of a "long history of drug abuse before his imprisonment."[103] The omnipresence of this explanation tallies with the generally favorable reception that lethal injection received in the press.

Accounts of botched electrocutions were paired in news reports with discussions of the ongoing transition to lethal injection. The *Times-Union* closed its story on William Vandiver's electrocution by commenting that "Meanwhile, Rep. Chester F. Dobis, D-Merrillville, said he and Rep. John W. Donaldson, R-Lebanon, would introduce the first day of the 1986 session a bill allowing death row inmates to choose lethal injection. 'From everything I've read on the subject, it is an absolutely painless way,' Dobis said."[104] As in this case, botched electrocutions most often served only to build support for lethal injection as an allegedly more humane method of state killing. As long as electrocution persisted in some jurisdictions, lethal injection largely escaped critique in the mainstream press.

As noted in Chapter 3, the mounting controversy surrounding electrocution came to a head in the late 1990s in Florida with the executions of Jesse Joseph Tafero in 1990, Pedro Medina in 1997, and Allen Lee Davis in 1999. Once again, newspaper coverage of these executions offered up opposing opinions from prison officials and death penalty opponents and referenced lethal injection as an alternative method. The *Tampa Tribune* highlighted lax upkeep of the electric chair before the Medina incident: "Prison workers interviewed after Medina's electrocution could not say how old the [copper wire] screen was and did not remember it being replaced or cleaned between executions. Sponges were not always replaced, either."[105] Meanwhile, Governor Lawton Chiles insisted that "there was no suffering at all by Mr. Medina." "'That's just so clear,' he said."[106]

In response to the Davis execution, his defense attorney was paraphrased in the *St. Petersburg Times* as claiming, "Corrections officials had once again botched an execution by failing to deliver enough voltage needed to kill a prisoner, especially one of Davis's large size, quickly and painlessly." State officials unequivocally denied the allegation: "DOC spokesman Morris, while declining to specify exact voltage levels, said corrections officers followed their electrocution procedures 'to the letter.'"[107] As to the question of changing methods, after Medina's botch Governor Chiles, while saying that "he [would] not push for the state to offer lethal injection as an alternative this legislative session," did say that "he would like to study the matter further."[108]

Newspapers treated the Davis execution as yet another chapter in the problematic history of Florida's electric chair. Beyond that, they raised no questions about the legitimacy of capital punishment. In his own analysis of the coverage of Davis's botched execution, Greer similarly concludes: "Thus, whilst most expressed horror at the barbarity of the spectacle, and many called for a suspension of all further executions by electric chair, the vast majority of responses were reported in a manner which criticized the technological administration of state killing, but remained silent about its wider practice."[109]

By the time of Medina's execution in 1997, Florida was a holdout in retaining electrocution as its primary method of execution. Today, as we noted previously, no state uses electrocution as its sole method of execution. The national prominence of botched electrocutions played a significant role in the transition to lethal injection.[110]

With electrocution all but eliminated, lethal injection quickly lost its position in news reports as the "more humane" method of state killing. Though difficulties with lethal injections were not new, reporters began to attribute more significance to botches, two of which garnered national attention in 2006. On May 2 in Ohio, technicians struggled for twenty-two minutes to find a vein in Joseph Clark's arm. A few minutes after the flow of lethal drugs began, Clark raised his head and proclaimed, "It don't work." His vein had collapsed. After thirty more minutes of searching for a usable site, during which time witnesses heard groaning from behind the curtain, the sentence was carried out.

Clark's execution bears a striking resemblance to the botched lethal injection of Stephen Morin in 1985. However, coming almost twenty years later, Clark's execution provoked a backlash that dwarfed the brief mention Morin had received in the *Dallas Morning News*. The report of the execution in the *New York Times* led: "It took almost 90 minutes to execute Joseph L. Clark in an Ohio prison yesterday, in what critics of the death penalty said was the latest in a series of botched executions nationwide." The *Times* quoted law professor Eric Freedman, who asserted that "today's botched execution makes perfectly clear that the first generation of drug protocols needs to be succeeded by a second generation, just as the electric chair became technologically obsolete and therefore vanished."[111]

Unsurprisingly, the reporter juxtaposed these arguments with statements from a prison spokeswoman, who "speculated that Mr. Clark's veins might have been damaged by drug abuse." The spokeswoman also promised that "we are going to review our policies and our protocol." Still, despite the typical back-and-forth, lethal injection was treated as a subject of genuine controversy rather than the largely accepted, humane replacement for electrocution.

Seven months later, the botched execution of Angel Diaz sparked an even bigger controversy. Florida's lethal injection team mistakenly placed the catheter so that the drugs were injected into the soft tissue of Diaz's arm rather than into a vein. According to official witnesses, Diaz continued to move for nearly twenty-five minutes after the flow of drugs began, grimacing, blinking, and attempting to mouth words. He died only after a second dosage of drugs was administered, thirty-four minutes after the start of the execution.

Critics of lethal injection saw the Diaz botch as added evidence of problems in the standard three-drug protocol that most states still use.[112] The *Press-Register* of Mobile, Alabama, opened its coverage of Diaz's botched execution by presenting readers with an alarming possibility: "Death penalty foes have warned for years of the possibility that an inmate being executed by lethal injection could remain conscious, experiencing severe pain as he slowly dies. That day may have arrived."[113] The article went on to blame the execution team for incorrectly inserting the shunt into Diaz's arm. It quoted an anesthesiologist as saying that "someone should have realized what was happening." The *Tampa Tribune* went even further, quoting a death penalty opponent who remarked, "these chemicals are prohibited to put down animals with, yet we use them on human beings."[114]

In the last part of the twentieth century, newspapers focused on controversies concerning methods of execution, first electrocution and then lethal injection. Even as the intensity of their coverage drew attention to problems with those methods, their balanced approach to reporting muted the reach of the critiques that their reports offered. Readers were invited to focus on problems in the technologies of state killing, but the implications of botched executions for the continuing practice of capital punishment were left unexplored or left for the opinion page.

The Legacy of America's Botched Executions

Botched executions, from Joda Hamilton's double hanging to Romell Broom's failed lethal injection, are extraordinary events. They reveal the violence and disorder of capital punishment. Throughout the twentieth century, however, the cultural reception of these events in newspapers downplayed or excused even the most glaring failures. Reporters witnessed these events and filtered them for the public's consumption, most often drawing attention away from their implications for the continuing legitimacy of capital punishment.

Today, in the wake of any mishap in the death chamber, different perspectives vie for preeminence on the pages of newspapers. Death penalty opponents are given a voice, which is almost always counteracted with reassurances offered by state actors. In most cases, a debate is staged—but a resolution is not offered. Botched executions remain newsworthy events, but not events whose meanings newspapers trace back to the practice of state killing itself.

Botched executions are failures that demand explanation and justification. In the past, newspaper accounts have helped maintain America's death penalty by repairing the damage done: by simultaneously telling two different stories about the execution scene, by subduing the violence entirely through objective reporting, and by impartially presenting readers with an undecided, perhaps undecidable, debate. Newspapers have read and construed botched executions as unavoidable misfortunes rather than as symptoms of injustice crying out for rectification. Recuperation has meant identifying scapegoats, strange circumstances, and even alternative methods of execution when all else fails. Newspapers have not offered readers a "deeper 'witnessing'" of the execution scene and, in turn, of capital punishment itself.

The result is that the gruesome spectacles described in this book have not played a substantial role in the struggle to end capital punishment itself. Sometimes they have fueled movement from one method of state killing to another, but unlike issues of racial justice in the administration of the death penalty or advancements in the science of DNA which have fueled the innocence movement, botched executions have not moved sentiment, or galvanized opposition, to state killing itself. However, as long as state killing continues, executions will from time to time go awry and cause "something more than the mere extinguishment of life." In those moments, we are all implicated in the gruesome spectacles that are played out in our name.

Numbers of Botched Executions by Time Period and Method of Execution

Method	Total executions	Botched executions	Botched execution rate
		1900–2010	
All Methods	8,776	276	3.15%
Hanging	2,721	85	3.12%
Electrocution	4,374	84	1.92%
Lethal Gassing	593	32	5.4%
Lethal Injection	1,054	75	7.12%
Firing Squad	34	0	0%
		1900–1919	
All Methods	2,374	79	3.33%
Hanging	1,747	70	4.01%
Electrocution	616	9	1.46%
Lethal Gassing	0	0	n/a
Lethal Injection	0	0	n/a
Firing Squad	11	0	0%
		1920–1949	
All Methods	4,264	70	1.16%
Hanging	930	13	1.4%
Electrocution	2,948	36	1.22%
Lethal Gassing	372	21	5.65%
Lethal Injection	0	0	n/a
Firing Squad	14	0	0%
		1950–1979	
All Methods	919	23	2.5%
Hanging	41	2	4.88%
Electrocution	660	13	1.97%
Lethal Gassing	211	8	3.79%
Lethal Injection	0	0	n/a
Firing Squad	7	0	0%
		1980–2010	
All Methods	1,219	104	8.53%
Hanging	3	0	0%
Electrocution	150	26	17.33%
Lethal Gassing	10	3	30%
Lethal Injection	1,054	75	7.12%
Firing Squad	2	0	0%

Two executions that were botched between 1890 and 1900 are not included in this table. Execution numbers from the years 1900–1999 come from http://deathpenalty. procon.org/view.resource.php?resourceID=004087#VI. The website acquired data from the ESPY files. (The "Espy File" is a database of executions in the United States and the earlier colonies from 1608 to 2002. This list was compiled by M. Watt Espy and John Ortiz Smykla). Execution numbers from the years 2000–2010 are from http://www.deathpenaltyinfo.org/executions-year. Botched execution numbers come from Appendix B.

APPENDIX B

Botched Executions from 1890 to 2010

1. August 6, 1890. New York. **William Kemmler**. Electrocution. After the first shock failed to kill Kemmler, the executioners administered a second jolt. Kemmler began to bleed, and the room was filled with the smell of burnt flesh and hair.

2. July 27, 1893. New York. **William G. Taylor**. Electrocution. The electric chair in Auburn Prison failed to kill Taylor on the first shock. In fact, the prison dynamo broke down, and it took an hour to repair the system for the second, fatal jolt.

3. January 10, 1900. Pennsylvania. **James Eagan**. Hanging. Spectators to the execution were horrified by severe bleeding that "smeared the rope crimson." Doctors present confirmed death fifteen minutes after the drop.

4. February 10, 1900. New Jersey. **James Brown**. Hanging. The *New York Times* described his execution as "brutal and clumsy."

5. February 27, 1900. New York. **Antonio Ferraro**. Electrocution. The chair at Sing Sing Prison took five shocks over eight minutes before the attending physician could pronounce death.

6. April 25, 1900. Tennessee. **Sonnie Crain**. Hanging. His neck was not broken when he fell through the trap, and he strangled to death. He was cut down eight minutes after the sheriff sprung the trap.

Our archive of botched executions was compiled through extensive searches of newspaper databases (Access World News, Proquest Newspapers, Lexis-Nexis, America's Historical Newspapers, Alternative Press Watch, and Google's News Archive, in addition to the databases of several larger, individual publications). We began by conducting keyword searches and then proceeded to search every name in the ESPY file from 1890 to 2010.

Botched executions marked with * were also included in Michael Radelet's "Examples of Post-*Furman* Botched Executions." The descriptions of these executions are taken from his list. See Michael Radelet, "Examples of Post-*Furman* Botched Executions," October 1, 2010, http://www.deathpenaltyinfo.org/some-examples-post-furman-botched-executions.html.

We have revised the list of botched executions by treating separately executions carried out simultaneously in which each execution was botched.

7. May 8, 1900. New Jersey. **William Clifford**. Hanging. Before the execution Clifford expressed hope that the hangman would not bungle Clifford's execution like he had Brown's. After the drop, the rope nearly slipped off Clifford's neck, almost revealing his face to the horrified crowd. He eventually died by strangulation.

8. June 1, 1900. New Mexico. **Jose P. Ruiz**. Hanging. Ruiz did not break his neck during his fall, and it took twenty-three minutes for him to strangle to death.

9. June 30, 1900. District of Columbia. **Benjamin Snell**. Hanging. Snell, an especially heavy man, was nearly decapitated by the drop. The extra-wide rope cut through Snell's windpipe, carotid arteries, and vertebra, leaving his body hanging only on the muscles at the back of his neck.

10. August 31, 1900. North Carolina. **Tom Jones**. Hanging. Jones was hanged for murder in Raleigh, North Carolina. The trap door fell at 10:29 in the morning. Jones's neck was broken in the fall of about six and a half feet. However, he was not pronounced dead until 10:43. There was, according to the *Charlotte Observer*, "much struggling of the body and limbs." The failure of the execution to cause immediate death was attributed to Jones's light weight.

11. September 27, 1900. Tennessee. **A. Dillard Warren**. Hanging. Before the trap was sprung, the noose had to be adjusted because Warren said it wasn't right. When the trigger on the trap was pulled, the trap failed to release. Warren stated, "I reckon I had better get off." He got off the trap, and the scaffold was rearranged. The trap was sprung again, and this time Warren fell through. However, Warren grabbed at the rope with his tied hands, and the four-foot drop was not enough to break his neck. He strangled to death and was cut down after sixteen minutes.

12. September 28, 1900. North Carolina. **Art Kinsauls**. Hanging. Kinsauls was very light at only 110 pounds on the day of his execution. Sampson County had only a stepladder for its gallows, and the fall proved insufficient to break Kinsauls's neck. In addition, he was now bleeding profusely from partially healed wounds from a recent suicide attempt. Officials cut him down, forced him up the ladder again, and repeated the drop, this time with more success.

13. October 6, 1900. Oregon. **Coleman (Coalman) Gillespie**. Hanging. A six-foot drop failed to break Gillespie's neck, and he slowly strangled before the witnesses. Death was announced fifteen minutes after the drop.

14. October 26, 1900. South Carolina. **Warby Wine**. Hanging. A hitch in the mechanism in Orangeburg prevented a full and swift drop, and Wine eventually died by strangulation.

15. November 16, 1900. Arizona. **William Halderman**. Hanging. While his brother Thomas had his neck broken by the fall, William's neck was not broken. His death was caused by shock, nerve compression, and strangulation.

16.   November 16, 1900. Arizona. **Santiago Ortiz**. Hanging. Ortiz's neck was not broken but only partially dislocated by his fall.

17.   December 21, 1900. Virginia. **John Holden**. Hanging. After the drop, Holden, convicted of attempted rape, clearly remained conscious, drawing his legs into his body several times and twitching visibly. He eventually died by strangulation.

18.   January 25, 1901. Washington. **Martin Stickles**. Hanging. The force of the drop partially severed the convict's head from his shoulders. Blood covered his clothing.

19.   April 26, 1901. New Mexico. **"Black Jack" Tom Ketchum**. Hanging. The rope fully severed Ketchum's head. The outlaw's body fell to the ground doubled over, and horrified spectators watched blood spurt out intermittently.

20.   July 5, 1901. Florida. **William Williams, Jim Harrison, Belton Hamilton**, and **John Simmons**. Hanging. Four black men were hanged in Vernon. The drop broke only one neck; the other three strangled to death. Newspaper coverage from the time does not specify which convict broke his neck.

21.   July 5, 1901. Florida. **William Williams, Jim Harrison, Belton Hamilton**, and **John Simmons**. Hanging. Four black men were hanged in Vernon. The drop broke only one neck; the other three strangled to death. Newspaper coverage from the time does not specify which convict broke his neck.

22.   July 5, 1901. Florida. **William Williams, Jim Harrison, Belton Hamilton**, and **John Simmons**. Hanging. Four black men were hanged in Vernon. The drop broke only one neck; the other three strangled to death. Newspaper coverage from the time does not specify which convict broke his neck.

23.   August 6, 1901. Tennessee. **Nathan Caruthers**. Hanging. Caruthers fell smoothly, but the knot in the noose slipped to the back of his neck, and his neck did not break. Caruthers strangled to death, and his body quivered. He was cut down fourteen minutes after he fell.

24.   January 31, 1902. Oregon. **Joseph Wade**. Hanging. The drop failed to break his neck. Wade was pronounced dead fifteen minutes later.

25.   March 20, 1902. Mississippi. **Will Lanier**. Hanging. Full decapitation.

26.   April 4, 1902. Florida. **Moses Robertson**. Hanging. Robertson was hanged in Jacksonville. The drop did not break his neck, and the man dangled with legs twisting and kicking convulsively. One of his arms was loosened from the straps and Robertson was able to remove the black cap from his face. He waved it in the air several times. It was over fifteen minutes before he was pronounced dead.

27.   May 23, 1902. District of Columbia. **Elijah Chapman**. Hanging. His neck was not broken in the fall. Chapman's body twitched for several minutes after the trap was sprung.

28.   August 2, 1902. Florida. **George Robinson**. Hanging. At the drop, the

rope snapped and Robinson fell to the ground. Now bleeding from his mouth, nose, and neck but still conscious, he was led back up the scaffold. After a second drop with a new rope, he eventually died by strangulation.

29. September 19, 1902. South Dakota. **Ernest Loveswar**. Hanging. Loveswar was hanged in Sturgis. According to the *Minneapolis Journal*, the execution was "bunglingly performed." The first drop was a failure and Loveswar was hauled up through the trap. The noose was adjusted and he strangled slowly.

30. February 20, 1903. North Dakota. **Jacob L. Bassanella**. Hanging. The drop failed to break his neck. Bassanella drew his legs up to his chest three times. Death followed by strangulation in seven and a half minutes.

31. March 27, 1903. Oregon. **Alfred Belding**. Hanging. The condemned hit his head on the platform as he dropped through the trap. Nevertheless, his neck was broken.

32. July 31, 1903. Arizona. **Francisco Renteria**. Hanging. Renteria's neck was not broken by his fall, and he died by strangulation.

33. December 29, 1903. New York. **Frank White**. Electrocution. White, a black man, was put to death in the electric chair at the state prison in Auburn. Six contacts, each of 1,740 volts and 7 1/2 amperes, were required to kill him. After the fourth contact, a strange gurgling in his throat shocked and horrified both attending physicians and spectators. Even after the fifth contact, the stethoscope still measured cardiac action. During the fifth and final shock the electrode was said to have flashed brilliantly as the odor of burning flesh and hair filled the execution chamber.

34. February 23, 1904. Montana. **James Martin**. Hanging (upright jerker). The force of the counterweight drop proved insufficient to break the convict's neck. Martin pulled his knees up to his chest and took ten deep breaths after the cord was cut. Death took fifteen minutes.

35. April 22, 1904. Illinois. **Peter Neidermeyer**. Hanging. Neidermeyer, the leader of three "Chicago bandits," was hanged in that city. He was reported to have been "crazed" at the sight of the gallows and had to be carried to his death. Too weak to stand on his own, Neidermeyer was hung from a chair perched on the platform. The executioner neglected to ask the condemned man for any last words. As the trap fell, the chair was removed from behind and the body shot downward. The shroud covering Neidermeyer's face was however partly disarranged, and the "fearful muscular struggles" of the dying man continued for some fifteen minutes in full view of horrified spectators.

36. June 17, 1904. Ohio. **Mike Schiller**. Electrocution. Schiller's execution was termed "botched and brutal" under a Youngstown, Ohio, newspaper headline. Fifty witnesses were present in the Columbus death chamber. It was necessary to apply the current five times. After each, Schiller groaned, and his body stretched and strained at the straps of the electric chair. According to reporters,

he died on the final contact by partial cremation. At the points of contact, flesh sizzled and burned for several minutes.

37. July 28, 1904. Tennessee. **Ben Springfield**. Hanging. Springfield was hanged in the jail yard in Jackson. His neck was not broken by the fall, and he strangled to death.

38. March 23, 1905. Pennsylvania. **William J. Byers**. Hanging. Two attempts were needed to kill Byers at the gallows in a Pittsburgh jail yard that morning. When the trap fell the first time, the noose was unknotted and Byers fell to the ground. There was a red mark around the convicted man's neck, and he obviously struggled painfully as he was returned to his cell. Soon after, Byers was hanged for a second time. He was pronounced dead twelve minutes after the trap fell.

39. April 5, 1905. Tennessee. **James Scudder**. Hanging. The rope around Scudder's neck turned and failed to break his neck. He strangled to death.

40. May 5, 1905. Montana. **Herbert Metzger**. Hanging (upright jerker). The force of the counterweight drop proved insufficient to break the convict's neck. Metzger "convulsed" and "his shoulders drew upwards." Death took eleven and a half minutes.

41. May 8, 1905. Missouri. **William Rudolph**. Hanging. The drop failed to break Rudolph's neck, and he died by strangulation after fourteen minutes.

42. May 13, 1905. Virginia. **Cloyd Hale**. Hanging. The drop failed to break Hale's neck; death by strangulation followed in fourteen minutes.

43. June 3, 1905. Washington. **Henry Arao**. Hanging. Probably due to Arao's light weight, the drop failed to break his neck. Death followed by strangulation.

44. July 17, 1905. New York. **James Breen**. Electrocution. Breen was executed at Sing Sing Prison. During the first shock, water from a wet sponge from the helmet dropped down, forming an arc light above the collar of his shirt. The collar was slightly burned.

45. July 18, 1905. Tennessee. **Abraham Miles**. Hanging. Miles's neck was not broken by his fall. He convulsed and gurgled as he strangled to death on the rope.

46. October 7, 1905. New Jersey. **Paul Genz**. Hanging. Following the hanging of the convicted murderer Genz in the Hudson Country jail yard, the Reverend E. A. Murray reported that the man, with a prearranged movement of his fingers, signaled that he was still conscious after the drop. His botching precipitated widespread controversy in New Jersey over the continued use of hanging.

47. October 27, 1905. Florida. **Edward Lamb**. Hanging. Lamb was hanged in Bradentown. It was necessary to drop him twice before he was formally pronounced dead.

48. December 9, 1905. Vermont. **Mary Rogers**. Hanging. Rogers was

hanged for the murder of her husband in Windsor, Vermont. The noose was apparently left a bit too long because Rogers's toes touched the floor when the trap fell. Due to this mishap, it is questionable whether her neck was actually broken. Some reports note that Rogers was not cut down after the fall, but the noose was removed from around her neck—taking with it a piece of the woman's hair.

49.   December 22, 1905. New Jersey. **Edwin Tapley**. Hanging. Tapley was hanged for murder at the gallows in Jersey City. He died of strangulation.

50.   February 13, 1906. Minnesota. **William Williams**. Hanging. Williams was the last man to be hanged in Minnesota. The execution was marred by a miscalculation of rope length. The rope stretched and his feet touched the ground. In the end, Williams was hoisted up to strangle for over fifteen minutes.

51.   February 15, 1906. Pennsylvania. **Jacob Hauser**. Hanging. Hauser's death was termed "one of the most sickening executions ever witnessed in Pennsylvania" by a *Los Angeles Times* headline. His neck did not break with the fall, and he was left to strangle for ten minutes before he was pronounced dead.

52.   March 30, 1906. Maryland. **Issac Winder**. Hanging. Winder was hanged in Baltimore. It was by no means an easy affair. In sight of a riotous mob of two thousand, he reportedly fought five men with the force of a "maniac" in order to avoid the gallows. Winder sank down on the floor of the trap and refused to rise. It took six men to eventually string him up and kill him.

53.   April 20, 1906. Montana. **Lu Sing**. Hanging (upright jerker). The force of the counterweight drop proved insufficient to break the convict's neck. Death followed by strangulation in fifteen minutes.

54.   May 25, 1906. New Mexico. **John Medlock**. Hanging. Medlock's neck was not broken by his fall, and it took thirteen minutes for him to strangle to death.

55.   December 21, 1906. Missouri. **Joda Hamilton**. Hanging. The hanging of Hamilton was termed a "horror" by the *Lewiston Morning Tribune*. The twenty-year-old son of a farmer, he was put to death in Houston. The first rope broke, and spectators watched, horrified, as Hamilton writhed in pain on the ground below the gallows. Partially conscious, he was lifted and carried back to the gallows. Hamilton was pronounced dead shortly after the trap was sprung for the second time.

56.   January 10, 1907. Tennessee. **John Thomas**. Hanging. The fall did not break Thomas's neck. His legs and shoulders convulsed for several minutes as he strangled to death.

57.   January 19, 1907. Arizona. **Clement Leigh**. Hanging. Leigh was bleeding and appeared "ghastly" during his execution because he had hit his head against a metal projection in the bars of his cell when he learned he was to be executed.

58. February 15, 1907. Virginia. **Massie Hill**. Hanging. Hill was executed in the morning at the gallows in Farmville. After the trap was sprung, the rope snapped and Hill fell to the ground in front of the stairs leading up to the platform. He did not lose consciousness, and the noose was removed from his neck. When asked if he was much hurt, Hill responded that he was not but that if the officers wanted him to walk back up the stairs they would have to remove the strapping around his legs. The rope was adjusted once more and again the trigger was pulled. Hill's body shot down past the swinging door. The crowd looked on, horrified, as the rope again split into several pieces. Fifteen minutes later, Hill was pronounced dead on the ground where he lay.

59. April 29, 1907. Texas. **John Armstrong**. Hanging. Armstrong, a black man, was hanged in Columbus. When the trap was sprung, his feet touched the ground and it was necessary for the officers on the scaffold to hold him up.

60. July 20, 1907. Ohio. **Henry White**. Electrocution. White was executed in the state prison at Columbus. The *Free Lance* (of Fredericksburg, Virginia) called the electrocution a "horrible fiasco." The first two shocks failed to kill White. Witnesses watched as he writhed in agony, his strained muscles nearly bursting through the straps of the electric chair. With the third shock, a sheet of flame enveloped him. Nevertheless, the current was continued for several minutes. When it was finally stopped, physicians declared him dead.

61. August 28, 1907. Pennsylvania. **Carmine Renzo**. Hanging. Renzo was put to death in Indiana, Pennsylvania, in the first execution in that county for more than twenty years. The rope snapped on the first attempt. Renzo, half dead, was carried to the platform once more. The second attempt was a success.

62. January 3, 1908. Kentucky. **Clarence Sturgeon**. Hanging. The nineteen-year-old Sturgeon was hanged in Louisville. The condemned and witnesses were forced to wait for an excessive amount of time before the execution due to a malfunction with the machinery. Sturgeon's neck was not broken in the drop, and he strangled to death for seventeen minutes.

63. January 11, 1908. Tennessee. **Peter Turner**. Hanging. The night before his execution, Turner tried to commit suicide by slashing his wrists and neck, which caused his execution to be delayed by an hour. When Turner did fall through the trap, his neck wounds burst open, causing a considerable amount of blood to spurt out of his neck as he hung from the rope.

64. June 15, 1908. Montana. **George J. Rock**. Hanging (upright jerker). The force of the counterweight drop proved insufficient to break the convict's neck. Death followed by strangulation in ten minutes.

65. October 23, 1908. Louisiana. **Jacques Pierre**. Hanging. According to his hangman, it was apparently Pierre's "own fault" that his neck was not broken in the fall that was to kill him. Because Pierre moved his head after the noose was adjusted, the knot was slipped around the back of his neck.

66. February 26, 1909. Oregon. **C. Y. Timmons**. Hanging. During the

alleged crime that sent him to the gallows, Timmons suffered a severe razor wound to his neck that partially severed his trachea. This wound was not fully healed on the date of his execution, and the force of the fall reopened the wound. Blood poured out, drenching his body, and Timmons continued to breathe through the hole in his neck "for some time."

67. April 7, 1909. Montana. **William A. Hayes**. Hanging (upright jerker). The force of the counterweight drop proved insufficient to break the convict's neck. Hayes twitched convulsively and clutched at his neck. He strangled to death after eight minutes.

68. April 12, 1909. New York. **Barnard Carlin**. Electrocution. The execution, reportedly, would have been one of the quickest on record had it not been for a mishap just as the current was turned on. When the signal was given and the current turned on, there was no response from Carlin. It was soon determined that the electrode attached to Carlin's right leg had fallen to the floor—no circuit had been formed.

69. May 13, 1910. Washington. **Richard Quinn**. Hanging. He was eventually strangled, even after asking to be dropped again when his neck was not broken on the first attempt.

70. September 9, 1910. Oregon. **Isaac B. Harrell**. Hanging. The drop severed the right jugular vein, and "great quantities of blood spurted from his neck." He was pronounced dead after only three minutes, his death presumably hastened by loss of blood.

71. December 2, 1910. Arizona. **Rafael Barela**. Hanging. Barela's neck was not broken by his fall, and it took twenty minutes for him to strangle to death.

72. July 8, 1911. Kentucky. **James Buckner**. Electrocution. Buckner was put to death in the first electrocution to occur at the state penitentiary in Eddyville. It was a strange event—nearly taking the lives of two men instead of one. Prison physician R. H. Mors, apparently ignorant to the warning cries of other officers, narrowly escaped death by electrocution. Mors had approached Buckner to check his pulse before the current had been shut off.

73. January 6, 1912. Vermont. **Elroy Kent**. Hanging. Kent was hanged at the state prison in Windsor. When the trap fell, the rope snapped under the weight of the condemned man. The rope was reattached to the gallows, and Kent was made to hang for another seventeen minutes after the attending physician found a partial pulse. The body was then cut down. According the *Boston Globe* report, the rope that broke under the weight of Kent was reportedly the same rope that had stretched and allowed Mary Rogers (executed in 1905) to "fall to the ground."

74. May 24, 1912. Wyoming. **Joseph Seng**. Hanging. The drop failed to break Seng's neck. He died by strangulation in nine minutes and forty-five seconds.

75. June 9, 1913. District of Columbia. **Nathaniel Green**. Hanging. The *Washington Post* called the hanging execution of Green "revolting." Members of Congress were at the time considering the substitution of electrocution or shooting for hanging in the District. The Green execution provided "striking support."

76. April 24, 1913. Pennsylvania. **John Harris**. Hanging. Harris was executed in Uniontown. The rope was about three feet too long. With the rope around his neck, Harris fell to the ground in front of the scaffold; landing on his knees, he attempted to rise. The sheriff and his deputies quickly lifted Harris and held him hanging for eighteen minutes before he finally died of strangulation.

77. July 31, 1915. New York. **Charles Becker**. Electrocution. Becker was executed in the electric chair at Sing Sing. As the executioner pulled the lever and the current turned on, Becker's large body tautened and surged against the leather straps of the chair. As a result, the straps were loosened, and the ensuing scene reportedly horrified witnesses. Moreover, the heavy belt that is meant to be fastened across the chest of the condemned was instead fastened across his arms. With the jerk of Becker's body, the head and chin piece slipped, revealing his distorted face to the room of spectators. In the end, it took three shocks to kill him.

78. September 3, 1915. New York. **Thomas Tarpy**. Electrocution. The British veteran took five shocks from the electric chair at Sing Sing before he was pronounced dead. One of the guards exclaimed, "My God! What a Man!"

79. August 11, 1916. Wyoming. **Wilbur Palmer**. Hanging. The drop failed to break his neck. He died by strangulation in eight minutes.

80. September 13, 1916. Tennessee. **Mary the Elephant**. Hanging. On September 12, Mary, a large circus elephant, became enraged by a bull hook and killed one of her trainers in Erwin, Tennessee. Mayor Miller and Sheriff Hickman arrested the animal, and it was determined that the elephant would be hanged for her crime using a construction crane and heavy chain. The first chain broke and Mary fell to ground, breaking her rear hips. The second chain held, and Mary strangled to death.

81. December 5, 1919. Maryland. **George Cummings**. Hanging. Cummings, a black man, was hanged in Upper Marlboro. Cummings was pronounced dead sixteen minutes after the trap fell. The seven-foot drop was not sufficient to break the man's neck. He died of strangulation.

82. December 3, 1920. Delaware. **Lemuel Price**. Hanging. Spectators declared the execution to be a "horrible spectacle," Price having struggled at the end of the rope for many minutes until he finally died by strangulation.

83. June 18, 1921. Louisiana. **Felix Birbiglia**. Hanging. After the noose apparently slipped, the crowd outside the parish jail rushed the barriers, which

had been set up to keep the crowd away from the execution site, to see the miscarried execution. It took thirty minutes after the hanging had begun for Birbiglia to be pronounced dead.

84. August 27, 1921. Nevada. **Gee Jon**. Lethal Gas. Jon was the first man to be executed in a gas chamber in the United States. When a heater malfunctioned, the hydrocyanic acid entering the chamber through pipes did not properly heat. Some of it remained in its liquid form and pooled on the floor instead of wafting into the chamber as lethal gas. This caused the execution to last longer than it should. Furthermore, cracks in the gas chamber created a dangerous situation for witnesses and prison officials alike as the hydrocyanic acid seeped through holes in the walls.

85. February 7, 1922. New Jersey. **George Gares**. Electrocution. After the first electric shock was administered, there was a blinding flash and a sizzling sound as the electrode attached to Gares's leg fell to the ground. Witnesses turned their heads as the condemned man reportedly gasped and writhed. Eventually the electrode was reconnected, additional shocks were administered, and Gares was pronounced dead.

86. March 10, 1922. Arkansas. **James Wells**. Electrocution. It took an inexperienced executioner twelve attempts to kill Wells in the electric chair. The twelve shocks of electricity took a full twenty minutes to complete.

87. September 15, 1922. Iowa. **Eugene Weeks**. Hanging. Rain earlier in the morning had soaked the rope, causing it to stretch considerably after the drop. Although he eventually died of strangulation, Weeks's feet dragged along the ground for several minutes.

88. September 15, 1922. North Carolina. **Angus Murphy**. Electrocution. A witnessing reporter described steam issuing from under the helmet along with a crackling sound while the current was applied. Afterwards there was a strong odor of burnt flesh.

89. February 2, 1923. Arkansas. **F. G. Bullen**. Electrocution. One of the men in a quadruple execution in Arkansas needed to be "executed twice," according to the *New York Times*. Bullen was electrocuted and remained in the chair for five minutes. His body was removed from the chair and placed in a casket. When the undertaker noticed that Bullen appeared to still be breathing, he refused to take the body out of the room. Bullen was placed back in the chair and electrocuted again, after which he was pronounced dead.

90. March 2, 1923. Ohio. **Henry White**. Electrocution. It took a full five shocks to kill White. Prison officials stated that they could not remember ever before needing to use that many rounds of electricity to kill a man.

91. March 1, 1923. North Carolina. **Robert Williams**. Electrocution. Williams's electrocution caused state representative John S. Watkins to state that he would have steps taken to reinstate the use of hanging as a method of execution instead of the electric chair. The first shock given to Williams caused

the water-soaked helmet on his head to set on fire, and he also foamed at the mouth. After this shock, it was determined that Williams was not dead, so a second shock, lasting several minutes and apparently causing him great agony, was administered before he was pronounced dead.

92. February 8, 1924. Texas. **Charles Reynolds**, **Ewell Morris**, **George Washington**, **Mack Matthews**, and **Melvin Johnson**. Electrocution. The generator seemed to be weakening, as each of the five executions took longer than the last. The executioners took a break between the fourth and fifth executions, as the accumulated odor of burning flesh had sickened many of the forty witnesses.

93. February 8, 1924. Texas. **Charles Reynolds**, **Ewell Morris**, **George Washington**, **Mack Matthews**, and **Melvin Johnson**. Electrocution. The generator seemed to be weakening, as each of the five executions took longer than the last. The executioners took a break between the fourth and fifth executions, as the accumulated odor of burning flesh had sickened many of the forty witnesses.

94. October 8, 1926. California. **Alfonse Rincon**. Hanging. Rincon was put to death in a double hanging. His execution was marred when his head struck the side of the platform as he fell through the trap.

95. September 9, 1927. Maryland. **Otis Simmons**. Hanging. The executioner sprung the trap before the rope had been adjusted; as a consequence, the drop failed to break Simmons's neck. He was pronounced dead by strangulation fourteen minutes later.

96. May 29, 1928. District of Colombia. **Philip Jackson**. Electrocution. Jackson was the first man to be executed by electricity in the District. The current was turned on six separate times before he was pronounced dead. After each shock, Jackson continued to strain against the straps. The execution took seventeen minutes.

97. February 21, 1930. Arizona. **Eva Dugan**. Hanging. When the trap was opened, Dugan, the first female to be legally executed in Arizona, dropped more than six feet, and the noose severed her head.

98. February 24, 1931. Florida. **Nathan Burton**. Electrocution. Burton was placed in the electric chair, and the power was turned on. After fifty seconds of electric shock, a high-voltage wire going to the chair snapped, causing a glowing arc that illuminated the death room. Technicians disconnected the chair and tried to splice the wire, but by the time power was available again, a physician had already pronounced Burton dead.

99. December 17, 1931. North Carolina. **J. W. Ballard**. Electrocution. The electrodes covering seventeen-year-old James Ballard's head were pressed up against his left ear during the electrocution, and as a result his left ear was almost entirely burned off.

100. April 29, 1932. Kentucky. **Walter Holmes**. Electrocution. Resisting ex-

ecution in the electric chair in Eddyville, Holmes attacked and wounded guards with an iron pipe that he had removed from his cell. He was finally subdued.

101. April 28, 1933. Ohio. **Tony Rotunno**. Electrocution. Rotunno's heart was not yet stopped after three shocks. It took nine minutes in total before death was pronounced. His right leg began to smoke where the electrode was attached; the flesh turned a purple color; and the smell in the room was "acrid."

102. May 18, 1934. Louisiana. **John Capaci** and **George Dallao**. Hanging. The heads of both Capaci and Dallao were almost completely severed by the force of their drop. As a result, an official witness fainted.

103. May 18, 1934. Louisiana. **John Capaci** and **George Dallao**. Hanging. The heads of both Capaci and Dallao were almost completely severed by the force of their drop. As a result, an official witness fainted.

104. August 24, 1934. Kentucky. **Will Chaney**. Electrocution. After two charges of electricity were administered to the condemned, the electric chair broke down, unbeknownst to the physicians. The physicians checked Chaney's body after the second shock, concluded he was not dead, and asked for a third charge to be administered. However, officials informed the physicians that no charge could be administered until repairs were made to the chair. When physicians reexamined Chaney, they pronounced him dead.

105. February 2, 1935. Virginia. **Robert Mais**. Electrocution. Mais's frail body crashed against the straps due to the high voltage in the electric chair. It took twenty minutes to kill him.

106. March 21, 1935. Illinois. **Chester Novack**. Electrocution. After three shocks were administered, Novack appeared dead and was taken out of the chair. After a more careful examination, a physician detected signs of life. Officials restrapped the unconscious Novack back into the chair and administered two more shocks. According to the *St. Joseph News-Press*, they stated that his "resistance to the powerful electric current was extremely unusual."

107. June 21, 1935. Colorado. **Leonard Belongia**. Electrocution. It took twenty minutes to kill Belongia in the electric chair.

108. December 20, 1935. Georgia. **Marvin Honea**. Electrocution. It took five shocks in the electric chair to kill Honea.

109. January 31, 1936. Mississippi. **Allen Foster**. Lethal Gas. In the first use of a lethal gas chamber east of the Mississippi, Foster died a slow death. The gas chamber "failed to function in accordance with expectations," according to the *New York Times*. Foster was conscious for a full three minutes after the hydrocyanic gas was released into the chamber, and it took eleven minutes for him to die. The partial failure of the gas chamber led newspapers, state officials, and others to question the switch from the electric chair to lethal gas.

110. April 4, 1936. New Jersey. **Bruno Hauptmann**. Electrocution. Just before Hauptmann was pronounced dead, there came a curl of smoke from

where the leg electrode was attached—a suggestion that the voltage had been too great.

111.   July 7, 1936. Arizona. **Earl Gardner**. Hanging. Officials quickly assembled a makeshift scaffold on which to hang Gardner. A small man, he hit the side of the trap and his noose slipped out of place as his body fell. He hung by the neck for thirty-three minutes, moaning and kicking in pain, before he was pronounced dead.

112.   July 10, 1936. North Carolina. **Henry Grier**. Electrocution. In Raleigh, Grier escaped the chair momentarily and attempted suicide by leaping off the side of a corridor to the prison basement.

113.   April 23, 1938. Texas. **John Vaughn** and **Johnnie Banks**. Electrocution. As Vaughn was delivering his last words (protesting his innocence) in the death chamber, the prison warden entered and revealed that the generator for the electric chair had broken. Since the prison was unable to carry out the execution, the governor of Texas reprieved the two men for a week. They were ultimately executed on April 30 and 29, respectively.

114.   April 23, 1938. Texas. **John Vaughn** and **Johnnie Banks**. Electrocution. As Vaughn was delivering his last words (protesting his innocence) in the death chamber, the prison warden entered and revealed that the generator for the electric chair had broken. Since the prison was unable to carry out the execution, the governor of Texas reprieved the two men for a week. They were ultimately executed on April 30 and 29, respectively.

115.   December 2, 1938. California. **Albert Kessel** and **Robert Lee Cannon**. Lethal Gas. Kessel and Cannon were executed at San Quentin in California's first use of poison gas. Cannon's death took twelve minutes and Kessel's fifteen and a half. Spectators were reportedly "sickened."

116.   December 2, 1938. California. **Albert Kessel** and **Robert Lee Cannon**. Lethal Gas. Kessel and Cannon were executed at San Quentin in California's first use of poison gas. Cannon's death took twelve minutes and Kessel's fifteen and a half. Spectators were reportedly "sickened."

117.   December 8, 1938. Ohio. **Anna Marie Hahn**. Electrocution. Hahn died in Ohio's electric chair in Columbus. A bluish stream of smoke curled upward from the electrode connected to her right leg.

118.   July 7, 1939. North Carolina. **Bricey Hammonds**. Lethal Gas. Hammonds, a one-legged Native American, was put to death in a gas chamber. He appeared to scream for a full five minutes after the gas was released, an unusually long time to remain conscious.

119.   August 2, 1939. Massachusetts. **Wallace Green**. Electrocution. As the usual executioner was ill, "Mr. X," a substitute, was brought in. "Mr. X" was "not an expert." It took the executioner five separate shocks, over the span of about twenty minutes, to kill Green. A second man was killed after Green, but

he needed only three shocks as the voltage to the chair had been increased after it took so long to kill Green. Green's execution brought outrage from Herbert C. Parsons, head of the Massachusetts Council for the Abolition of the Death Penalty, who denounced the botch as an "example of inhumanity," according to the *New York Times*.

120. December 21, 1939. New York. **Everett McDonald**. Electrocution. A mishap occurred during McDonald's execution. After a second shock, one of the electrodes on his leg fell off. The executioner put the electrode back on and administered the third and final shock.

121. April 10, 1942. California. **Henry James** and **Dewey Clark**. Lethal Gas. The two men, executed together at San Quentin, each took fourteen minutes to die in the lethal gas chamber.

122. April 10, 1942. California. **Henry James** and **Dewey Clark**. Lethal Gas. The two men, executed together at San Quentin, each took fourteen minutes to die in the lethal gas chamber.

123. May 8, 1942. Maryland. **Wilbur Pritchett**. Hanging. In "the bloodiest hanging in Maryland history," Pritchett was put to death for rape. The weight of his body caused the noose to all but sever his head from the rest of his body. Blood spurted out in an eight-foot circle, and Pritchett whirled around on the end of the rope for several minutes.

124. November 13, 1942. California. **Delmar Arnold**. Lethal Gas. It took Arnold, a twenty-one-year-old black man, twelve minutes to die in the San Quentin gas chamber.

125. March 19, 1943. Washington. **Chester Montgomery**. Hanging. After entering the death chamber, Montgomery fought off prison guards until they strapped him to an emergency board before hanging him.

126. May 14, 1943. California. **Warren Cramer**. Lethal Gas. Cramer died thirteen minutes after entering the gas chamber at San Quentin.

127. October 8, 1943. Colorado. **George Honda**. Lethal Gas. Honda attempted suicide, or hara-kiri, at his execution, but was stopped by bystanders.

128. November 26, 1943. North Carolina. **John Redfern**. Lethal Gas. The state executioner was forced to throw poison by hand when a mechanism in the state prison's lethal gas chamber jammed and was unable to release cyanide, as Redfern sat strapped into the chair inside.

129. February 23, 1945. Iowa. **William Jasper Jarrett**. Hanging. Jarrett was nearly decapitated by his fall through the trap at the state prison gallows.

130. May 3, 1946. Louisiana. **Willie Francis**. Electrocution. The electric chair failed to kill Francis after it had been improperly set up by an intoxicated prison guard and inmate. A shock of electricity went through Francis's body, but he did not die. He could be heard screaming, "I'm not dying," and "Take it off! Let me breathe," despite the fact that the first shock of electricity was sup-

posed to render the convict unconscious. He survived two separate shocks of electricity, and the execution was then stopped by the sheriff, who unstrapped Francis from the chair. After a failed appeal to the Supreme Court, Francis was finally executed a year and a week later, on May 9, 1947.

131.   May 13, 1946. Louisiana. **George Edwards**. Electrocution. Using the same chair that had failed to kill Willie Francis the week before, officials at the prison in Leesville botched the execution of Edwards. The generator supplying power to the electric chair caught fire when the executioner threw the switch. Witnesses realized that the chair was nonfunctional, and feared that the execution had failed. Prison officials said that if more than one shock had been necessary to kill him, they would not have been able to execute him. However, prison doctors pronounced Edwards dead a minute after the first shock.

132.   June 14, 1946. Alabama. **Joe Lodies Mincey**. Electrocution. Mincey wrapped sheets around the bars of his cell, preventing prison officials from unlocking his cell to take him to the electric chair. He also threw a bucket of water through the bars onto prison guards. After an hour of negotiating with guards, Mincey finally agreed to walk to the execution chamber. Once in the chamber, he started a battle with seven prison officials, including Gray, a 268-pound prison guard captain. The battle lasted five minutes. Mincey's struggles delayed his execution by more than an hour.

133.   August 16, 1946. Massachusetts. **Raphael Skopp**. Electrocution. It took six shocks in the electric chair at Charleston State Prison to kill Skopp. The unusual number of shocks was necessary because of his large, rugged physique.

134.   April 11, 1947. Tennessee. **Albert Duboise**. Electrocution. Duboise was already strapped into the chair when prison officials in Nashville discovered it was broken. He waited fifteen minutes while workmen repaired a broken power line before he was executed.

135.   July 11, 1947. South Carolina. **J. C. Sims**. Electrocution. A spurt of yellow flame shot from Sims's neck after the state electrician pulled the switch on the electric chair.

136.   July 23, 1947. North Carolina. **Bert Grant**. Electrocution. Grant took an "unusually long" time to die after the current was turned on: three minutes and fifty seconds. Reportedly, more current than normal was necessary to insure his death.

137.   September 5, 1947. Texas. **Arthur Adams**. Electrocution. Adams waited an extra hour to be executed because a connection on the electric chair broke.

138.   October 31, 1947. North Carolina. **Grady Brown** and **J. C. Brooks**. Lethal Gas. Brown and Brooks were in the Raleigh gas chamber for more than eleven minutes before both were pronounced dead.

139.   October 31, 1947. North Carolina. **Grady Brown** and **J. C. Brooks**. Lethal Gas. Brown and Brooks were in the Raleigh gas chamber for more than eleven minutes before both were pronounced dead.

140.   April 23, 1948. North Carolina. **Booker T. Anderson** and **Buster Hooks**. Lethal Gas. Death took eleven minutes.

141.   April 23, 1948. North Carolina. **Booker T. Anderson** and **Buster Hooks**. Lethal Gas. Death took eleven minutes.

142.   August 21, 1948. Ohio. **Donald Frohner**. Electrocution. The eighteen-year-old Frohner was executed in Columbus. The electrode attached to Frohner's right ankle began to smoke violently shortly after the switch was pulled. It burst into a bright red and purple flame. The current was then switched off. When it was turned back on, the electrode caught fire once more. It burned until Frohner was pronounced dead.

143.   December 3, 1948. South Carolina. **Matthew Jamison**. Electrocution. The initial shock lasted for six minutes and one second, a record for the state of South Carolina. Jamison was still alive, and more shocks were required to kill him. A nurse fainted.

144.   March 4, 1949. Alabama. **Phillip Cobb**. Electrocution. Cobb was slated to be executed on this date, but he received an eleventh-hour reprieve due to equipment failure. Electricians testing the chair shortly before his execution was to begin determined that the chair was not functioning properly. One of the power cables was worn out, so power was not reaching the electrodes. Cobb's electrocution was delayed a week; he was executed on March 11.

145.   March 18, 1949. North Carolina. **Emmett Garner**. Lethal Gas. It took fourteen minutes for Garner to die in a Raleigh gas chamber.

146.   August 12, 1949. Maryland. **Eugene James**. Hanging. The noose was not tight enough around James's neck to break it. He strangled to death slowly, screaming as he hung at the end of the rope.

147.   December 9, 1949. North Carolina. **Audie Brown, Monroe Medlin,** and **Allen T. Reid**. Lethal Gas. Reid and Brown were executed together in the gas chamber; it took twelve minutes for Brown and thirteen minutes for Reid to die. Medlin was executed immediately after the two other men; his gassing took eleven minutes.

148.   December 9, 1949. North Carolina. **Audie Brown, Monroe Medlin,** and **Allen T. Reid**. Reid and Brown were executed together in the gas chamber; it took twelve minutes for Brown and thirteen minutes for Reid to die. Medlin was executed immediately after the two other men; his gassing took eleven minutes.

149.   December 9, 1949. North Carolina. **Audie Brown, Monroe Medlin,** and **Allen T. Reid**. Reid and Brown were executed together in the gas chamber; it took twelve minutes for Brown and thirteen minutes for Reid to die. Medlin

was executed immediately after the two other men; his gassing took eleven minutes.

150.   December 20, 1949. North Carolina. **Leander Jacobs** and **Hector Chavis**. Lethal Gas. It took eleven minutes for Jacobs and Chavis to die in the gas chamber.

151.   December 20, 1949. North Carolina. **Leander Jacobs** and **Hector Chavis**. Lethal Gas. It took eleven minutes for Jacobs and Chavis to die in the gas chamber.

152.   June 2, 1950. South Carolina. **Charles Butler**. Electrocution. It took five shocks to kill the 230-pound Butler.

153.   March 23, 1951. North Carolina. **Curtis Shedd**. Lethal Gas. Shedd died after eleven minutes in the gas chamber.

154.   December 10, 1951. Washington. **Grant Rio**. Hanging. Rio was executed in Walla Walla. He was pronounced dead after hanging for nineteen minutes.

155.   May 10, 1952. Ohio. **James C. Edwards**. Electrocution. Edwards briefly escaped from the guards in the execution chamber and fought back fiercely while they forced him into the chair.

156.   January 3, 1953. Washington. **Turman Wilson**. Hanging. The drop failed to break his neck. Wilson gasped and moaned for several minutes, and a trickle of blood appeared from beneath his hood. He was dead in ten minutes.

157.   June 19, 1953. New York. **Ethel Rosenberg**. Electrocution. In these notorious executions, Mr. Rosenberg was dead after the standard three shocks, but Mrs. Rosenberg's heart continued to beat. The executioners at Sing Sing killed her with another two shocks, during which a "ghastly plume of smoke" rose from her head.

158.   February 20, 1953. California. **Leandress Riley**. Lethal Gas. Riley's execution became a major newspaper headline when he went to his death fighting. After attempting suicide, the condemned was finally subdued, handcuffed, and dragged into the gas chamber. However, once restrained, Riley somehow managed to get free from the chair's straps. When the gas finally entered the chamber, Riley held his breath for minutes before dying.

159.   March 5, 1954. South Carolina. **Shelton H. Gainey**. Electrocution. Six charges lasting four minutes were required to end Gainey's life.

160.   May 7, 1954. South Carolina. **Raymond Carney**. Electrocution. During the initial shock, the bolts holding the electric chair's front legs to the floor were jerked out of their casings. The chair was still held down by the rear legs for the rest of the execution. Carney was still alive after the standard three shocks, and two more were required to kill him.

161.   July 15, 1955. North Carolina. **Richard Scales**. Lethal Gas. Convicted

of slaying a housewife, Scales took fifteen minutes to die after he began breathing in the lethal gas in the gas chamber.

162.   December 3, 1955. South Carolina. **Clay Daniels**. Electrocution. Daniels leapt from the electric chair before the straps could be put on his arms, and battled six guards for approximately twenty minutes. Eventually, they were able to force him back into the chair. It then took six minutes and fifty-five seconds, the longest amount of time in South Carolina history up to this date, to kill Daniels with electric shocks.

163.   December 23, 1955. Kentucky. **Chester Merrifield**. Electrocution. Merrifield passed out when placed in the electric chair and was shocked and killed before he regained consciousness.

164.   April 6, 1956. California. **Robert Pierce**. Lethal Gas. With blood gushing from a self-inflicted wound at his throat, Pierce died in the gas chamber at San Quentin. He fought and cursed up until the moment of his death. Blood splattered on the four guards who dragged him to the death chamber.

165.   September 7, 1956. West Virginia. **Robert Hopkins**. Electrocution. Hopkins's execution in the electric chair lasted fourteen minutes. Three minutes after the first switch was thrown, three physicians found that Hopkins was still alive. A second switch was thrown and he was pronounced dead at 9:12 P.M.

166.   March 5, 1957. Georgia. **Jennings E. Fields**. Electrocution. Just before heading to the death chamber in Reidsville, Fields slit both of his wrists in a futile suicide attempt. He attacked one of the five guards who were required to force him into the chair.

167.   May 30, 1957. Maryland. **Eddie Lee Daniels**. Lethal Gas. Before going unconscious, Daniels let out a loud cry. It took him fourteen minutes to die.

168.   June 7, 1957. South Carolina. **Willie Marion Daniels**. Electrocution. A small black and white kitten disrupted Daniels's execution at the prison in Columbia. As the physician was checking for a heartbeat, the kitten ran between the legs of witness chairs and approached the condemned man, circling the electric chair several times.

169.   June 25, 1959. Nebraska. **Charles Starkweather**. Electrocution. The execution required five charges before Starkweather was pronounced dead.

170.   May 2, 1960. California. **Caryl Chessman**. Lethal Gas. Chessman told reporters he would nod his head if the execution hurt. Witnesses to his execution said he nodded his head for minutes. Just minutes after his execution began the prison warden received a phone call staying his execution, but it was too late. It took Chessman nine minutes to die.

171.   May 12, 1960. New York. **Pablo Vargas**. Electrocution. Vargas put up a "desperate resistance" in the death chamber. It ultimately took eight guards to force him into the death chair.

172.   June 15, 1961. Indiana. **Richard Kiefer**. Electrocution. Kiefer was given

six shocks in the Fort Wayne electric chair before he was pronounced dead by a prison physician and another doctor from Michigan City. It was Indiana's first execution in ten years, the previous execution being that of Robert Watts on January 16, 1951.

173. August 24, 1961. Nevada. **Thayne Archibald**. Lethal Gas. Executed in the Nevada gas chamber, it took Archibald several minutes to lose consciousness once the gas was released. Archibald struggled, gasped, and thrashed his head about violently for several minutes before finally succumbing to the fumes and losing consciousness.

174. April 13, 1967. California. **Aaron Mitchell**. Lethal Gas. Mitchell was executed in the San Quentin gas chamber. It took twelve minutes after the gas was released for him to die. A four-hundred-person vigil composed of death penalty opponents was held outside the prison the night of his execution.

175. *August 10, 1982. Virginia. **Frank J. Coppola**. Electrocution. Although no media representatives witnessed the execution and no details were ever released by the Virginia Department of Corrections, an attorney who was present later stated that it took two fifty-five-second jolts of electricity to kill Coppola. The second jolt produced the odor and sizzling sound of burning flesh, and Coppola's head and leg caught on fire. Smoke filled the death chamber from floor to ceiling.

176. *April 22, 1983. Alabama. **John Evans**. Electrocution. After the first jolt of electricity, sparks and flames erupted from the electrode attached to Evans's leg. The electrode burst from the strap holding it in place and caught on fire. Smoke and sparks also came out from under the hood in the vicinity of his left temple. Two physicians entered the chamber, and they detected a heartbeat. The electrode was reattached to Evans's leg, and another jolt of electricity was applied. This resulted in more smoke and burning flesh. Again the doctors found a heartbeat. Ignoring the pleas of Evans's lawyer, a third jolt of electricity was applied. The execution took fourteen minutes and left Evans's body charred and smoldering.

177. *September 2, 1983. Mississippi. **Jimmy Lee Gray**. Lethal Gas. Officials had to clear the room eight minutes after the gas was released when Gray's desperate gasps for air repulsed witnesses. His attorney, Dennis Balske of Montgomery, Alabama, criticized state officials for clearing the room when the inmate was still alive. Said noted death penalty defense attorney David Bruck, "Jimmy Lee Gray died banging his head against a steel pole in the gas chamber while the reporters counted his moans (eleven, according to the Associated Press)." Later it was revealed that the executioner, Barry Bruce, had been drunk.

178. December 14, 1983. Louisiana. **Robert Williams**. Electrocution. Williams's execution in the electric chair lasted fourteen minutes. It took five jolts of electricity to kill him, sending smoke and sparks into the execution chamber.

179. March 1, 1984. Louisiana. **Johnny Taylor**. Electrocution. During the electrocution, two curls of smoke appeared were the electrodes had been applied to Taylor's leg.

180. March 16, 1984. North Carolina. **James Hutchins**. Lethal Injection. The first man executed in North Carolina since 1961, it took Hutchins fifteen minutes to die after the drug series began to flow through his veins.

181. May 11, 1984. Florida. **James Adams**. Electrocution. Adams was sentenced to die in the electric chair. When officers attempted to screw the headpiece onto his head, they found that one of the two nuts they had would not fit into the headpiece. The officers had to "scramble around" for several minutes, according to the *Sarasota Herald Tribune*, to find a different nut that would properly secure the headpiece onto the condemned.

182. November 9, 1984. Florida. **Timothy Palmes**. Electrocution. Palmes was put to death in the electric chair. During the execution, smoke curled up from his right leg, where the electrode was attached.

183. November 11, 1984. North Carolina. **Velma Barfield**. Lethal Injection. Barfield was sentenced to death by lethal injection. It took fourteen minutes for her to die after the drugs were first administered.

184. *December 12, 1984. Georgia. **Alpha Otis Stephens**. Electrocution. "The first charge of electricity . . . failed to kill him, and he struggled to breathe for eight minutes before a second charge carried out his death sentence." After the first two-minute power surge, there was a six-minute pause so his body could cool before physicians could examine him (and declare that another jolt was needed). During that six-minute interval, Stephens took twenty-three breaths. A Georgia prison official said, "Stephens was just not a conductor" of electricity.

185. *March 13, 1985. Texas. **Stephen Peter Morin**. Lethal Injection. Because of Morin's history of drug abuse, the execution technicians were forced to probe both of his arms and one of his legs with needles for nearly forty-five minutes before they found a suitable vein.

186. May 29, 1985. Florida. **Marvin Francois**. Electrocution. Ten minutes passed before Francois was declared dead, admittedly four minutes longer than in past electrocutions at the state prison.

187. June 25, 1985. Texas. **Charles Milton**. Lethal Injection. Milton's execution took twenty-three minutes.

188. October 16, 1985. Indiana. **William E. Vandiver**. Electrocution. After the first administration of 2,300 volts, Vandiver was still breathing. The execution eventually took seventeen minutes and five jolts of electricity. Vandiver's attorney, Herbert Shaps, witnessed the execution and observed smoke and a burning smell. He called the execution "outrageous." The Department of Corrections admitted the execution "did not go according to plan."

189. April 15, 1986. Florida. **Daniel Thomas**. Electrocution. Prison officials struggled to get Thomas into the electric chair. It took five corrections officers and two medical officers to force Thomas into the chair. One official received a kick to the groin and a minor bite wound in the process.

190. April 22, 1986. Florida. **David Funchess**. Electrocution. The jolts of electricity sent smoke rising from Funchess's hands into the chamber.

191. *August 20, 1986. Texas. **Randy Woolls**. Lethal Injection. A drug addict, Woolls helped the execution technicians find a usable vein for the execution.

192. January 30, 1987. Texas. **Ramon Hernandez**. Lethal Injection. Hernandez's execution was delayed due to officials' difficulty locating a vein to insert the needle.

193. *June 24, 1987. Texas. **Elliot Rod Johnson**. Lethal Injection. Because of collapsed veins, it took nearly an hour to complete Johnson's execution.

194. January 7, 1988. Texas. **Robert Streetman**. Lethal Injection. Streetman was already being strapped to a gurney in the death chamber when confused state officials decided to delay his execution.

195. *December 13, 1988. Texas. **Raymond Landry**. Lethal Injection. Landry was pronounced dead forty minutes after being strapped to the execution gurney and twenty-four minutes after the drugs first started flowing into his arms. Two minutes after the drugs were administered, the syringe came out of his vein, spraying the deadly chemicals across the room toward witnesses. The curtain separating the witnesses from the inmate was then pulled and not reopened for fourteen minutes while the execution team reinserted the catheter into the vein. Witnesses reported "at least one groan." A spokesman for the Texas Department of Corrections, Charles Brown, said, "There was something of a delay in the execution because of what officials called a 'blowout.' The syringe came out of the vein, and the warden ordered the (execution) team to reinsert the catheter into the vein."

196. *May 24, 1989. Texas. **Stephen McCoy**. Lethal Injection. He had such a violent physical reaction to the drugs (heaving chest, gasping, choking, back arching off the gurney, etc.) that one of the witnesses (male) fainted, crashing into and knocking over another witness. Houston attorney Karen Zellars, who represented McCoy and witnessed the execution, thought the fainting would catalyze a chain reaction. The Texas attorney general admitted the inmate "seemed to have a somewhat stronger reaction," adding, "The drugs might have been administered in a heavier dose or more rapidly."

197. *July 14, 1989. Alabama. **Horace Franklin Dunkins Jr**. Electrocution. It took two jolts of electricity, nine minutes apart, to complete the execution. After the first jolt failed to kill Dunkins (who was mildly retarded), the captain of the prison guard opened the door to the witness room and stated, "I believe

we've got the jacks on wrong." Because the cables had been connected improperly, it was impossible to dispense sufficient current to cause death. The cables were reconnected before a second jolt was administered. Death was pronounced nineteen minutes after the first electric charge. At a postexecution news conference, Alabama prison commissioner Morris Thigpen said, "I regret very very much what happened. [The cause] was human error."

198. *May 4, 1990. Florida. **Jesse Joseph Tafero**. Electrocution. During the execution, six-inch flames erupted from Tafero's head, and three jolts of power were required to stop his breathing. State officials claimed that the botched execution was caused by "inadvertent human error"—the inappropriate substitution of a synthetic sponge for a natural sponge that had been used in previous executions. They attempted to support this theory by sticking a part of a synthetic sponge into a "common household toaster" and observing that it smoldered and caught fire.

199. June 25, 1990. Arkansas. **R. Gene Simmons**. Lethal Injection. Simmons was pronounced dead seventeen minutes after the initial injection was administered.

200. *September 12, 1990. Illinois. **Charles Walker**. Lethal Injection. Because of equipment failure and human error, Walker suffered excruciating pain during his execution. According to Gary Sutterfield, an engineer from the Missouri State Prison who was retained by the state of Illinois to assist with Walker's execution, a kink in the plastic tubing going into Walker's arm stopped the deadly chemicals from reaching Walker. In addition, the intravenous needle was inserted pointing at Walker's fingers instead of his heart, prolonging the execution.

201. September 21, 1990. Florida. **James William Hamblen**. Electrocution. A large amount of white smoke puffed up from around his right leg as the current was turned on for the first time. His leg turned yellow and purple where the electrode was attached.

202. *October 17, 1990. Virginia. **Wilbert Lee Evans**. Electrocution. When Evans was hit with the first burst of electricity, blood spewed from the right side of the mask on his face, drenching his shirt with blood and causing a sizzling sound as blood dripped from his lips. Evans continued to moan before a second jolt of electricity was applied. The autopsy concluded that Evans suffered a bloody nose after the voltage surge elevated his high blood pressure.

203. April 24, 1991. Florida. **Roy Harich**. Electrocution. On the third charge, white smoke began to rise from his left leg. He was pronounced dead after the current was shut off.

204. *August 22, 1991. Virginia. **Derick Lynn Peterson**. Electrocution. After the first cycle of electricity was applied, and again four minutes later, prison physician David Barnes inspected Peterson's neck and checked him with

a stethoscope, announcing each time, "He has not expired." Seven and a half minutes after the first attempt to kill the inmate, a second cycle of electricity was applied. Prison officials later announced that in the future they would routinely administer two cycles before checking for a heartbeat.

205. *January 24, 1992. Arkansas. **Rickey Ray Rector**. Lethal Injection. It took medical staff more than fifty minutes to find a suitable vein in Rector's arm. Witnesses were kept behind a drawn curtain and not permitted to view this scene, but they reported hearing Rector's eight loud moans during the process. During the ordeal, Rector (who suffered from serious brain damage) helped the medical personnel find a vein. The administrator of the state's Department of Corrections medical programs said (paraphrased by a newspaper reporter), "the moans did come as a team of two medical people that had grown to five worked on both sides of his body to find a vein." The administrator said, "That may have contributed to his occasional outbursts." The difficulty in finding a suitable vein was later attributed to Rector's bulk and his regular use of antipsychotic medication.

206. *March 10, 1992. Oklahoma. **Robyn LeRoy Parks**. Lethal Injection. Parks had a violent reaction to the drugs used in the lethal injection. Two minutes after the drugs were dispensed, the muscles in his jaw, neck, and abdomen began to react spasmodically for approximately forty-five seconds. Parks continued to gasp and violently gag until death came, some eleven minutes after the drugs were first administered. *Tulsa World* reporter Wayne Greene wrote that the execution looked "painful and ugly," and "scary." "It was overwhelming, stunning, disturbing—an intrusion into a moment so personal that reporters, taught for years that intrusion is their business, had trouble looking each other in the eyes after it was over."

207. March 20, 1992. Alabama. **Larry Gene Heath**. Electrocution. The current caused smoke to rise from Heath's left leg. Witnesses noticed a faint burning odor.

208. *April 6, 1992. Arizona. **Donald Eugene Harding**. Lethal Gas. Death was not pronounced until ten and a half minutes after the cyanide tablets were dropped. During the execution, Harding thrashed and struggled violently against the restraining straps. A television journalist, Cameron Harper, who witnessed the execution said that Harding's spasms and jerks lasted six minutes and thirty-seven seconds. "Obviously, this man was suffering. This was a violent death . . . an ugly event. We put animals to death more humanely." Another witness, newspaper reporter Carla McClain, said, "Harding's death was extremely violent. He was in great pain. I heard him gasp and moan. I saw his body turn from red to purple." One reporter who witnessed the execution suffered from insomnia and assorted illnesses for several weeks; two others were "walking vegetables" for several days.

209. *April 23, 1992. Texas. **Billy Wayne White**. Lethal Injection. White was pronounced dead some forty-seven minutes after being strapped to the execution gurney. The delay was caused by difficulty finding a vein; White had a long history of heroin abuse. During the execution, White attempted to assist the authorities in finding a suitable vein.

210. *May 7, 1992. Texas. **Justin Lee May**. Lethal Injection. May had an unusually violent reaction to the lethal drugs. According to one reporter who witnessed the execution, May "gasped, coughed and reared against his heavy leather restraints, coughing once again before his body froze." Associated Press reporter Michael Graczyk wrote, "Compared to other recent executions in Texas, May's reaction was more violent. He went into a coughing spasm, groaned and gasped, lifted his head from the death chamber gurney and would have arched his back if he had not been belted down. After he stopped breathing, his eyes and mouth remained open."

211. December 15, 1993. Texas. **Clifford Phillips**. Lethal Injection. Phillips's execution was delayed due to officials' difficulty in locating a vein.

212. March 3, 1994. Virginia. **Johnny Watkins Jr**. Electrocution. Witnesses of Watkins's execution were recorded as saying that smoke was "prevalent."

213. *May 10, 1994. Illinois. **John Wayne Gacy**. Lethal Injection. After the execution began, the lethal chemicals unexpectedly solidified, clogging the intravenous tube that led into Gacy's arm, and prohibiting any further passage. Blinds covering the window through which witnesses observed the execution were drawn, and the execution team replaced the clogged tube with a new one. Ten minutes later, the blinds were reopened and the execution process resumed. It took eighteen minutes to complete. Anesthesiologists blamed the problem on the inexperience of prison officials who were conducting the execution, saying that proper procedures taught in "IV 101" would have prevented the error.

214. May 17, 1994. Maryland. **Frederick Thanos**. Lethal Injection. Thanos's arms were so scarred by drug use that executioners could find no usable veins in them. Instead, they had to tear his pants and inject the drugs through a vein in the prisoner's leg.

215. June 15, 1994. North Carolina. **David Lawson**. Lethal Gas. As executioners attempted to put a mask on his face, Lawson, already strapped into the chair in the gas chamber, began to scream, "I'm human! I'm human! Don't kill me!"

216. September 2, 1994. Nevada. **Harold Otey**. Electrocution. Otey was shocked four times because he did not appear to die after the first shock. Witnesses said they saw smoke rise from his left knee after the third shock.

217. August 2, 1994. Texas. **Robert Drew**. Lethal Injection. Drew coughed and gasped and tears streamed down his face as the needle was inserted into his arm.

218. December 11, 1994. Texas. **Raymond Kinnamon**. Lethal Injection.

While the lethal drugs were administered, Kinnamon rose up from the gurney and tried to free his hands from their restraints.

219. *May 3, 1995. Missouri. **Emmitt Foster**. Lethal Injection. Seven minutes after the lethal chemicals began to flow into Foster's arm, the execution was halted when the chemicals stopped circulating. With Foster gasping and convulsing, the blinds were drawn so the witnesses could not view the scene. Death was pronounced thirty minutes after the execution began, and three minutes later the blinds were reopened so the witnesses could view the corpse. According to William "Mal" Gum, the Washington County coroner who pronounced death, the problem was caused by the tightness of the leather straps that bound Foster to the execution gurney; it was so tight that the flow of chemicals into the veins was restricted. The coroner entered the death chamber twenty minutes after the execution began, diagnosed the problem, and told the officials to loosen the strap so the execution could proceed. Foster did not die until several minutes after a prison worker finally loosened the straps. In an editorial, the *St. Louis Post-Dispatch* called the execution "a particularly sordid chapter in Missouri's capital punishment experience.

220. September 22, 1995. North Carolina. **Phillip Lee Ingle**. Lethal Injection. It took Ingle thirteen minutes to die once the lethal drugs entered his body.

221. December 4, 1995. Florida. **Jerry White**. Electrocution. White was put to death in the electric chair. He screamed loudly as the current went through his body, despite claims that the condemned is always rendered unconscious with the first shock. His screams led fellow inmate Philip Atkins, who was to die an hour after White, to appeal his own case, stating that since White had screamed, the electric chair had malfunctioned. Atkins's appeal was denied, and he was executed the next day, December 5.

222. *January 23, 1996. Virginia. **Richard Townes Jr**. Lethal Injection. This execution was delayed for twenty-two minutes while medical personnel struggled to find a vein large enough for the needle. After unsuccessful attempts to insert the needle into the arms, the needle was finally inserted into the top of Townes's right foot.

223. *July 18, 1996. Indiana. **Tommie J. Smith**. Lethal Injection. Because of his unusually small veins, it took one hour and nine minutes for Smith to be pronounced dead after the execution team began sticking needles into his body. For sixteen minutes, the execution team failed to find adequate veins, and then a physician was called. Smith was given a local anesthetic and the physician twice attempted to insert the tube in Smith's neck. When that failed, an angio-catheter was inserted in Smith's foot. Only then were witnesses permitted to view the process. The lethal drugs were finally injected into Smith forty-nine minutes after the first attempts, and it took another twenty minutes before death was pronounced.

224. December 6, 1996. Florida. **John Mills Jr**. Electrocution. As Mills was

being electrocuted, a puff of white smoke rose up from his leg where an electrode was attached.

225. *March 25, 1997. Florida. **Pedro Medina**. Electrocution. A crown of foot-high flames shot from the headpiece during the execution, filling the execution chamber with a stench of thick smoke and gagging the two dozen official witnesses. An official then threw a switch to manually cut off the power and prematurely end the two-minute cycle of 2,000 volts. Medina's chest continued to heave until the flames stopped and death came. After the execution, prison officials blamed the fire on a corroded copper screen in the headpiece of the electric chair, but two experts hired by the governor later concluded that the fire was caused by the improper application of a sponge (designed to conduct electricity) to Medina's head.

226. *May 8, 1997. Oklahoma. **Scott Dawn Carpenter**. Lethal Injection. Carpenter was pronounced dead some eleven minutes after the lethal injection was administered. As the drugs took effect, Carpenter began to gasp and shake. "This was followed by a guttural sound, multiple spasms and gasping for air" until his body stopped moving, three minutes later.

227. *June 13, 1997. South Carolina. **Michael Eugene Elkins**. Lethal Injection. Because Elkins's body had become swollen from liver and spleen problems, it took nearly an hour to find a suitable vein for the insertion of the catheter. Elkins tried to assist the executioners, asking, "Should I lean my head down a little bit?" as they probed for a vein. After numerous failures, a usable vein was finally found in his neck.

228. *April 23, 1998. Texas. **Joseph Cannon**. Lethal Injection. It took two attempts to complete the execution. After making his final statement, the execution process began. A vein in Cannon's arm collapsed and the needle popped out. Seeing this, Cannon lay back, closed his eyes, and exclaimed to the witnesses, "It's come undone." Officials then pulled a curtain to block the view of the witnesses, reopening it fifteen minutes later, when a weeping Cannon made a second final statement and the execution process resumed.

229. August 14, 1998. North Carolina. **Zane Brown Hill**. Lethal Injection. The execution began at 2:01 A.M. Hill was not pronounced dead until 2:24 A.M. Although authorities admitted that the execution took longer than usual, no explanation was given.

230. *August 26, 1998. Texas. **Genaro Ruiz Camacho**. Lethal Injection. The execution was delayed approximately two hours due in part to problems finding suitable veins in Camacho's arms.

231. *October 5, 1998. Nevada. **Roderick Abeyta**. Lethal Injection. It took twenty-five minutes for the execution team to find a vein suitable for the lethal injection.

232. *July 8, 1999. Florida. **Allen Lee Davis**. Electrocution. "Before he was

pronounced dead . . . the blood from his mouth had poured onto the collar of his white shirt, and the blood on his chest had spread to about the size of a dinner plate, even oozing through the buckle holes on the leather chest strap holding him to the chair." His execution was the first in Florida's new electric chair, built especially so it could accommodate a man Davis's size (approximately 350 pounds). Later, when another Florida death row inmate challenged the constitutionality of the electric chair, Florida Supreme Court justice Leander Shaw commented that "the color photos of Davis depict a man who—for all appearances—was brutally tortured to death by the citizens of Florida." Justice Shaw also described the botched executions of Jesse Tafero and Pedro Medina, calling the three executions "barbaric spectacles" and "acts more befitting a violent murderer than a civilized state." Justice Shaw included pictures of Davis's dead body in his opinion. The execution was witnessed by a Florida State senator, Ginny Brown-Waite, who at first was "shocked" to see the blood, until she realized that the blood was forming the shape of a cross and that it was a message from God saying he supported the execution.

233. October 21, 1999. North Carolina. **Arthur Martin Boyd Jr.** Lethal Injection. It took eighteen minutes for Boyd to die.

234. November 16, 1999. Texas. **Desmond Jennings**. Lethal Injection. It took a team of five specially trained men to bring an uncooperative Jennings from his cell to the death chamber and strap him to the gurney.

235. *May 3, 2000. Arkansas. **Christina Marie Riggs**. Lethal Injection. Riggs dropped her appeals and asked to be executed. However, the execution was delayed for eighteen minutes when prison staff couldn't find a suitable vein in her elbows. Finally, Riggs agreed to the executioners' requests to have the needles in her wrists.

236. *June 8, 2000. Florida. **Bennie Demps**. Lethal Injection. It took execution technicians thirty-three minutes to find suitable veins for the execution. "They butchered me back there," said Demps in his final statement. "I was in a lot of pain. They cut me in the groin; they cut me in the leg. I was bleeding profusely. This is not an execution, it is murder." The executioners had no unusual problems finding one vein, but because Florida protocol requires a second, alternate intravenous drip, they continued to work to insert another needle, finally abandoning the effort after their prolonged failures.

237. *June 28, 2000. Missouri. **Bert Leroy Hunter**. Lethal Injection. Hunter had an unusual reaction to the lethal drugs, repeatedly coughing and gasping for air before he lapsed into unconsciousness. An attorney who witnessed the execution reported that Hunter had "violent convulsions. His head and chest jerked rapidly upward as far as the gurney restraints would allow, and then he fell quickly down upon the gurney. His body convulsed back and forth like this repeatedly. . . . He suffered a violent and agonizing death."

238. August 16, 2000. Texas. **John Thomas Satterwhite**. Lethal Injection. Satterwhite's execution was delayed due to officials' difficulty locating a vein to insert the needle.

239. December 7, 2000. Alabama. **Edward Castro**. Lethal Injection. Castro's execution lasted thirteen minutes.

240. *December 7, 2000. Texas. **Claude Jones**. Lethal Injection. Jones was a former intravenous drug abuser. His execution was delayed thirty minutes while the execution team struggled to insert an intravenous line into a vein. One member of the execution team commented, "They had to stick him about five times. They finally put it in his leg." Wrote Jim Willett, the warden of the Walls Unit and the man responsible for conducting the execution: "The medical team could not find a vein. Now I was really beginning to worry. If you can't stick a vein then a cut-down has to be performed. I have never seen one and would just as soon go through the rest of my career the same way. Just when I was really getting worried, one of the medical people hit a vein in the left leg. Inside calf to be exact. The executioner had warned me not to panic as it was going to take a while to get the fluids in the body of the inmate tonight because he was going to push the drugs through very slowly. Finally, the drug took effect and Jones took his last breath."

241. *November 7, 2001. Georgia. **Jose High**. Lethal Injection. High was pronounced dead some one hour and nine minutes after the execution began. After attempting to find a usable vein for "15 to 20 minutes," the emergency medical technicians under contract to do the execution abandoned their efforts. Eventually, one needle was stuck in High's hand, and a physician was called in to insert a second needle between his shoulder and neck.

242. August 24, 2002. South Carolina. **Anthony Green**. Lethal Injection. It took twenty minutes for Green to die by lethal injection after the drugs were administered.

243. December 11, 2002. Mississippi. **Jessie Derrell Williams**. Lethal Injection. Officials at the state penitentiary had trouble finding a vein. Mississippi Department of Corrections officer Claire Papizan said the trouble may have been caused by dehydration, as Williams had refused food and drink at all three meals before his execution.

244. December 14, 2002. Alabama. **Anthony Keith Johnson**. Lethal Injection. In Alabama's first lethal injection, it took officials twenty-seven minutes for Johnson to be pronounced dead.

245. September 12, 2003. North Carolina. **Henry Lee Hunt**. Lethal Injection. Hunt was pronounced dead nearly seventeen minutes after the lethal combination of drugs started flowing.

246. January 14, 2004. Ohio. **Lewis Williams**. Lethal Injection. Loudly proclaiming his innocence and begging for God's mercy, Williams forcibly re-

sisted prison guards' efforts to transport him from his cell and strap him to the gurney. At least nine guards were involved in restraining Williams during his desperate last stand. The Ohio state prison director described the incident as "disturbing and traumatic."

247. February 3, 2004. Ohio. **John Glenn Roe**. Lethal Injection. Guards struggled to find a suitable vein, delaying the execution by about twenty minutes. They eventually placed the needle in Roe's wrist.

248. July 20, 2004. Ohio. **Scott Mink**. Lethal Injection. Prison officials took over twenty minutes to insert the intravenous lines. Mink's "brittle" veins kept collapsing after the needle was inserted.

249. September 9, 2004. Virginia. **James Edward Reid**. Lethal Injection. Medical technicians required twelve minutes to insert the needle in Reid. In the end, they had to resort to using a vein in his upper groin.

250. November 4, 2004. Texas. **Robert Brice Morrow**. Lethal Injection. Prison officials were unable to find a suitable vein in Morrow's arm, delaying the execution briefly. Instead they had to use veins on the tops of his hands for each needle.

251. January 19, 2005. California. **Donald Jay Beardslee**. Lethal Injection. Prison officials hunted for a usable vein for sixteen minutes.

252. May 6, 2005. North Carolina. **Earl J. Richmond Jr**. Lethal Injection. Richmond was pronounced dead a full nineteen minutes after the lethal drugs entered his vein.

253. August 31, 2005. Missouri. **Timothy Johnston**. Lethal Injection. With the needle already in his arm, Johnston writhed and rolled on the gurney before the drugs were administered.

254. November 4, 2005. Delaware. **Brian D. Steckel**. Lethal Injection. Steckel was pronounced dead a full fourteen minutes after the lethal drugs entered his vein.

255. December 3, 2005. California. **Stanley "Tookie" Williams**. Lethal Injection. Prison officials spent twelve minutes searching for a vein. At one point, Williams winced, raised his head off the gurney, and asked, "Still can't find it?"

256. January 17, 2006. California. **Clarence Ray Allen**. Lethal Injection. The elderly inmate, seventy-six years old at the time of his execution, did not die after the first round of drugs. Prison officials had to administer a second dose of potassium chloride, and death came eighteen minutes after the drugs first began to flow.

257. *May 2, 2006. Ohio. **Joseph L. Clark**. Lethal Injection. It took twenty-two minutes before the execution technicians found a vein suitable for insertion of the catheter. But three or four minutes thereafter, as the vein collapsed and Clark's arm began to swell, he raised his head off the gurney and said five times, "It don't work. It don't work." The curtains surrounding the gurney were then

closed while the technicians worked for thirty minutes to find another vein. Media witnesses later reported that they heard "moaning, crying out and guttural noises." Finally, death was pronounced almost ninety minutes after the execution began. A spokeswoman for the Ohio Department of Corrections told reporters that the execution team included paramedics, but not a physician or a nurse.

258. May 24, 2006. Texas. **Jesus Ledesma Aguilar**. Lethal Injection. Aguilar's execution by lethal injection lasted fourteen minutes.

259. July 20, 2006. Virginia. **Brandon Hedrick**. Electrocution. Smoke.

260. October 25, 2006. Florida. **Daniel Harold Rolling**. Lethal Injection. Rolling's execution took thirteen minutes.

261. *December 13, 2006. Florida. **Angel Diaz**. Lethal Injection. After the first injection was administered, Diaz continued to move and was squinting and grimacing as he tried to mouth words. A second dose was then administered, and thirty-four minutes passed before Diaz was declared dead. At first a spokesperson for the Florida Department of Corrections claimed that this was because Diaz had some sort of liver disease. After performing an autopsy, the medical examiner, Dr. William Hamilton, stated that Diaz's liver was undamaged but that the needle had gone through his vein and out the other side, so that the deadly chemicals were injected into soft tissue rather than the vein. Two days after the execution, Governor Jeb Bush suspended all executions in the state and appointed a commission "to consider the humanity and constitutionality of lethal injections."

262. March 20, 2007. Texas. **Charles Anthony Nealy**. Lethal Injection. Technicians' inability to find a suitable vein delayed Nealy's execution twenty minutes.

263. *May 24, 2007. Ohio. **Christopher Newton**. Lethal Injection. According to the Associated Press, "prison medical staff" at the Southern Ohio Correctional Facility struggled to find veins on each of Newton's arms during the execution. Newton, who weighed 265 pounds, was declared dead almost two hours after the execution process began. The execution "team" stuck Newton at least ten times with needles before getting the shunts in place were the needles are inserted.

264. *June 26, 2007. Georgia. **John Hightower**. Lethal Injection. It took approximately forty minutes for nurses to find a suitable vein to administer the lethal chemicals to Hightower, and death was not pronounced until 7:59, fifty-nine minutes after the execution process began.

265. May 6, 2008. Georgia. **William Earl Lynd**. Lethal Injection. Officials did not pronounce death until seventeen minutes after the lethal drugs began flowing into Lynd's veins.

266. *June 4, 2008. Georgia. **Curtis Osborne**. Lethal Injection. After a fifty-five-minute delay while the U.S. Supreme Court reviewed Osborne's final

appeal, prison medical staff began the execution by trying to find suitable veins in which to insert the intravenous line. The executioners struggled for thirty-five minutes to find a vein, and it took fourteen minutes after the fatal drugs were administered before death was pronounced by two physicians who were inside the death chamber.

267. June 3, 2009. Ohio. **Daniel Wilson**. Lethal Injection. Technicians took approximately fifteen minutes to place a needle in Wilson's right arm. Blood oozing from the injection site saturated a paper towel during the procedure.

268. *September 15, 2009. Ohio. **Romell Broom**. Lethal Injection. Efforts to find a suitable vein and to execute Broom were terminated after more than two hours during which the executioners were unable to find a usable vein in his arms or legs. During the failed efforts, Broom winced and grimaced with pain. After the first hour's lack of success, Broom on several occasions tried to help the executioners find a good vein. At one point, he covered his face with both hands and appeared to be sobbing, his stomach heaving. Finally, Ohio Governor Ted Strickland ordered the execution to stop, and announced plans to attempt the execution anew after a one-week delay so that physicians could be consulted for advice on how the man could be killed more efficiently. The executioners blamed the problems on Mr. Broom's history of intravenous drug use. As of October 1, 2010, Mr. Broom remained on Ohio's death row.

269. January 7, 2010. Ohio. **Vernon Smith**. Lethal Injection. Prison officials had trouble finding a vein into which they could insert the intravenous line during Smith's execution. This caused the execution to take twenty-eight minutes.

270. February 16, 2010. Florida. **Martin Grossman**. Lethal Injection. It took Grossman fifteen minutes to die by lethal injection.

271. March 18, 2010. Virginia. **Paul Powell**. Electrocution. Powell elected to die in the electric chair rather than by lethal injection—the two methods available to Virginia death row inmates. During the first shock, smoke curled from Powell's right leg. During a second shock, smoke and sparks emitted from his leg. His knee also swelled and turned purple.

272. April 20, 2010. Ohio. **Darryl Durr**. Lethal Injection. Several days before his execution, Durr's lawyers put forth a last-minute plea stating that Durr was allergic to the anesthetic that would be used in his execution. He was executed anyway. During the execution, about two minutes after the drugs began to flow through his veins, Durr picked up his head and shoulders off the table, despite the fact that he was restrained. He grimaced, then fell back down, and his throat contracted spasmodically. His reaction sparked controversy over whether he was having an allergic reaction or simply fighting death.

273. May 19, 2010. Mississippi. **Paul Woodward**. Lethal Injection. It took

prison officials at Mississippi State Penitentiary thirty or forty minutes to find a suitable vein in Woodward's arm.

274. May 20, 2010. Virginia. **Darick Walker**. Lethal Injection. Prison officials had trouble inserting one of the intravenous lines into Walker's arm. His last words were: "I don't think y'all done this right, took y'all too long to hook it up. You can print that. That's it."

275. July 13, 2010. Ohio. **William Garner**. Lethal Injection. Garner was sentenced to death by lethal injection. Nine minutes after the lethal chemicals entered Garner's veins, prison officials opened the curtains around his body. This usually signals the end of an execution and the announcement of the time of death. However, the coroner said he heard "faint heart sounds." Prison officials waited another five minutes before pronouncing Garner dead. Prison officials said they would reexamine the procedure for determining when the curtain is pulled and death is determined.

276. *September 27, 2010. Georgia. **Brandon Joseph Rhode**. Lethal Injection. After the Supreme Court rejected his appeals, "Medics then tried for about 30 minutes to find a vein to inject the three-drug concoction." It then took fourteen minutes for the lethal drugs to kill him. The execution had been delayed six days because a prison guard had given Rhode a razor blade, which Rhode used to attempt suicide.

Acknowledgments

We are grateful to the Mellon Foundation and Amherst College's Dean of the Faculty, Gregory Call, whose support made our collaboration possible. We benefited from the generous critiques and comments offered by colleagues at the Annual Meeting of the Association of Law, Culture, and the Humanities and faculty workshops at Chicago-Kent School of Law and Quinnipiac Law School. Special thanks to our Stanford University Press editor, Michelle Lipinski, for her enthusiastic support and helpful editing.

An earlier version of Chapter 1 was published in Austin Sarat, *When the State Kills: Capital Punishment and the American Condition* (Princeton, 2001) and an earlier version of Chapter 6 was published as Austin Sarat, Katherine Blumstein, Aubrey Jones, Heather Richard, Madeline Sprung-Keyser, and Robert Weaver, "Botched Executions and the Struggle to End Capital Punishment: A Twentieth-Century Story," 38 *Law and Social Inquiry* (2013), 694–720. We are grateful for permission to use this material here.

Finally, even though our subject is an unrelentingly difficult and painful one, our collaboration has been a wonderful experience for all of us.

A Note on Collaboration

Several years ago, with the support of the Mellon Foundation, Amherst College launched an initiative to encourage research collaborations between students and faculty in the humanities and the humanistic social sciences. For a long time, students interested in the sciences have had the opportunity to do research *with* faculty. They have worked in labs, analyzed data, attended conferences, and coauthored articles. But until recently there was no parallel for students in the humanities and humanistic social sciences. The Mellon initiative changed things, and this book is a result of that new opportunity for student-faculty collaboration.

In the spring semester of 2011, I offered a research tutorial on America's Death Penalty to six Amherst undergraduates. My goal was to introduce them to the various research traditions that have informed work on capital punishment and equip them to do scholarship in the area. During the semester, I invited my students to work with me on a project on the history of botched executions; five of the six students accepted my invitation. Over the next eighteen months, we constructed an archive of the botched executions that occurred during the period from 1890 to 2010. We developed a conceptual framework and an analysis plan, interpreted the cultural meaning of America's botched executions, presented our work at a meeting of the Association for the Study of Law, Culture, and the Humanities, and ultimately coauthored three articles.

Four of these students, whose names appear on the title page of this book, continued to work with me on the project on which this book is based. We met regularly to review the progress of our work, discussed and debated different approaches and interpretations, and exchanged memos and drafts. Our joint efforts extended beyond their graduation from Amherst College. While the conventions of publishing did not allow all five of our names to appear on the front cover, our collaborative work is manifest on every page of this book.

Austin Sarat

Notes

Chapter 1

1. See Claude Moore, "The Story of Art Kinsauls," *Our Heritage* (October 18, 1991), http://files.usgwarchives.net/nc/wayne/heritage/kinsauls.txt.

2. Ibid.

3. Ibid.

4. Ibid.

5. "Murderer Hanged Twice," *Washington Post* (September 29, 1900).

6. Ibid.

7. See, for example, "Flames Erupt During Florida Execution: Gruesome Scene Renews Debate on Electrocutions," *USA Today* (March 26, 1997), 3A.

8. "Flames Erupt in Electric Chair's Death Jolt; Execution: Fire Shoots from Florida Man's Head, Renewing Capital Punishment Debate," *Los Angeles Times* (March 26, 1997), 1.

9. "Retire 'Chair' Use Lethal Injection," *Sun-Sentinel* (Ft. Lauderdale, FL) (March 26, 1997), 22A.

10. "Inmate Catches Fire in Florida Electric Chair: 'You Could Smell the Acrid Smoke,'" *Houston Chronicle* (March 26, 1997), 6A.

11. *Jones v. Butterworth*, 701 So. 2d 76, 77 (1997).

12. "Inmate Catches Fire," 6A.

13. "Retire 'Chair' Use Lethal Injection," 22A.

14. See Robert Johnson, *Death Work: A Study of the Modern Execution Process* (Pacific Grove, CA: Brooks/Cole, 1990).

15. Several scholars have written about the history of the death penalty and its medicalization, sterilization, and privatization. For example, Deborah Denno has written extensively on the medical appearances associated with lethal injection, as well as the changes in middle-class culture in the twentieth century that left American citizens in search of cleaner, more humane methods of execution. See Deborah Denno, "The Lethal Injection Quandary: How Medicine Has Dismantled the Death Penalty," 76 *Fordham Law Review* (2007), 49–128. In addition, Stuart Banner writes that the early twentieth century saw

"the continual centralization and professionalization of punishment" and the development of new technologies of execution. Stuart Banner, *The Death Penalty: An American History* (Cambridge, MA: Harvard University Press, 2002).

16. See Charles Ogletree and Austin Sarat, eds., *The Road to Abolition? The Future of Capital Punishment in the United States* (New York: NYU Press, 2009).

17. Abernathy argues that "contrary to what logic seems to dictate, the attempt over time has been to make the penalty of death gentle, hidden, and antiseptic." See Jonathan Abernathy, "The Methodology of Death: Reexamining the Deterrence Rationale," 27 *Columbia Human Rights Law Review* (1996), 422.

18. "Those Left Grief-Stricken by Bombing Cry for Vengeance," *St. Louis Post-Dispatch* (June 4, 1997), News, 1A.

19. Ibid.

20. As Berg and Radelet suggest, any effort to accurately count botched executions is likely to "underestimate the true number of state killings that have been botched. . . . Given the relative privacy in which executions are carried out and the reluctance of prison personnel to admit and publicise bungles, other cases of botched executions for which no public record exists . . . are quite possible." See Marian J. Berg and Michael L. Radelet, "On Botched Executions," in *Capital Punishment: Strategies for Abolition*, Peter Hodgkinson and William A Schabas, eds. (Cambridge, UK: Cambridge University Press, 2004), 145–46.

21. Ibid., 144.

22. We, like Berg and Radelet, "consider our compilation of cases a catalogue of examples of botched executions, not a definitive list." Ibid., 146.

23. Banner, *Death Penalty*, 206.

24. Chris Greer, "Delivering Death: Capital Punishment, Botched Executions and the American News Media," in *Captured by the Media: Prison Discourse in Popular Culture*, Paul Mason, ed. (Portland, OR: Willan, 2006), 84. "One route," Berg and Radelet argue, "towards the demise of the executioner is to document and publicise the inhumanity and barbarity of the ways in which his work is conducted. People who otherwise support the death penalty may grow uncomfortable with their positions if confronted with direct evidence that executions are bloody, painful and/or torturous." See Berg and Radelet, "On Botched Executions," 144.

25. Thomas Metzger, *Blood and Volts: Edison, Tesla, and the Electric Chair* (Brooklyn, NY: Autonomedia, 1996).

26. See Allen Huang, "Hanging, Cyanide Gas, and the Evolving Standards of Decency: The Ninth Circuit's Misapplication of the Cruel and Unusual Clause of the Eighth Amendment," 74 *Oregon Law Review* (1995), 995.

27. Dissenting opinion by Justice Shaw in *Jones v. Butterworth*, 87.

28. Judge Reinhardt dissenting in *Campbell v. Wood*, 18 F3d 662, 701 (1994).

29. Michel Foucault, *Discipline and Punish* (New York: Vintage Press, 1977), 50.

30. Petrus Spierenburg, *The Spectacle of Suffering* (Cambridge, UK: Cambridge University Press, 1984). Also V.A.C. Gatrell, *The Hanging Tree: Execution and the English People 1770–1868* (New York: Oxford University Press, 1994), ch. 2.

31. Foucault, *Discipline and Punish*, 48–49.

32. Foucault, *Discipline and Punish*, 58.

33. See Johnson, *Death Work*, 5. Also Susan Blaustein, "Witness to Another Execution," *Harper's Magazine* (May 1994), 53; and Richard Trombley, *The Execution Protocol: Inside America's Capital Punishment Industry* (New York: Crown, 1992).

34. See Hugo Adam Bedau, *The Death Penalty in America* (New York: Oxford University Press, 1982), 13.

35. Michael Madow, "Forbidden Spectacle: Executions, the Public and the Press in Nineteenth-Century New York," 43 *Buffalo Law Review* (1995), 466, 469.

36. Huang, "Hanging, Cyanide Gas," 997.

37. Ian Gray and Moira Stanley, *A Punishment in Search of a Crime: Americans Speak Out Against the Death Sentence* (New York: Avon Books, 1989), 19–20.

38. The numbers add up to more than thirty-two (the number of states using capital punishment) because statutes often permit more than one means of execution.

39. *In re Kemmler*, 136 U.S. 436, 444 (1890).

40. Abernathy, "Methodology of Death," 404.

41. Ibid.

42. William Bowers with Glenn L. Pierce and John F. McDevitt, *Legal Homicide: Death as Punishment in America, 1864–1982* (Boston: Northeastern University Press, 1984), 12.

43. *Hill v. Lockhart*, 791 F. Supp. 1388, 1394 (1992). See also *Ex Parte Kenneth Granviel*, 561 S.W. 2d 503, 513 (1978). The court found that "The Texas Legislature substituted death by lethal injection as a means of execution in lieu of electrocution for the reason it would be a more humane and less spectacular form of execution." As Justice Anstead argued in *Provenzano*, "[J]ust as electrocution may have been originally evaluated in comparison with hanging, we know today that the overwhelming majority of death penalty jurisdictions have long since rejected use of the electric chair and have turned to lethal injection as a more humane punishment." See *Provenzano v. Moore*, 744 So. 2d 413, 446 (1990).

44. Kristina Beard, "Five Under the Eighth: Methodology Review and the Cruel and Unusual Punishments Clause," 51 *University of Miami Law Review* (1997), 445. During the term that began in October 1999, the Court agreed to hear a case from Florida on the constitutionality of electrocution. That case was

dismissed when Florida passed legislation authorizing the use of lethal injection.

45. *Wilkerson v. Utah*, 99 U.S. 130 (1878).

46. *In re Kemmler.*

47. Ibid., 447.

48. Ibid.

49. See Giorgio Agamben, *Homo Sacer: Sovereign Power and Bare Life*, Daniel Heller-Roazen, trans. (Stanford, CA: Stanford University Press, 1998) 83. Also Peter Fitzpatrick, "'Always More to Do': Capital Punishment and the (De) Composition of Law," in *The Killing State: Capital Punishment in Law, Politics, and Culture*, Austin Sarat, ed. (New York: Oxford University Press, 1999), 128–29.

50. *Louisiana ex rel. Francis v. Resweber*, 329 U.S. 459 (1947). For an interesting description of the case see Arthur Miller and Jeffrey Bowman, *Death by Installments: The Ordeal of Willie Francis* (Westport, CT: Greenwood Press, 1988).

51. *Francis v. Resweber*, 460, n. 12.

52. Francis also alleged that a second execution would violate the due process clause of the Fourteenth Amendment. Ibid., 462.

53. Indeed Willie Francis makes virtually no appearance in Reed's opinion. We learn little about him except that he was a "colored citizen of Louisiana." Ibid., 460. Neglect of the real-life experiences and feelings of the people whose fate is decided by law is characteristic of a wide range of legal decisions. See John Noonan, *Persons and Masks of the Law* (New York: Farrar, Straus and Giroux, 1976).

54. *Francis v. Resweber*, 464.

55. Ibid.

56. Ibid., 462.

57. Ibid.

58. Ibid., 464.

59. Ibid., 464.

60. Ibid., 480, n. 2.

61. Ibid., 480.

62. See ibid., 481, n. 2.

63. Ibid., 474.

64. Ibid., 475.

65. See Alan Hyde, *Bodies of Law* (Princeton, NJ: Princeton University Press, 1997), ch. 11. See also Austin Sarat, ed., *Pain, Death, and the Law* (Ann Arbor: University of Michigan Press, 2001).

66. *Campbell v. Wood.*

67. *Fierro v. Gomez*, 865 F. Supp. 1387 (1994).

68. *Provenzano v. Moore*, 737 So. 2d 551, Corrected Opinion (1999).

69. Gary E. Hood, "Campbell v. Wood: The Death Penalty in Washington State: 'Hanging' on to a Method of Execution," 30 *Gonzaga Law Review* (1994–95), 170.

70. Hood, "Campbell v. Wood," 171.

71. Timothy V. Kaufman-Osborn, *From Noose to Needle: Capital Punishment and the Late Liberal State* (Ann Arbor: University of Michigan Press), 99, 103.

72. More specifically, before 1993, no autopsy was ever performed on anyone hanged in Washington; no official records were kept since the responsibility for carrying out executions was expropriated by the state in 1904; and from 1909 to 1982, Washington had on its books an obscenity statute that criminalized the publication of detailed newspaper accounts of state executions. Kaufman-Osborn, *From Noose to Needle*, 119.

73. Deborah W. Denno, "Is Electrocution an Unconstitutional Method of Execution? The Engineering of Death over the Century," 35 *William and Mary Law Review* (1993–94), 685–86. In his *Book of Executions in America*, Frederick Drimmer refers to at least one incident at Walla Walla in the early 1960s in which an inmate's "head was nearly ripped off, spraying the witnesses in the front row with blood." Frederick Drimmer, *Until You Are Dead: The Book of Executions in America* (New York: Carol, 1990), 133.

74. Kaufman-Osborn, *From Noose to Needle,*118. Kaufman-Osborn further notes that the total number of persons executed under the terms of the 1959 army procedures when it was adopted by the Washington State Department of Corrections was zero.

75. Kaufman-Osborn, *From Noose to Needle*, 104. Citing the "Report of the Committee to Inquire into the Execution of Capital Sentences" (1886).

76. Ibid., 115.

77. Ann Japenga, "Mystery Hangman Sets Off a Washington Controversy," *Los Angeles Times* (April 12, 1989).

78. Ibid., 87. Citing "Report of the Committee" (1886).

79. *Campbell v. Wood*, 682.

80. Ibid.

81. For a discussion of that hearing which claimed that "the question of whether hanging is a form of cruel and unusual punishment is curiously absent," see Timothy Kaufman-Osborn, "The Metaphysics of the Hangman," in *Studies in Law, Politics, and Society*, vol. 20, Austin Sarat and Patricia Ewick, eds. (Stamford, CT: JAI Press, 2000), 35–70.

82. *Campbell v. Wood*, 683.

83. Ibid.

84. Ibid., 684.

85. Ibid.

86. Ibid., 687.

87. Ibid.

88. Ibid., 693.

89. Ibid., 701.

90. Ibid., 708.

91. Ibid., 702.

92. Ibid.

93. Ibid., 712.

94. Kaufman-Osborn, *From Noose to Needle*, 93. Citing "Killer Struggles with Guards Before Hanging," *Los Angeles Times* (May 28, 1994).

95. *Fierro v. Gomez*, 1391.

96. Ibid., 1413.

97. Ibid., 1407.

98. Ibid., 1410–11.

99. Ibid., 1412.

100. Ibid., 1396.

101. Ibid., 1398.

102. Ibid., 1401.

103. Ibid., 1400.

104. Ibid., 1403.

105. Ibid., 1404.

106. Ibid.

107. This approach was followed in an Arizona case which found lethal gas to be unconstitutional. See *LaGrand v. Stewart*, 173 F.3d 1144 (1999).

108. *Provenzano v. Moore*, 413.

109. Ibid.

110. Ibid., 414.

111. Ibid., 434.

112. Ibid., 438.

113. Ibid., 443.

114. Ibid., 447, 451.

115. Ibid., 452.

116. Elaine Scarry, *The Body in Pain: The Making and Unmaking of the World* (New York: Oxford University Press, 1985), 3.

117. Ibid., 4.

118. Ibid., 6.

119. Ibid., 13.

120. Ibid., 15.

121. Ibid.

122. The movement from representing death to representing pain as the touchstone in judicial considerations of methods of executions may be less clear

than we have so far made it out to be. Pain, as Scarry reminds us, is frequently used as a "symbolic substitute for death." Ibid., 31. She argues that the world-destroying experience of physical pain is an imaginative substitute for "what is unfeelable in death." Pain and death are, she suggests, "the most intense forms of negation, the purest expression of the anti-human, of annihilation, of total aversiveness, though one is an absence and the other a felt presence." In her view, then, when the courts speak about pain they are neither eliding nor displacing the subject of death. They are speaking to, and about it, in one of the most powerful ways available to human language.

123. Hyde, *Bodies of Law*, 192.

124. Ibid., 193.

125. Ibid., 194.

126. Ibid.

127. Ibid.

128. As Abernathy puts it, "[T]he shifts from public to private executions and toward more humane means of killing have been designed to comfort the punisher, not the condemned." "Methodology of Death," 423. Alternatively, they may be explained as efforts to reduce administrative inconveniences associated with continued use of methods of state killing not at the cutting edge of technologies for taking life. As Judge Harding noted when he called on the Florida legislature to authorize the use of lethal injection, "Florida death row inmates almost routinely challenge electrocution as a cruel and unusual punishment. . . . Such challenges consume an inordinate amount of the time and resources expended by inmates' counsel, State counsel, and judicial personnel. Furthermore, each time an execution is carried out, the courts wait in dread anticipation of some 'unforeseeable accident' that will set in motion a frenzy of inmate petitions and other filings." *Provenzano v. Moore*, 419, 420.

129. *Provenzano v. Moore*, 415.

130. Walter Benjamin, "Critique of Violence," in *Reflections: Essays, Aphorisms and Autobiographical Writing*, Edmund Jephcott, trans. (New York: Schocken Books, 1986).

131. We have not included execution by firing squad, because there were only thirty-four such executions during the course of the twentieth century.

Chapter 2

1. In the 1840s, *The United States Magazine and Democratic Review*, published by periodical editor and lawyer John O'Sullivan, ran dozens of articles advocating the abolition of the death penalty. John Cyril Barton, "Antigallows Activism in Antebellum American Literature," in *Demands of the Death: Executions, Storytelling, and Activism in the United States*, Katy Ryan, ed. (Iowa City: University of Iowa Press, 2012), 150.

2. Timothy V. Kaufman-Osborn, *From Noose to Needle: Capital Punishment and the Late Liberal State* (Ann Arbor: University of Michigan Press, 2002), 75.

3. Barton, "Antigallows Activism," 150. Citing Nathaniel Hawthorne, "Earth's Holocaust," in *The Centenary Edition of the Works of Nathaniel Hawthorne,* William Charvat, Roy Harvey Pearce, and Claude M. Simpson, eds. (Columbus: Ohio State University Press, 1974), 392.

4. "Methods of Execution," *Death Penalty Information Center* (2013), http://www.deathpenaltyinfo.org/methods-execution#state. Both states have lethal injection as the primary method of execution.

5. John Laurence, *A History of Capital Punishment* (New York: Citadel Press, 1960), 6–9.

6. Brian Bailey, *Hangmen of England* (London: W.H. Allen, 1989), 1.

7. Charles Duff, *A Handbook on Hanging* (New York: New York Review of Books, 2001 [1928]), 5.

8. Some 75,000 people are thought to have been executed by the English noose and axe between 1530 and 1630. Execution rates declined steadily until 1750, when they once again started to increase and stayed high. It is estimated that approximately 7,000 people were put to death between 1770 and 1880. Crowds of 3,000 to 7,000 spectators were common, although some reports claim audiences of up to 100,000 at Tyburn and Newgate in London. V.A.C. Gatrell, *The Hanging Tree: Execution and the English People, 1770–1868* (Oxford, UK: Oxford University Press, 1994), 30, 7.

9. Ibid., 41. Kaufman-Osborn, *From Noose to Needle,* 90. (The "special merit" of hanging was that it was thought to be "peculiarly degrading.")

10. Kaufman-Osborn, *From Noose to Needle,* 63.

11. Ibid.

12. Gatrell, *Hanging Tree,* 51.

13. Kaufman-Osborn, *From Noose to Needle,* 64.

14. Gatrell, *Hanging Tree,* 52. Citing *M. Mison's Memoirs and Observations in His Travels over England* (London: Printed for D. Brown, etc. 1719 [1698]).

15. Ibid., 93. See also Frederick Drimmer, *Until You Are Dead* (New York: Kensington, 1992), 126. Citing Negley K. Teeters and Jack H. Hedblom, *Hang by the Neck: The Legal Use of Scaffold and Noose, Gibbet, Stake, and Firing Squad from Colonial Times to Present* (Springfield, IL: Charles C. Thomas, 1967).

16. Stuart Banner, *The Death Penalty: An American History* (Cambridge, MA: Harvard University Press, 2002), 44.

17. Banner, *Death Penalty,* 45.

18. Ibid., 70.

19. Gatrell, *Hanging Tree,* 51.

20. Kaufman-Osborn, *From Noose to Needle,* 70.

21. Gatrell, *Hanging Tree*, 45.

22. Kaufman-Osborn, *From Noose to Needle*, 75–76.

23. Ibid., 77.

24. Koestler continues, "not to mention various forms of mutilation and lacerations, jaws torn off by hitting the edge of the trap, gashes torn in the neck, heads partly or entirely torn off, and people being hanged twice or even three times in succession." Arthur Koestler, *Reflections on Hanging* (New York: Macmillan, 1957), 139–40.

25. Gatrell, *Hanging Tree*, 45–46.

26. Kaufman-Osborn, *From Noose to Needle*, 82.

27. Louis P. Masur, *Rites of Execution: Capital Punishment and the Transformation of American Culture, 1776–1865* (New York: Oxford University Press, 1989), 4.

28. Kathryn Preyer, "Penal Measures in the American Colonies: An Overview," 26 *American Journal of Legal History* 4 (October 1982), 353.

29. America's first death penalty abolitionists and reformers included such prominent thinkers as Benjamin Franklin, Thomas Jefferson, James Madison, John Quincy Adams, Lydia Maria Child, Wendell Phillips, and Margaret Fuller. John Cyril Barton, "The Anti-Gallows Movement in Antebellum America," in *Research in English and American Literature,* vol. 23, Brook Thomas, ed. (Tubingen, Germany: Gunter Narr Verlag, 2006), 139.

30. David Brion Davis, "The Movement to Abolish Capital Punishment in America, 1787–1861," *American Historical Review* 63 (October 1957), 33.

31. Leviticus 24:17: "And he that killeth a man shall surely be put to death." Banner, *Death Penalty*, 104. Citing Benjamin Rush, "An Enquiry into the Justice and Policy of Punishing Murder by Death," *Essays, Literary, Moral and Philosophical* (March 9, 1787).

32. John Greenleaf Whittier, "The Human Sacrifice" (1843) in *The Complete Poetical Works of John Greenleaf Whittier* (Boston, 1894), 355–56.

33. Banner, *Death Penalty*, 99.

34. Barton, "Antigallows Activism," 139. In October 1845, a national society met in Philadelphia and elected George M. Dallas, the sitting vice president of the United States, as its president. By 1850, societies were reported in Tennessee, Ohio, Alabama, Louisiana, Indiana, Iowa, and Pennsylvania, in addition to those in Massachusetts and New York. Davis, "Movement to Abolish Capital Punishment," 42.

35. Banner, *Death Penalty*, 131, 134. Banner emphasizes that while by the time of the Civil War the North had been through decades of death penalty debate and reform, the South had not. He writes, "In the South, capital punishment still existed on paper for a wide range of crimes committed by whites and still existed in practice for an even wider range committed by blacks." Ibid., 143.

36. Ibid., 96–97.

37. Banner, *Death Penalty*, 24. Over 30,000 people watched from the surrounding hillside as Jesse Strang was hanged in Albany, New York, in 1827, and 50,000 were said to have crowded around the gallows when John Johnson was executed in New York City four years earlier. Ibid., 25. More than a hundred years later, 20,000 people descended upon the town of Owensboro, Kentucky, when in 1936 Rainey Bethea became the last man in the United States to be publicly executed. Headlines around the country proclaimed, "Death Makes a Holiday: 20,000 Revel over Hanging" and "Ghostly Carnival Precedes Hanging." In 1938, Kentucky lawmakers cited the negative publicity surrounding Bethea's hanging as the basis of their decision to finally end public executions in the state. "After 75 Years, Last Public Hanging Still Haunts City," Fox News (August 12, 2011), http://www.foxnews.com/us/2011/08/12/after-75-years-last-public-hanging-haunts-city/.

38. Ibid., 11.

39. Masur, *Rites of Execution*, 95.

40. Kaufman-Osborn, *From Noose to Needle*, 83.

41. Masur, *Rites of Execution*, 116.

42. Davis, "Movement to Abolish Capital Punishment," 33; Banner, *Death Penalty*, 154.

43. Masur, *Rites of Execution*, 94. *Quasi*-private because relatively large numbers of people were still able to witness jail yard executions, at least during the first half of the nineteenth century. Crowds often numbered in the hundreds. The 1845 (botched) hanging of Samuel Zepphon in Pennsylvania's Moyamensing Prison yard, for example, was attended by over one hundred spectators. Sometimes thousands would gather outside the prison on hanging day. Ibid., 93–94, 113. Masur makes the argument that "In principle, private executions were supposed to protect the sensibilities of all citizens, eliminate a scene of public chaos and confusion, and permit the prisoner to die quietly penitent; in practice, they became a theatrical event for an assembly of elite men who attended the execution by invitation while the community at large was excluded." This excluded public, in turn, would read about prison executions in the morning paper. Ibid., 111.

44. Barton, "Antigallows Activism," 140. Reformers tended to view the campaigns against slavery and the gallows as essentially inseparable. As Masur explains, both slavery and capital punishment "represented systems of brutality that coerced individuals, and both institutions merited attack." Masur, *Rites of Execution*, 157.

45. Masur, *Rites of Execution*, 160.

46. Gatrell, *Hanging Tree*, 46. Citing the *Daily Telegraph and Daily News* (May 27, 1868).

47. Banner, *Death Penalty*, 171. The upright jerker was used in several New

Jersey counties in the 1850s and 1860s. It arrived in Pittsburgh by 1866, in Charleston, South Carolina, by 1872, in Chicago by 1874, and in Plymouth, Massachusetts, by 1875. Ibid.

48. Ibid., 172. Citing J. Edwards Remault, *The "Car-Hook" Tragedy* (Philadelphia: Barclay & Co. Publishers, 1873), 73 (Commentary of the "Life, Trial, and Execution of William Foster"). Remault's criticism of the "brutal process of elevating or 'jerking' them up" and impassioned call for a return to the drop followed under the subheading, "The Science of Strangulation."

49. Kaufman-Osborn, *From Noose to Needle*, 87.

50. Even more specifically, "The lesion referred to is a bilateral fracture of the second cervical vertebra, the axis (C2) with associated anterior sublaxation or dislocation of the vertebral body, resulting in fatal injury to the spinal cord. It is characterized by fracture-dislocation of the second cervical vertebra as a result of hyperextension and distraction of the neck." Catherine Hellier and Robert Connolly, "Cause of Death in Judicial Hanging: A Review and Case Study," *Medicine, Science, and the Law* 49, no. 1 (2009), 18.

51. Kaufman-Osborn, *From Noose to Needle*, 87.

52. Ibid.

53. Drimmer, *Until You Are Dead*, 127.

54. Banner, *Death Penalty*, 170–71. Kaufman-Osborn highlights the "multiple and infernally ambiguous" constituents in a judicial hanging when he discusses the complexity and convolution involved in knot placement:

> For example, placement of the knot on the left side of the neck near the chin has the effect of throwing the head backward and so increasing the likelihood that the condemned's spinal cord will be severed. But this asymmetrical placement almost certainly will not occlude both carotid arteries, and so, should the hangman's fracture not occur, may leave the victim acutely conscious of the process of dying. The achievement of unconsciousness is best accomplished by placing the knot squarely at the back of the neck so as to achieve an even distribution of pressure on right and left arteries. But that position will throw the condemned's head forward and so almost certainly will not cause cervical dislocation. (Kaufman-Osborn, *From Noose to Needle*, 122)

55. Koestler, *Reflections on Hanging*, 140. Frederick Drimmer describes the complicated search for a suitable hangman before Charles Campbell's first scheduled execution in early 1989. "A spokesman for the Department of Corrections," Drimmer writes, "declared that there were only two hangmen left in the United States, and that one of them had suffered a nervous breakdown." While dozens of Washington's citizens volunteered to serve as Campbell's executioner, none proved to be technically competent. In the end, a qualified person was reportedly hired from outside the state. Drimmer, *Until You Are Dead*, 130.

56. Maryland, early in its history, found it so difficult to hire a hangman that a series of capital criminals was pardoned in exchange for serving a term as executioner. In the late nineteenth century, as untrained local officials felt increasing pressure to execute prisoners efficiently and humanely, some sought methods that would effectively remove their agency from the process. A newspaper account of the 1889 hangings of Tim and Pete Barrett in Grand Forks, South Dakota, emphasizes that "The traps rests upon two bolts each, and the rope which sprung them was located in one of the adjacent cages, so that spectators did not observe who pulled the fatal bolt." "Trap Sprung! Tim and Pete Barrett Meet Their Doom on the Scaffold This Morning," *Grand Forks [SD] Herald (The Daily Herald)* 15, no. 118 (March 22, 1889), 1. In the early 1890s, a number of gallows designs were implemented that allowed the condemned to hang themselves. Banner, *Death Penalty*, 36, 174.

57. Banner, *Death Penalty*, 36–38.

58. Kaufman-Osborn, *From Noose to Needle*, 123.

59. Banner, *Death Penalty*, 47. Citing Alonzo Calkins, *Felonious Homicide: Its Penalty, and the Execution Thereof, Judicially* (New York: Russell Brothers, 1873); Ryk James and Rachel Nasmyth-Jones, "The Occurrence of Cervical Fractures in Victims of Judicial Hangings," *Forensic Science International* 54 (1992).

60. Hellier and Connolly, "Cause of Death in Judicial Hanging," 20.

61. Kaufman-Osborn, *From Noose to Needle*, 123.

62. Harold Hillman, "The Possible Pain Experienced During Execution by Different Methods," *Perception* 22 (1993), 746.

63. Gatrell, *Hanging Tree*, 46–47. Citing *The Guardian* (December 15, 1990).

64. Kaufman-Osborn, *From Noose to Needle*, 91.

65. The Bald Knobbers was a group of motivated vigilantes in the southern part of the state of Missouri, who were active during the period 1883–1889.

They are commonly depicted wearing hoods with horns, a distinction that evolved during the rapid proliferation of the group into neighboring counties apart from its Taney County origins. The group got its name from the grassy bald knob summits of the Ozark Mountains in the area. The hill where they first met is called Snapp's Bald, located just north of Kirbyville, Missouri. (Wikipedia, http://en.wikipedia.org/wiki/Bald_Knobbers)

66. "A Gallows Butchery, Three Bald Knob Murderers Hanged at Ozark, Missouri," *Philadelphia Inquirer* (May 11, 1889), 6.

67. "A Horrible Execution," *Dallas Morning News* (May 11, 1889), 1.

68. Ibid.

69. Banner, *Death Penalty*, 153.

70. Banner, *Death Penalty*, 153.

71. Drew Gilpin Faust, *The Republic of Suffering* (New York: Random House, 2008), xi. The country had had enough death: two percent of the population, approximately 620,000 men, had perished in four years time. Ibid.

72. Annulla Linders, "The Execution Spectacle and State Legitimacy: The Changing Nature of the American Execution Audience," 36 *Law and Society Review* 3 (2002), 630.

73. Ibid.

74. Banner, *Death Penalty,* 169.

75. David Garland, *Peculiar Institution: America's Death Penalty in an Age of Abolition* (New York: Oxford University Press, 2010), 146.

76. Markus Dubber, "The Pain of Punishment," 46 *Buffalo Law Review* (1996), 555.

77. "Dragged at a Mob's Heels, Brutal Lynching of a Michigan Negro Criminal," *Kansas City Star* (May 27, 1889), 1.

78. Ibid.; "Hung by a Masked Mob, The Horrible Fate of a Mulatto Brute," *Columbus [GA] Daily Enquirer* 31, no. 147 (May 28, 1889), 1; "Judge Lynch Visits Michigan," *Philadelphia Inquirer* 125, no. 6 (May 28, 1889), 6.

79. Garland, *Peculiar Institutions,* 33.

80. Ibid.

81. David Garland, "Penal Excess and Surplus Meaning: Public Torture Lynchings in 20th Century America," 39 *Law and Social Review* (December 2005), 795.

82. "A Gallows Expert Talks," *Omaha Daily Herald* 24, no. 240 (May 31, 1889), 5.

83. Ibid.

84. Ibid.

85. "Wise County, Virginia," http://www.wisecounty.org/.

86. "Negro Hanged—George Robinson Pays the Death Penalty," *The Post* (August 7, 1902).

87. "Wise County Sesquicentennial Corner: Hangings in the County—Another Hanging . . . This Time Twice!" *Clinch Valley Times* (St. Paul, VA) (August 9, 2006).

88. Ibid.

89. Ibid.

90. "Negro Hanged."

91. Ibid.

92. Ibid.

93. "Hanging at Wise Court House—George Robinson Hung. The Rope Broke," *Clinch Valley News* (St. Paul, VA) (August 8, 1902).

94. Ibid.

95. "Wise County Sesquicentennial Corner."

96. "Hanging at Wise Court House."

97. "Negro Hanged."

98. "Thousand People Witness Hanging—Execution at Wise Court House, Va.—First Drop Rope Broke," *Atlanta Constitution* (August 2, 1902).

99. "Hanging at Wise Court House."

100. "Wise County Sesquicentennial Corner."

101. "The Rope Broke and George Robinson Was Hanged the Second Time," *Hickman [KY] Courier* (August 8, 1902).

102. "Hangman's Rope Too Long," *Washington Post* (April 25, 1913).

103. "Rope Too Long; Execution of Man Bungled," *Evening True American* (Trenton, NJ) (April 24, 1913).

104. "Bungled Hanging Scenes Revolting," *Evening News* (Providence, RI) (April 24, 1913).

105. "Hangman's Rope Too Long."

106. "Rope Too Long."

107. "Bungled Hanging Scenes Revolting."

108. "Rope Too Long."

109. "Sheriff Pulls Hanging Man from Ground," *Tacoma [WA] Times* (April 24, 1913).

110. "Hangman's Rope Too Long."

111. "Rope Too Long."

112. "Hangman's Rope Too Long."

113. "Bungled Hanging Scenes Revolting."

114. Ibid.

115. "Hangman's Rope Too Long."

116. "Bloody Try for Freedom at Montana Prison 30 Years Ago Recalled by Former Warden Conley," *Three Forks [MT] News* (March 24, 1938).

117. Ibid.

118. "Two Swung from Deer Lodge Gallows for the Brutal Slaying of a Prison Guard and Murderous Knife Attack on Warden Conley," *Roundup [MT] Record-Tribune & Winnett Times* (February 13, 1941).

119. "A Look Back: The Murder of a Deputy Warden," *Silver State Post* (Deer Lodge, MT) (January 4, 2012).

120. "Two Swung from Deer Lodge Gallows."

121. "Bloody Try for Freedom."

122. "Hayes Concerned in the Death of Prison Officer," *Anaconda [MT] Standard* (April 3, 1909).

123. "Bloody Try for Freedom."

124. "Hayes Concerned in the Death of Prison Officer."

125. Ibid.

126. "A Look Back."

127. Ibid.

128. "Two Swung from Deer Lodge Gallows."

129. Ibid.

130. Ibid.

131. Ibid.

132. "A Look Back."

133. "Hayes Concerned in the Death of Prison Officer."

134. "Two Swung from Deer Lodge Gallows."

135. Ibid.

136. "A Look Back."

137. *State v. Hayes*, 38 Mont. 219, 99 Pac. 434.

138. "Rock Pays Penalty for Atrocious Deed," *Post Express* (Lincoln, NE) (June 18, 1908).

139. Ibid.

140. Ibid.

141. Ibid.

142. Ibid.

143. Ibid.

144. Ibid.

145. Ibid.

146. "Two Swung from Gallows at State Penitentiary a Dozen Years Ago for Murderous Assault on Warden and Deputy," *Times-Optimist* (Gilman, MT) (May 13, 1921).

147. "Two Swung from Deer Lodge Gallows."

148. "Two Swung from Gallows."

149. A significant number of newspaper accounts focus specifically on the "disagreeable task" of hanging a woman; that is, on the history of women executed in the United States. "First Woman Is Hanged in Arizona," *Daily Boston Globe* (February 22, 1930), 2. One *Los Angeles Times* article, "Ghosts Haunt Hanging Scene," for example, reports that Eva Dugan was the twenty-seventh woman to be executed in the country since its foundation. The article also lists each woman executed and emphasizes that at the time of Dugan's hanging, there was only one known case where an innocent woman was put to death. "Ghosts Haunt Hanging Scene," *Los Angeles Times* (February 22, 1930), 2.

150. "Blood-Stained Wrench, Mathis Clue," *Arizona Daily Star* (January 24, 1927).

151. "Crime: Cheerful Eva," *Time* (magazine) (March 3, 1930).

152. Ibid.

153. "Eva, Unshaken, Goes to Death," *Prescott [AZ] Evening Courier* (February 21, 1930), 4.

154. L. Kay Gillespie, *Executed Women of the 20th and 21st Centuries* (Lanham, MD: University Press of America, 2009), 5. Citing the *San Francisco Chronicle* (February 22, 1930).

155. Lowell Parker, *Arizona Republican* (March 23, 1976).

156. "Eva, Unshaken, Goes to Death," 4.

157. "Insanity Plea for Mrs. Dugan," *Prescott [AZ] Evening Courier* (February 14, 1930), 1.

158. Gillespie, *Executed Women*, 3. Citing the *Arizona Republican* (February 21, 1930).

159. "Crime: Cheerful Eva."

160. "Arizona Woman Slayer Calm in Shadow of Rope," *Chicago Daily Tribune* (February 21, 1930), 5.

161. Gillespie, *Executed Women*, 5. Citing the *San Francisco Chronicle* (February 21, 1930).

162. "Eva Dugan Sings Upon Death Walk," *Sarasota [FL] Herald Tribune* (February 21, 1930), 1.

163. "Mrs. Eva Dugan Goes to Death on Gallows," *Mount Airy [NC] News* (February 27, 1930), 2.

164. "Mother of Two Children Hanged for Killing Man," *Evening Independent* (St. Petersburg, FL) (February 21, 1930), 1.

165. "Eva, Unshaken, Goes to Death," 4.

166. Ibid.

167. Gillespie, *Executed Women*, 3. Citing the *Arizona Republican* (February 21, 1930).

168. "Mrs. Eva Dugan Goes to Death on Gallows," 2.

169. "Hang Woman in Arizona for Murder," *Greensburg [PA] Daily Tribune* (February 21, 1930), 1.

170. "Mrs. Eva Dugan Goes to Death on Gallows," 2.

171. "Arizona Hangs Its First Woman, Mrs. Eva Dugan," *Milwaukee Journal* (February 21, 1930), 1.

172. "Arizona Death Penalty History: Florence Prison," Arizona Department of Corrections (2013). Available at http://www.azcorrections.gov/adc/history/History_DeathPenalty.aspx.

173. Gillespie, *Executed Women*, 6. Citing the *Ogden [UT] Standard Examiner* (February 22, 1930).

174. "Mrs. Dugan Dies Game: Murder Atoned on Gallows," *Los Angeles Times* (February 22, 1930), 1.

175. See for example, "Mrs. Dugan Smiles While Black Hood Is Placed on Head," *Ludington [MI] Daily News* (February 21, 1930), 8 (continued from p. 1); "Eva Dugan Sings Upon Death Walk," *Sarasota [FL] Herald Tribune* (February 21, 1930), 1. Reports vary significantly as to the exact time at which the trap was sprung: 4:20 A.M., 4:17 A.M., 5:11 A.M., and 5:02 A.M., for example. Nonetheless, 4:11 A.M. is the time that the majority of newspapers list.

176. "Eva, Unshaken, Goes to Death," 1.

177. "Mrs. Eva Dugan Goes to Death on Gallows," 2.

178. Gillespie, *Executed Women*, 5. Citing Delbert Cosulich, *Tucson Daily Citizen* (February 21, 1930).

179. "Eva, Unshaken, Goes to Death," 1.

180. Gillespie, *Executed Women*, 6. Citing an article about the Reverend Hofmann from the *Arizona Republican* (June 20, 1972).

181. "Woman Killer Is Hanged on Gallows Today," *Daily Times* (Beaver, PA) (February 21, 1930), 1.

182. Gillespie, *Executed Women*, 7.

183. Ibid.

184. Linders, "Execution Spectacle and State Legitimacy," 629.

185. Banner, *Death Penalty*, 167.

Chapter 3

1. "Killed by an Electric Shock," *New York Times* (August 11, 1881), 5. See also Craig Brandon, *The Electric Chair: An Unnatural American History* (Jefferson, NC: McFarland, 1999), 12–14; Mark Essig, *Edison and the Electric Chair: A Story of Light and Death* (New York: Walker, 2003); Richard Moran, *Executioner's Current: Thomas Edison, George Westinghouse, and the Invention of the Electric Chair* (New York: Knopf, 2002).

2. Essig, *Edison and the Electric Chair*, 91.

3. "Killed by an Electric Shock," 5.

4. George B. Snow, "Obituary. Dr. Alfred Porter Southwick," *The Dental Cosmos; a Monthly*.

5. Brandon, *Electric Chair*, 16.

6. Ibid., 14. *Record of Dental Science* 40, no. 7 (July 1898), 597–98.

7. Ibid., 20.

8. Ibid., 20–22.

9. Ibid., 72.

10. Denise LeBeau, "Gas Chambers: A History and Overview," Animal Law Coalition (August 20, 2007), http://animallawcoalition.com/gas-chambers-a-history-and-overview; see also "To Protect Cats and Dogs," *New York Tribune* (March 13, 1894).

11. Brandon, *Electric Chair*, 32.

12. Ibid., 36.

13. David B. Hill, "Governor Hill's Initial Gubernatorial Address," in *Messages from the Governors: Comprising Executive Communications to the Legislature and Other Papers Relating to Legislation from the Organization of the First Colonial Assembly in 1683 to and Including the Year 1906*, Charles Z. Lincoln, ed. (Albany, NY: Published by Authority of the State, January 6, 1885).

14. Michael Lumer and Nancy Tenney, "The Death Penalty in New York: An Historical Perspective" 4 *Journal of Law and Policy* 81 (1995–96), 84.

15. Brandon, *Electric Chair,* 51.

16. Ibid., 105. Citing the "Report of the New York State Commission" (1888) at 35.

17. "Report of the Commission to Investigate and Report the Most Humane and Practical Method of Carrying into Effect Sentences of Death in Capital Cases" (January 17, 1888), 85, http://books.google.com/books?id=3aEoAQAAMAAJ&pg=PA95&lpg=PA95&dq=report+of+the+gerry+commission+january+17,+1888&source=bl&ots=siVsPkANcR&sig=WgBjXIWl61eby-rk6z9XOZld3FM&hl=en&sa=X&ei=8PzYULO1I-LHoQGM9YBw&ved=0CEcQ6AEwAQ#v=onepage&q=report%20of%20the%20gerry%20commission%20january%2017%2C%201888&f=false.

18. Brandon, *Electric Chair,* 54.

19. Moran, *Executioner's Current,* 72.

20. "Commission Report," 79.

21. Ibid., 80–84.

22. Despite Edison's personal opposition to capital punishment, when he received a letter from Dr. Alfred Southwick requesting his assistance and his facility to do research for New York's death penalty commission, Edison readily agreed.

23. "Commission Report," 95.

24. Brandon, *Electric Chair,* 68.

25. Essig, *Edison and the Electric Chair,* 51–52, 113, 134, 141.

26. See "Edison's Miracle of Light-AC-DC: What's the Difference?" *PBS-The American Experience* (1999–2000), http://www.pbs.org/wgbh/amex/edison/sfeature/acdc.html for a detailed explanation of the differences between alternating and direct current.

27. Ibid.

28. Essig, *Edison and the Electric Chair,* 135. Citing from "A Warning from the Edison Electric Light Co." (February 1888).

29. Brandon, *Electric Chair,* 74.

30. Ibid., 26.

31. Ibid., 74.

32. Ibid., 72.

33. Ibid., 70.

34. Ibid., 75.

35. See for example, Kentucky Electrocution State Protocol, which calls only for two shock cycles: "501 KAR 16:340. Electrocution Protocol," Kentucky Justice and Public Safety Cabinet and Department of Corrections, http://www.lrc.state.ky.us/kar/501/016/340.htm; see also Stephen Trombley, *Execution Protocol: Inside America's Capital Punishment Industry* (New York: Anchor, 1993).

36. Essig, *Edison and the Electric Chair,* 245.

37. "Kemmler's Death," *Abilene [KS] Weekly Reflector* (August 7, 1890), 1.

38. "Horrible Death Scene," *Anaconda [MT] Standard* (August 7, 1890), 1.

39. "Kemmler's Doom," *Arizona Republican* (August 7, 1890), 1.

40. "Horrible Death Scene," 1.

41. "Electricizing Is Considered to Be a Ghastly Failure," *St. Paul Daily Globe* (August 7, 1890), 6.

42. "Kemmler Executed: The Work Done in a Most Bungling Manner," *Columbus [NE] Journal* (August 13, 1890), 1.

43. "Far Worse than Hanging," *New York Times* (August 7, 1890), 1.

44. "Kemmler's Doom," 1.

45. Ibid.

46. "In the Death Chair," *New York Herald* (August 7, 1890).

47. "First Taking of Human Life by Electricity," *Manufacturers and Farmer's Journal* (Providence, RI) (August 7, 1890), 3.

48. Ibid.

49. "In the Death Chair."

50. "Kemmler's Case," *Bayonne [NJ] Herald* (August 9, 1890).

51. "In the Death Chair."

52. "Hacked to Death While Insane," *Washington Post* (March 31, 1889).

53. T. D. Crothers, "The Kemmler Case," *Times and Register* (October 26, 1889).

54. "Tortured to Death," *Washington Post* (August 6, 1890).

55. Brandon, *Electric Chair*, 91.

56. Ibid., 93.

57. "Kemmler the First," *New York Times* (May 15, 1889), 3.

58. "The New Execution Law," *New York Times* (July 10, 1889).

59. "In the Death Chair."

60. *In re Kemmler,* 7 N.Y.S. 145 (1889).

61. "In the Death Chair."

62. Ibid.

63. "New Execution Law."

64. Ibid.

65. Ibid.

66. Ibid.

67. Ibid.

68. Ibid.

69. "Electric Light and Power Cases: Kemmler vs. Durston" (QE003), in *Litigation Series-The Edison Papers* (Courtesy of Thomas Edison National Historic Park, 1888–89), http://edison.rutgers.edu/NamesSearch/DocDetImage.php3.

70. Thomas Alva Edison, "Legal Statements and Testimony" (QE003), in

Litigation Series-The Edison Papers (Courtesy of Thomas Edison National Historic Park, July 23, 1889) (QE003A0623; TAEM 115:945), http://edison.rutgers. edu/NamesSearch/DocDetImage.php3, 2515.

71. "New Execution Law."

72. *In re Kemmler,* 7 N.Y.S. 145 (1889).

73. Ibid.

74. *In re Kemmler,* 136 U.S. 436.

75. Ibid.

76. "Jackson Executed; First in District's New Death Chair," *Washington Post* (May 30, 1928), 18.

77. "Assailant of Mrs. Welling to Die Tomorrow," *Cumberland [MD] Evening Times* (May 28, 1928), 1.

78. "Jackson Executed," 18.

79. "Assailant of Mrs. Welling to Die Tomorrow," 1.

80. "Jackson Executed," 18.

81. "Assailant of Mrs. Welling to Die Tomorrow," 1.

82. "Jackson Executed," 18.

83. Ibid.

84. Ibid.

85. "Say Confession Was Obtained by 3rd Degree," *The Afro American* (Baltimore, MD) (April 23, 1927), 2.

86. "Negro Attacks Phone Operator," *Miami News* (February 19, 1927).

87. Ibid.

88. "Congress Will Seek Assailant of 'Phone Girl,'" *Sarasota [FL] Herald-Tribune* (February 20, 1927).

89. "Say Confession Was Obtained by 3rd Degree," 2.

90. Ibid.

91. Ibid.

92. Ibid.

93. "Coolidge Asked to Save Convicted Moron from Chair," *The Afro American* (Baltimore, MD) (April 28, 1928).

94. Ibid.

95. "Inquiry Asked into Sanity of Rapist," *The Afro American* (Baltimore, MD) (May 14, 1928), 2.

96. Ibid.

97. Ibid.

98. "Coolidge Asked to Save Convicted Moron."

99. "Newspaper Men Save Slayer at 11th Hour," *Afro American* (Baltimore, MD) (July 9, 1927), 1.

100. "Coolidge Asked to Save Convicted Moron."

101. "Condemned Man Puts Up Fight at Death's Door," *Spokane [WA] Daily Chronicle* (December 3, 1955).

102. "Man Battles 6 for 20 Minutes at Electric Chair," *St. Petersburg Times* (December 3, 1955).

103. "Convict Battles 7 Guards 20 Min. at Death Chair," *Washington Post* (December 3, 1955).

104. Ibid.

105. "Man Fights Off Guards 20 Min. at Electrocution," *Los Angeles Times* (December 3, 1955).

106. "Convict Battles 7 Guards."

107. Ibid.

108. "Man Fights Off Guards."

109. "Convict Battles 7 Guards."

110. Thelma Smith, "Execution Date Is Set for Negro Men Guilty of Raping White Girl," *Florence [SC] Morning News* (September 9, 1955).

111. "Girl Raped, Date Badly Hurt in Area's Lover's Lane Attack," *Florence [SC] Morning News* (August 14, 1955).

112. Ibid.

113. "Brothers Die for Raping Girl," *Gastonia [NC] Gazette* (September 9, 1955), 9.

114. Smith, "Execution Date Is Set."

115. "Girl Raped, Date Badly Hurt."

116. Ibid.

117. Ibid.

118. Ibid.

119. Ibid.

120. Ibid.

121. Ibid.

122. Ibid.

123. Ibid.

124. Smith, "Execution Date Is Set."

125. "Convicted Killer Executed in Faulty Chair—Policeman's Killer Electrocuted in Faulty Chair," *San Francisco Chronicle* (May 5, 1990), C11.

126. "Tafero Execution Scheduled," *Sun Sentinel* (Ft. Lauderdale, FL) (May 4, 1990), 1.

127. Michael deCourcy Hinds, "Making Execution Human (Or Can It Be?)," *New York Times* (October 13, 1990).

128. "Execution Protestors Begin March," *Globe and Mail* (Toronto) (May 7, 1990), 2.

129. Cynthia Barnett, "Tafero Meets Grisly Fate in Chair," *Gainesville [FL] Sun* (May 5, 1990), 1. See also Cynthia Barnett, "A Sterile Scene Turns Grotesque," *Gainesville [FL] Sun* (May 5, 1990), 1.

130. Ibid. See also Sydney Freedberg, "The Story of Old Sparky," *St. Petersburg Times* (September 25, 1999).

131. Ibid.

132. *Tafero v. State*, 242 So. 2d 470 (1971).

133. Ibid.

134. "Two Violent Murders, One Violent Execution" (Editorial), *Palm Beach Post* (May 8, 1990).

135. *Tafero v. State*, 403 So. 2d 355 (1981).

136. Ibid.

137. Ibid.

138. Ibid.

139. Ibid.

140. Ibid.

141. "Two Violent Murders."

142. Claudia Whitman, "Jesse Tafero (Florida) Case Chart," *Grassroots Investigation Project* (sponsored by Equal Justice USA), http://www.lairdcarlson.com/grip/Tafero%20Case%20Chart.htm.

143. Ibid.

144. Ibid.

145. Ibid.

146. *Tafero v. State*, 403 So. 2d 355 (1981).

147. "Convicted Killer Executed," C11.

148. Charles Holmes, "Report Says Human Error to Blame in Flawed Execution." *Palm Beach Post* (May 9, 1990).

149. "Convicted Killer Executed," C11.

150. "Execution Protestors Begin March," 2.

151. Michael Griffin, "Medina's Fiery Execution Starts Uproar," *Orlando Sentinel* (March 26, 1997).

152. Ibid.

153. Ibid.

154. Ibid.

155. Ibid.

156. "Inmates Head Burns During Execution," *Telegraph-Herald* (Dubuque, IA) (March 26, 1997).

157. Ibid.

158. Ron Word (AP), "Killer's Execution Ends in Fire, Smoke—State: Inmate Was Already Dead," *Sun Sentinel* (Ft. Lauderdale, FL) (March 26, 1997).

159. Ibid.

160. Ibid.

161. Brett Kallestad (AP), "Fiery Medina Execution Blamed on Human Error," *Ocala [FL] Star-Banner* (April 12, 1997).

162. Griffin, "Medina's Fiery Execution Starts Uproar."

163. Alan Judd, "Electric Chair Is on Trial," *Gainesville [FL] Sun* (April 16, 1997).

164. Word, "Killer's Execution Ends in Fire, Smoke."

165. *Medina v. Singletary*, 59 F.3d 1095 (1995).

166. Ibid.

167. *Medina v. Florida,* Legal Brief–Case No. 63-680, Florida Supreme Court (December 6, 1983).

168. Ibid., 2.

169. Ibid., 3.

170. Ibid., 7.

171. Ibid.

172. Ibid., 11.

173. *Medina v. Singletary*, 59 F.3d 1095 (1995).

174. Ibid.

175. Ibid.

176. Ibid.

177. *Medina v. State,* 690 So. 2d 1255 (1997).

178. Ibid.

179. Ibid.

180. Word "Killer's Execution Ends in Fire, Smoke."

181. Margaret Talev, "Medina Dead When Mask Flamed Up," *Tampa Tribune* (April 1, 1997).

182. Kallestad, "Fiery Medina Execution Blamed on Human Error."

183. Talev, "Medina Died When Mask Flamed Up."

184. *Provenzano v. Florida,* 744 So. 2d 413 (1999).

185. Deborah Denno, "Is Electrocution an Unconstitutional Method of Execution? The Engineering of Death over the Century," 35 *William and Mary Law Review* (1993–94), 652–53.

186. *Bryan v. Moore,* 528 U.S. 960; 120 (2000).

187. Deborah W. Denno, "Adieu to Electrocution," 26 *Ohio Northern University Law Review* (2000), 665.

188. Because Florida passed a lethal injection law, the Court did not review the constitutionality of the electric chair.

189. See "Botched, Gruesome Electrocutions Mandate Switch to Lethal Injections," *Sun Sentinel* (Ft. Lauderdale, FL) (June 30, 1997), 8A. Prompted by an impending Supreme Court hearing on the constitutionality of electrocution, in January 2000 the Florida legislature passed a law making lethal injection the default method of execution in that state. Electrocution will be used only on the written request of those condemned to die.

190. Ibid.

191. *Provenzano v. Moore,* Case No. 95, 973, Corrected Opinion (September 24, 1999), Supreme Court of Florida, 56.

192. Quoted in the dissenting opinion of Justice Shaw in *Provenzano v. Moore,* 57.

193. Section 922.105 (1), Fla. Stat. (Supp. 1998).

194. Tennessee and Kentucky moved towards death by lethal injection in 2000. See "Methods of Execution," *Death Penalty Information Center (DPIC)* (Bureau of Justice Statistics, Capital Punishment, 2011; updated by DPIC), http://www.deathpenaltyinfo.org/methods-execution.

195. Ibid.

196. *State v. Mata*, 275 Neb. 1, 745 N.W. 2d 229 (2008).

197. Ibid. Italics added.

198. Ibid.

Chapter 4

1. Nevada, "Assembly Bill No. 230—Messrs. Hart and Bartlett," *Laws, statutes, etc.: Statutes of the State of Nevada Volume 1920–1921* (March 28, 1921), 387, http://books.google.com/books?id=dAyxAAAAIAAJ&pg=PR19&lpg=PR19&dq=nevada+state+legislative+assembly+1921&source=bl&ots=QwSROoLiow&sig=CdnWsdNeiGHMtSBBVA2Z05yxjok&hl=en&sa=X&ei=ckHfUfuAFZTb4APC54CADg&ved=0CEIQ6AEwBg#v=onepage&q=bill%20230&f=false

2. "Lethal Gas for Death Penalty Is Passed by Legislature of Nevada," *Springfield [MA] Republican* (March 15, 1921), 2.

3. "Nevada Governor Signs Gas Bill," *Springfield [MA] Republican* (March 28, 1921), 16.

4. Nevada, "Assembly Bill No. 230," 387.

5. "Nevada Governor Signs Gas Bill," 16.

6. Scott Christianson, *The Last Gasp: The Rise and Fall of the American Gas Chamber* (Berkeley: University of California Press, 2010), 9. See also Adam Hoschild, *Bury the Chains: Prophets and Rebels in the Fight to Free an Empire's Slaves* (Boston: Houghton Mifflin, 2005); Claude Ribbe, *Napoleon's Crimes: A Blueprint for Hitler* (Oxford, UK: Oneworld Publications, 2007).

7. *The New England Medical Gazette: Monthly Medical Journal of Homeopathic Medicine* 32 (Boston: 1897), 35, http://books.google.com/books?id=vrpXAAAAMAAJ&pg=PA35&lpg=PA35&dq=allegheny+medical+society+AND+%22death+penalty%22&source=bl&ots=CIkZ6gEQth&sig=e1HwLbQJKbYEse9_AFFdlPnr5mc&hl=en&sa=X&ei=_H3fUZOPMoT_4AOZnYDQBw&ved=0CCoQ6AEwAA#v=onepage&q=allegheny%20medical%20society%20AND%20%22death%20penalty%22&f=false. See also Christianson, *Last Gasp*, 30.

8. J. Chris Lange, M.D. (of Pittsburg), "Asphyxiation by Carbonic Acid as the Death Penalty," *Pennsylvania Medical Journal* 1, no. 1 (Pittsburg: June 1897), 108–9, http://books.google.com/books?id=irI1AQAAMAAJ&pg=PA108&lpg=PA108&dq=allegheny+medical+society+AND+%22death+penalty%22&source=bl&ots=4_OWWZS_tL&sig=1NXzgJnDpiyLovpLaKB05rBnDrE&hl=en&s

a=X&ei=_H3fUZOPMoT_4AOZnYDQBw&ved=oCCwQ6AEwAQ#v=onep age&q=humane&f=false.

9. Ibid., 109.

10. Denise LeBau, "Gas Chambers: A History and Overview," *Animal Law Coalition* (August 20, 2007), http://animallawcoalition.com/gas-chambers-a-history-and-overview/.

11. "To Protect Cats and Dogs," *New York Tribune* (March 13, 1894).

12. "Waging War on Worthless Curs," *Baltimore American* (July 7, 1910), 16.

13. Christianson, *Last Gasp*, 31. See also "72,000 Cats Killed in Paralysis Fear," *New York Times* (July 26, 1916).

14. Robert Harris and Jeremy Paxman, *A Higher Form of Killing: The Secret History of Chemical and Biological Warfare* (New York: Random House, 2002), 3.

15. Ibid., 9–10.

16. Ibid., 6.

17. Ibid.

18. Ibid., 11.

19. Ibid., 15.

20. Ibid., 20.

21. Ibid., 21.

22. Ibid., 30–34.

23. Christianson, *Last Gasp*, 43.

24. Ibid.

25. James E. Mills, "Chemical Warfare," 10 *Foreign Affairs* 444 (1931–32).

26. *State v. Gee Jon*, 46 NEV. 418; 211 (1923), 676.

27. Ibid.

28. Loren B. Chan, "Example for the Nation: Nevada's Execution of Gee Jon," *Nevada Historical Society Quarterly*, ed. John M. Townley (State of Nevada, Summer 1975), 91–106, http://nsla.nevadaculture.org/statepubs/epubs/210777-1975-2Summer.pdf.

29. *State v. Gee Jon*, 46 NEV. 418; 211 (1923), 676.

30. Ibid.

31. Ibid.

32. Ibid; see also "Condemned Men Will Die By Gas," *Springfield Republican* (January 28, 1922), 14.

33. Nevada Supreme Court, *In the Supreme Court of the State of Nevada: The State of Nevada Plaintiffs and Respondents v. Gee Jon and Hughie Sing Defendants and Appellants* (1922).

34. Ibid.

35. Chan, "Example for the Nation."

36. Ed Vogel, "Nevada Gas Chamber Marks Historic Point," *Las Vegas Review-Journal* (February 21, 1994), 1B.

37. "First Gas Execution Date Fixed," *Los Angeles Times* (January 31, 1924), 11; see also "Gee Jon, First to Be Executed, Was Bad Chinese Tongman," *Oxnard [CA] Daily Courier* (February 14, 1924).

38. Ibid.

39. Ibid.

40. "First Gas Execution Date Fixed," 11.

41. Scott Christianson, "A Notorious Nevada First," *Nevada Magazine* (November/December 2010), http://nevadamagazine.com/issues/read/a_notorious_nevada_first/.

42. Ibid.

43. "The First Gas Execution Today," *Nevada [MO] Daily Mail* (February 8, 1924), 1; see also Vogel, "Nevada Gas Chamber," 1b.

44. "Gas Execution Is Inaugurated," *Los Angeles Times* (February 9, 1924), 3. Although Thomas Russell, a young Mexican American man who murdered an Indian girl, was supposed to be executed at the same time, the Pardon Board lowered his sentence to life imprisonment just thirteen hours before the execution.

45. Ibid.

46. Ibid.

47. Ibid; "First Lethal Gas Execution Held," *Spokane Daily Chronicle* (February 8, 1924), 1.

48. http://cameochemicals.noaa.gov/chemical/881

49. "Chinese Dies Quickly from Lethal Fumes," *Evening Independent* (St. Petersburg, FL) (February 8, 1924), 1.

50. "First Lethal Gas Execution Takes Life of Young Chinese After Six Minutes Inside Air Proof Chamber," *Evening Independent* (February 9, 1924), 12; Chan, "Example for the Nation."

51. "First Lethal Gas Execution Takes Life of Young Chinese," 12.

52. Ibid.

53. Ibid.

54. "Gas Execution Is Inaugurated," 3.

55. Christianson, *Last Gasp*, 83.

56. Ibid., 85; "Gas Death Chamber Ready for Slayer," *Boston Daily Globe* (May 21, 1926).

57. Ibid.

58. "Build Death House," *Pittsburgh Press* (November 30, 1928), 27.

59. "Nevada Speeding Gas Death House," *Telegraph-Herald Times-Journal* (Dubuque, IA) (December 27, 1928).

60. Ibid.

61. "Man Executed in Gas Chamber," *Reading [PA] Eagle* (June 1, 1930).

62. Ibid.

63. The first gassing in Nevada's newly constructed death house, the execution of Bob White, was botched.

64. See "Table 1: American Gas Chamber Executions, 1924–1999," in Christianson, *Last Gasp*, 3; see also therein, ch. 5, 178–79.

65. Trina N. Seitz, "The Killing Chair: North Carolina's Experiment in Civility and the Execution of Allen Foster," *North Carolina Historical Review* 81, no. 1 (January 2004), 38.

66. Ibid., 57. Citing *News and Observer* (Raleigh, NC) (May 2, 1935).

67. "Negro Is Executed in N.C. Gas Chamber," *Ottawa [Canada] Citizen* (January 25, 1936).

68. Ibid.

69. Seitz, "Killing Chair," 59.

70. Ibid.

71. Ibid., 60.

72. Ibid., 62.

73. Ibid., 63. Citing John Parris, *News and Observer* (Raleigh, NC) (January 24, 1936).

74. "Execution Not Speedy," *Saskatoon [Canada] Star-Phoenix* (January 25, 1936).

75. "Poison Gas Used to Execute Negro," *St. Petersburg Times* (January 25, 1936).

76. Seitz, "Killing Chair," 64. Citing the *News and Observer* (Raleigh, NC) (January 25, 1936).

77. Ibid., 63.

78. "Poison Gas Used to Execute Negro," *St. Petersburg Times* (January 25, 1936).

79. Seitz, "Killing Chair," 64. Citing the *News and Observer* (Raleigh, NC) (January 25, 1936).

80. "No Improvement," *Bladen [NC] Journal* (January 30, 1936).

81. Seitz, "Killing Chair," 64.

82. Ibid., 65.

83. Ibid.

84. Seitz, "Killing Chair," 72. There were no executions in North Carolina between 1962 and 1983. The state adopted lethal injection during the 1983 General Assembly term but retained lethal gas as an option until 1999.

85. "Convicted Police Killer Is Executed in California," *News and Courier* (Charleston, SC) (April 13, 1967), 7-D.

86. Daryl E. Lembke, "Mitchell Executed as Pickets March," *Boston Globe* (April 13, 1967), 1.

87. Ibid.

88. "Execution Eve Death Try Fails," *Boston Globe* (April 12, 1967), 2.

89. "Convicted Police Killer Is Executed," 7-D.

90. "Execution Eve Death Try Fails," 2.

91. Sydney Kossen, "California Executes Prisoner for First Time in Four Years," *Washington Post, Times Herald* (April 14, 1967), A3.

92. Kathleen A. O'Shea and Ann Patrick Conrad, *Women and the Death Penalty in the United Sates, 1900–1998* (Westport, CT: Greenwood, 1999), 74–76.

93. Lembke, "Mitchell Executed," 1.

94. "Convicted Police Killer Is Executed," 7-D.

95. "Execution Eve Death Try Fails," 2.

96. Lembke, "Mitchell Executed," 1.

97. "Execution Eve Death Try Fails," 2.

98. Kossen, "California Executes Prisoner," A3.

99. Ibid.

100. "So They Say," *Owosso [MI] Argus-Press* (May 2, 1967), 4.

101. "Execution Eve Death Try Fails," 2.

102. "300 Protest Execution at Prison Gate as Killer Dies," *Los Angeles Times* (April 13, 1967), 3.

103. "Family, Pickets Conduct Vigil of Hope for Killer," *Los Angeles Times* (April 13, 1967), 3.

104. "Execution Eve Death Try Fails," 2.

105. "So They Say," 4.

106. Lembke, "Mitchell Executed," 1.

107. Kossen, "California Executes Prisoner," A3.

108. Ibid.

109. Ibid.

110. Lembke, "Mitchell Executed," 1.

111. "Family, Pickets Conduct Vigil," 3.

112. Ibid.

113. "300 Protest Execution at Prison Gate as Killer Dies," 5.

114. Ibid.

115. "Miss. Child Killer Dies Gasping and Choking," *Philadelphia Daily News* (United Press International) (September 2, 1983).

116. "Mississippi Executes Killer of 3-Year-Old," *Miami Herald* (Associated Press) (September 3, 1983), 3.

117. "Miss. Child Killer Dies," *Philadelphia Daily News*.

118. "Father Says Execution Won't Erase His Memories," *New York Times* (September 3, 1983), 2.

119. "Mississippi Executes Killer," 3.

120. Dan Lohwasser, "Prompt Execution Disputed," *Philadelphia Inquirer* (September 3, 1983), 2.

121. Ibid.

122. Ibid.

123. Ibid.

124. "Child's Murderer Is Executed in Mississippi Prison," *Washington Post* (September 2, 1983).

125. "Killer Dies in Miss. Gas Chamber," *Philadelphia Inquirer* (Inquirer Wire Services) (September 2, 1983).

126. Ivan Solotaroff, *The Last Face You'll Ever See: The Culture of Death Row* (New York: HarperCollins, 2001), 75.

127. Ibid.

128. Jo Gray, "15-Year Vigil Concludes for Parents of Slain Girl," *Kingman [AZ] Daily Miner* (September 2, 1983).

129. Ibid.

130. Solotaroff, *Last Face You'll Ever See*, 74.

131. Lohwasser, "Prompt Execution Disputed," 2.

132. Solotaroff, *Last Face You'll Ever See*, 74.

133. "Child's Murderer Is Executed."

134. "Child Killer Jimmy Lee Gray Executed in Miss.," *Lewiston [ID] Daily News* (September 3, 1983).

135. R. Shipp, "Killer of 3-Year-Old Mississippi Girl Dies After Justices Reject Plea," *New York Times* (September 2, 1983), 2.

136. "Killer Dies in Miss. Gas Chamber."

137. Solotaroff, *Last Face You'll Ever See*, 74.

138. Ibid.

139. Ibid.

140. Ibid.

141. Quoted in ibid., 77.

142. Ibid.

143. Shipp, "Killer of 3-Year-Old Mississippi Girl Dies," 2.

144. *Gray v. Lucas*, 710 F.2d 1048, 1061 (1983).

145. "Mother Wants Son Executed," *Gadsden [AL] Times* (January 20, 1977).

146. Ibid.

147. "Father Says Execution Won't Erase His Memories," 2.

148. "Mississippi Executes Killer," 3.

149. "Father Says Execution Won't Erase His Memories," 2.

150. "Mississippi Executes Killer," 3.

151. "Child's Murderer Is Executed."

152. "Killer Dies in Miss. Gas Chamber."

153. Ibid.

154. Ibid.

155. "Father Says Execution Won't Erase His Memories," 2.

156. Ibid.

157. Ibid.

158. "Killer Dies in Miss. Gas Chamber."

159. "West Arizona Executes Slayer," *Sun Sentinel* (Fort Lauderdale, FL) (April 7, 1992).

160. Neil Bibler, "State Executes Harding Today: Obscene Gesture Is Final Statement," *Prescott [AZ] Courier* (April 6, 1992).

161. Ibid.

162. "West Arizona Executes Slayer."

163. "Arizona Conducts First Execution in 29 Years," *New York Times* (April 7, 1992).

164. Joan Dayan, "The Blue Room in Florence," 85 *Yale Law Review* (1997), 27–46.

165. "Methods of Execution: Gas Chamber," in *The Death Penalty* (Death Penalty Curriculum, Michigan State University Comm Tech Lab and Death Penalty Information Center, 2002–2004), http://deathpenaltycurriculum.org/student/c/about/methods/gaschamber.htm.

166. Bibler, "State Executes Harding Today."

167. "Option Allowed for Executions—Condemned Will Get Choice," *Daily Breeze* (Torrance, CA) (August 29, 1992).

168. Bibler, "State Executes Harding Today."

169. Sam Stanton, "Grim Rite of Death Awaiting Harris," *Sacramento Bee* (April 15, 1992).

170. "Further Information on UA 442/91 (AMR 51/68/91, 16 December and Follow-Ups AMR 51/03/92, 3 January and AMR 51/17/92, 6 February)- USA (Arizona): Death Penalty: Donald Eugene Harding," Amnesty International (1992), http://www.amnesty.org/es/library/asset/AMR51/043/1992/es/a47621b7-edbd-11dd-a95b-fd9a617f028f/amr510431992en.html.

171. Ibid.

172. Ibid.

173. Ibid.

174. Ibid.

175. Bibler, "State Executes Harding Today."

176. Ibid.

177. "Donald Eugene Harding," Death Row: AZCentral (June 22, 2004), http://www.azcentral.com/specials/special32/articles/06230622EXEharding-ON.html.

178. *Harding v. Lewis,* 834 F.2d 853, No. 86-2057 (1987).

179. Ibid.

180. Ibid.

181. Ibid.

182. Ibid.

183. Ibid.

184. Ibid.

185. Ibid.

186. Ibid.

187. Ibid.

188. "Donald Eugene Harding."

189. *Harding v. Lewis*, 834 F.2d 853, No. 86-2057 (1987).

190. Ibid.

191. Ibid.

192. Ibid.

193. Ibid.

194. *State v. Harding*, 137 ARIZ. 278, 670 P.2D 383 (1983).

195. "Arizona Needs Permit to Use Gas Chamber," *Orlando Sentinel* (May 27, 1991).

196. Sister Helen Prejean, *The Death of Innocents* (Norwich, UK: Canterbury Press, 2006), 235.

197. Christianson, *Last Gasp*, 185–90.

198. Walter LaGrand was executed in the gas chamber even though he had the option of choosing lethal injection.

Chapter 5

1. Robbie Byrd, "Informal Talks Opened Door to Lethal Injection." *The Huntsville [TX] Item* (October 3, 2007).

2. "History of Lethal Injection Protocol," *Berkeley Law* (History Document Kit), 16, http://www.law.berkeley.edu/clinics/dpclinic/LethalInjection/LI/documents/kit/history.

3. Ibid., 17.

4. Ibid., 18.

5. Ibid., 19.

6. Ibid., 22.

7. Ibid., 19.

8. Deborah Denno, "The Future of Execution Methods," in *The Future of America's Death Penalty: An Agenda for the Next Generation of Capital Punishment Research*, Charles S. Lanier, William J. Bowers, and James R. Acker, eds. (Durham, NC: Carolina Academic Press, 2009), 490. Emphasis added.

9. "History of Lethal Injection Protocol," 24.

10. Denno, "Future of Execution Methods," 488.

11. For examples of lethal injection protocols, see Montana Department of Corrections, Montana State Prison Execution Technical Manual, January 16, 2013, found at http://www.cor.mt.gov/content/Resources/Reports/ETManual.

pdf. Also see "Lethal Injection Procedures," found at http://www.cdcr.ca.gov/reports_research/lethal_injection.html; and "Lethal Injection," found at http://www.deathpenalty.org/article.php?id=52.

12. Ellen Kreizberg and David Richter, "But Can It Be Fixed? A Look at Constitutional Challenges to Lethal Injection Executions," Santa Clara University School of Law, Legal Studies Research Paper Series, working paper no. 07-28 (June 2007), 106.

13. "History of Lethal Injection Protocol," 16. Citing "Brief for the Fordham University School of Law, Louis Stein Center for Law and Ethics as *Amicus Curiae* in Support of Petitioners," *Baze v. Rees*, no. 07-5439 (November 13, 2007), 16.

14. Ibid., 17.

15. Ibid.

16. Denno, "Future of Execution Methods," 488.

17. Jonathan I. Groner, "Lethal Injection: A Stain on the Face of Medicine," *British Medical Journal* 325 (2002), 1026–28.

18. Denno, "Future of Execution Methods," 488.

19. Ibid.

20. Ibid.

21. Ibid.

22. Ibid.

23. Quoted in ibid.

24. Ibid.

25. Ibid. Emphasis added.

26. Ibid.

27. According to the Death Penalty Information Center, "Most states use a 3-drug combination for lethal injections. . . . Seven states have used a single-drug method for executions—a lethal dose of an anesthetic (Arizona, Georgia, Idaho, Ohio, South Dakota, Texas, and Washington). Four other states have announced use of one-drug lethal injection protocols, but have not carried out such an execution (Arkansas, Kentucky, Louisiana, and Missouri)." Found at http://www.deathpenaltyinfo.org/state-lethal-injection.

28. Identifying a botched lethal injection is somewhat problematic because the medicalization of the process and the three-drug protocol, which until recently has been the standard, work to prevent the body from registering signs of suffering.

29. Frank Romanelli et al., "Issues Surrounding Lethal Injection as a Means of Capital Punishment," *American Journal of Pharmaceutical Education* (August 10, 2011), 1429. In *Nelson v. Campbell,* the Supreme Court ruled that sec. 1983 is an appropriate vehicle for challenging the constitutionality of specific death penalty procedures. The Court held that Alabama death row inmate Nelson could use sec. 1983 to challenge the "cut-down" procedure—in which an in-

mate's skin is scraped away to provide easier access for execution personnel to a usable vein—as cruel and unusual.

30. Ibid.

31. The Court's involvement was largely unprecedented. *Baze* presented the Court with its first opportunity since 1878 to evaluate an execution method under the Eighth Amendment. Denno, "Future of Execution Methods," 486.

32. "Foreseeable and Unnecessary Risk: Lethal Injection and the Three-Drug Protocol," *Baze v. Rees Resource Kit* (University of California, Berkeley, School of Law, Death Penalty Clinic), http://www.law.berkeley.edu/clinics/dp-clinic/LethalInjection/LI/documents/kit/Kit.pdf.

33. *Baze v. Rees*, 128 S. Ct. 1520 (2008), 1531–37.

34. Harvey Gee, "Eighth Amendment Challenges After *Baze v. Rees*: Lethal Injection, Civil Rights Lawsuits, and the Death Penalty," 31 *Boston College Third World Law Journal* (2011), 217.

35. Ibid.

36. Ibid., 233.

37. Ibid., 234.

38. Ibid., 237.

39. Ibid., 231.

40. Ibid., 239.

41. Shortages of the drugs needed for lethal injection have plagued the method since its initiation. More recently, in August 2013, the Texas Department of Criminal Justice released a statement confirming that Texas had a dwindling supply of pentobarbital, the single drug the state uses for its lethal injection procedures. According to the statement, the supply "will expire" in September. See Molly Hennessy-Fiske, "Texas Faces Possible Shortage of Execution Drug," *Los Angeles Times* (August 1, 2013).

42. Andrew Welsh-Huggins, "Shortage of Drugs Hold Up Some U.S. Executions," MSNBC (September 27, 2010), http://www.msnbc.msn.com/id/39385026/ns/health-health_care/t/shortage-drug-holds-some-us-executions/.

43. Christina Ng, "Videotaped Execution by Lethal Injection Set for Thursday," ABC (July 21, 2011), http://abcnews.go.com/US/videotaped-execu-tion-lethal-injection-set-thursday/story?id=14118367/.

44. "Ga. Postpones Scheduled Videotaped Execution," CBS (July 21, 2011), http://www.cbsnews.com/stories/2011/07/21/national/main20081334.shtml/.

45. Ibid.

46. Erica Goode, "Video of a Lethal Injection Reopens Questions on the Privacy of Executions," *New York Times* (July 23, 2011), http://www.nytimes.com/2011/07/24/us/24video.html?_r=3&pagewanted=all/.

47. Diane Jennings, "Recording of Execution in Georgia Likely to Lead to Similar Requests in Texas," *Montreal Gazette* (July 27, 2011),

48. William E. Schmidt, "First Woman Is Executed In U.S. Since 1962,"

New York Times (November 3, 1984), 1. http://www.montrealgazette.com/technology/FILMING+EXECUTIONS/5166946/story.html/.

49. Fred Grimm, "2 Roses, Then Matronly Killer Dies: Grandmother Is First Woman Executed Since 1962," *Miami Herald* (November 3, 1984), 1A.

50. Ashley Halsey, "Death Came Quietly to N.C. Woman," *Philadelphia Inquirer* (November 3, 1984), 3D.

51. Bella Stumbo "Velma Barfield: Cold Killer or Loving Grandma?" *Los Angeles Times* (September 19, 1984), 22.

52. Kathy Sawyer, "Women Executed for Murder," *Washington Post* (November 2, 1984), A1.

53. Stumbo, "Velma Barfield," 22.

54. Ibid.

55. Tom Minehart, "Mourners: Barfield's Faith in God Was Inspiring," *Gainesville [FL] Sun* (November 4, 1984), 12D.

56. Sawyer, "Women Executed," A1.

57. Stumbo, "Velma Barfield," 22.

58. Ibid.

59. The names of Barfield's victims were Stuart Taylor, Dolly Taylor Edwards, John Henry Lee, and Barfield's mother, Lillian McMillan Bullard. The murders spanned a period of seven years. Barfield was not suspected until Taylor's death. Joseph B. Ingle, "Final Hours—The Execution of Velma Barfield," *Loyola of Los Angeles Law Review* (November 1, 1989), 221–22.

60. Stumbo, "Velma Barfield," 22.

61. Ibid.

62. "Velma Barfield Dies by Injection Today," *Altus [OK] Times* (November 4, 1984), 16.

63. Minehart, "Mourners," 12D.

64. "Velma Barfield Executed, Hunt Sees Deterrent Value," *Lewiston [ME] Daily Sun* (November 3, 1984), 3.

65. Stumbo, "Velma Barfield," 22.

66. Ibid.

67. Minehart, "Mourners," 12D.

68. Stumbo, "Velma Barfield," 22.

69. Ingle, "Final Hours," 222.

70. Ibid.

71. Stumbo, "Velma Barfield," 22.

72. Ingle, "Final Hours," 222–23.

73. Ibid., 228.

74. Ibid., 229.

75. Ibid., 230.

76. "Velma Barfield Executed," 3; "Velma Barfield Dies by Injection Today," 16.

77. Schmidt, "First Woman Is Executed In U.S. Since 1962," 1.

78. "The Execution of Velma," *Robesonian* (Lumberton, NC) (December 30, 1984), 8A.

79. "Appeals Seek to Avert Barfield Execution," *Los Angeles Times* (October 30, 1984), B5.

80. "Woman Executed in North Carolina," *Lexington [KY] Herald-Leader* (November 2, 1984), A12.

81. Sawyer, "Women Executed," A1.

82. "Velma Barfield Dies by Injection Today," 16.

83. "Woman Executed in North Carolina," A12.

84. Grimm, "2 Roses, Then Matronly Killer Dies," 1A.

85. "Velma Barfield Dies by Injection Today," 16.

86. "Barfield, 42, Is Executed," *Daily Breeze* (Torrance, CA) (November 2, 1984), A2.

87. Michael Hirsley, "Executions Earn South Dubious Distinction of 'Death Belt,'" *Lakeland [FL] Ledger* (November 4, 1984), 19A.

88. "Woman Executed in North Carolina," A12.

89. "Velma Barfield Dies by Injection Today," 16.

90. Grimm, "2 Roses, Then Matronly Killer Dies," 1A.

91. "Eyewitness Gives Account of Execution," *Mount Airy [NC] News* (November 2, 1984), 10A, 14A.

92. Sawyer, "Women Executed for Murder," A1.

93. "Velma Barfield Dies by Injection Today," 16.

94. "Velma Barfield Executed," 3.

95. "Barfield, 42, Is Executed," A2.

96. "Eyewitness Gives Account of Execution," 10A, 14A.

97. Grimm, "2 Roses, Then Matronly Killer Dies," 1A.

98. "Velma Barfield Executed," 3.

99. Grimm, "2 Roses, Then Matronly Killer Dies," 1A.

100. Stumbo, "Velma Barfield," 22.

101. "Pajama-clad Velma Barfield Is Executed in North Carolina," *The Vindicator* (Youngstown, OH) (November 2, 1984), cover page.

102. "Velma Barfield Executed," 3.

103. "Eyewitness Gives Account of Execution," 10A, 14A.

104. "Velma Barfield Executed," 3.

105. "Eyewitness Gives Account of Execution," 10A, 14A.

106. "Velma Barfield Executed," 3.

107. "Mrs. Barfield's Skin, Eyes Removed for Transplants," *Lexington [KY] Herald-Leader* (November 3, 1984), A2.

108. Hirsley, "Executions Earn South Dubious Distinction," 19A.

109. Grimm, "2 Roses, Then Matronly Killer Dies," 1A.

110. Her husband was Thomas Burke, who was alleged to have passed away in a house fire.

111. Ann Peters, "Velma Barfield Executed in N.C.," *Philadelphia Daily News* (November 2, 1984), 3.Minehart, "Mourners," 12D.

112. "Clinton to Be on Hand for Killer's Execution," *Orlando Sentinel* (January 25, 1992), A6.

113. Marshall Frady, "Annals of Law and Politics: Death in Arkansas" *New Yorker* (February 22, 1993), 129.

114. Ibid., 107.

115. Ibid.

116. Ibid.

117. Ibid., 108.

118. Ibid., 109.

119. Ibid., 110.

120. Ibid., 112.

121. Ibid., 105–33, 150.

122. Ronald Smothers, "The 1992 Campaign: Death Penalty; Clinton Weighs Clemency for Killer Scheduled to Die," *New York Times* (May 7, 1992), A24.

123. Frady, "Annals of Law and Politics," 111.

124. Ibid.

125. Ibid., 112.

126. Ibid.

127. Ibid., 115.

128. Ibid., 114.

129. Ibid.

130. Frady, "Annals of Law and Politics," 115.

131. Peter Applebome, "The 1992 Campaign," *New York Times* (January 25, 1992), A8.

132. Frady, "Annals of Law and Politics," 115.

133. Mike Allen, "Debate Rages on Executing Inmate in Wheelchair," *New York Times* (October 30, 1992), B16.

134. Applebome, "1992 Campaign."

135. Frady, "Annals of Law and Politics," 118.

136. "Sale of Warrant Aids Death Foes," *The Bulletin* (Bend, OR) (August 7, 1992), C11.

137. Applebome, "1992 Campaign."

138. Frady, "Annals of Law and Politics," 108.

139. Smothers, "1992 Campaign," A24.

140. Mike Barnicle, "More than Just a Politician," *Boston Globe* (January 26, 1992), 21.

141. "Campaign," *Eugene [OR] Register-Guard* (May 15, 1992), 2.

142. Frady, "Annals of Law and Politics," 105–33, 150.

143. Ibid., 122.

144. Ibid.

145. Ibid., 128.

146. Ibid., 131.

147. Ibid.

148. Ibid.

149. Applebome, "1992 Campaign."

150. Frady, "Annals of Law and Politics," 131.

151. Allen, "Debate Rages on Executing Inmate in Wheelchair," B16.

152. Frady, "Annals of Law and Politics," 132.

153. "Sale of Warrant Aids Death Foes," C11.

154. Allen, "Debate Rages on Executing Inmate in Wheelchair," B16.

155. "Governor Delays Ohio Execution After Vein Troubles," *Bennington [VT] Banner* (September 15, 2009).

156. "Lawyer: Ohio Execution on Hold After Vein Troubles," *Associated Press Archive* (September 15, 2009).

157. Andrew Welsh-Huggins, "Ohio Inmate 'Traumatized' After Failed Execution," *Associated Press Archive* (September 16, 2009).

158. Alan Johnson, "Effort to Kill Inmate Halted," *Columbus Dispatch* (September 16, 2009), A1.

159. Peter Krouse, "Death Row Inmate Romell Broom Receives Temporary Reprieve from Execution," *Plain Dealer* (Cleveland) (September 19, 2009).

160. Michael Scott, "'Dead Man' Author Prejean Deplores Failed Execution" *Plain Dealer* (Cleveland) (September 18, 2009), B3.

161. Romell Broom and Clare Nonhebel, *Survivor on Death Row* (UK: Clare Nonhebel, 2012), 46.

162. Ibid., 265.

163. Ibid., 142.

164. Ibid., 42.

165. Ibid., 46.

166. Ibid., 50.

167. Ibid.

168. Ibid., 273.

169. Ibid., 278.

170. Ibid., 112.

171. Ibid., 54.

172. Ibid., 289.

173. Ibid., 88.

174. Ibid.,102.

175. Welsh-Huggins, "Ohio Inmate 'Traumatized.'"

176. "Ohio Inmate Spends Long Day Near Death Chamber," *Associated Press Archive* (September 16, 2009).

177. "Lawyer: Ohio Execution on Hold After Vein Troubles."

178. "Ohio Inmate Spends Long Day Near Death Chamber."

179. "Governor Delays Ohio Execution After Vein Troubles."

180. Jon Craig, "Botched Execution Brings Reprieve for Ohio Killer," *USA Today* (September 16, 2009).

181. "Governor Delays Ohio Execution After Vein Troubles."

182. "Ohio Inmate Spends Long Day Near Death Chamber."

183. Andrew Stern, "Execution Fails over Inmate's Unsuitable Veins," Reuters (September 16, 2009).

184. "Ohio Inmate Spends Long Day Near Death Chamber."

185. Johnson, "Effort to Kill Inmate Halted," A1.

186. Welsh-Huggins, "Ohio Inmate 'Traumatized.'"

187. "Ohio Execution on Hold Due to Unsuitable Veins," *Associated Press: Today News* (September 15, 2009).

188. "Governor Delays Ohio Execution After Vein Troubles."

189. "Ohio Execution on Hold Due to Unsuitable Veins."

190. "Governor Delays Ohio Execution After Vein Troubles."

191. Craig, "Botched Execution Brings Reprieve."

192. Ibid.

193. "Governor Delays Ohio Execution After Vein Troubles."

194. "Ohio Inmate Spends Long Day Near Death Chamber."

195. Welsh-Huggins, "Ohio Inmate 'Traumatized.'"

196. Alan Johnson, "Freeze on Lethal Injections Sought," *Columbus Dispatch* (September 29, 2000).

197. Welsh-Huggins, "Ohio Inmate 'Traumatized.'"

198. Ibid.

199. Johnson, "Effort to Kill Inmate Halted," A1.

200. Frank Lewis, "Strickland Supports Death Penalty, Despite Problems with Recent Execution," *Portsmouth [OH] Daily Times* (September 18, 2009), A3.

201. Carol J. Williams, "Botched Execution in Ohio Raises Concerns About Lethal Injection," *Los Angeles Times* (September 18, 2009).

202. Krouse, "Death Row Inmate Romell Broom Receives Temporary Reprieve from Execution."

203. Scott, "'Dead Man' Author Prejean Deplores Failed Execution," B3.

204. Johnson, "Freeze on Lethal Injections Sought."

205. Bob Driehaus, "Inmate Will Testify About Failed Execution," *New York Times* (September 18, 2009), A15.

206. Johnson, "Freeze on Lethal Injections Sought."

207. Victoria Gill, "The Search for a Humane Way to Kill," BBC News (August 7, 2012).

208. Tim O'Neil, "Too-Tight Strap Hampered Execution—Coroner: Chemical Flow Was Impeded," *St. Louis Post-Dispatch* (May 5, 1995), 1B.

209. Phil Luciano, "A Poorly Executed Execution?" *Journal Star* (Peoria, IL) (May 13, 1995), B1. Foster's botched execution came almost exactly a year after the lethal injection of serial killer John Wayne Gacy in Illinois. As in Foster's case, the drugs suddenly stopped flowing into Gacy's blood stream midway through the process. Prison officials quickly replaced a clogged IV tube so that the execution could continue. In total, Gacy's execution took eighteen minutes.

210. Juan Ignacio Blanco, "Emmitt Foster," in *Murderpedia: The Encyclopedia of Murderers*, http://murderpedia.org/male.F/f1/foster-emitt.htm/.

211. "Missouri Executes Man for 1983 Killing," *Reading [PA] Eagle* (May 4, 1995), A9.

212. Ibid.

213. Ibid.

214. Ibid.

215. Ibid.

216. Terry Ganey, "Inmates Sue over Method of Execution," *St. Louis Post-Dispatch* (June 15, 1995), 1A.

217. Luciano, "Poorly Executed Execution?" B1.

218. O'Neil, "Too-Tight Strap Hampered Execution," 1B.

219. Hunter T. George II, "Convict Executed in Pennsylvania" *The Hour* (Norwalk, CT) (May 3, 1995), 14.

220. Luciano, "Poorly Executed Execution?" B1.

221. O'Neil, "Too-Tight Strap Hampered Execution," 1B.

222. "'Blessed' Release," *The Independent* (London) (May 4, 1995), 11.

223. Luciano, "Poorly Executed Execution?" B1.

224. O'Neil, "Too-Tight Strap Hampered Execution," 1B.

225. Tom Jackman, "Lawsuit Challenges Injections," *Kansas City Star* (June 15, 1995), C1.

226. Gary Fields and Maria Goodavage, "NYC Cops: Excess Force not Corruption," *USA Today* (June 16, 1995), 3A.

227. Luciano, "Poorly Executed Execution?" B1.

228. "Execution Denounced," *St. Louis Post-Dispatch* (May 7, 1995), 6C.

229. See Justice Scalia's opinion, *Callins v. Collins,* 510 U.S. 1141 (1994). Emphasis added.

Chapter 6

1. "Joda Hamilton Will Hang Today," *Nevada [MO] Daily Mail* (December 21, 1906).

2. Ibid.

3. "Hanged Twice," *San Francisco Call* (December 22, 1906), 10.

4. "Hamilton Hangs Twice," *Daily Tribune* (Beaver Falls, PA) (December 24, 1906), 7.

5. "Hang Boy Twice Before He Dies," *Los Angeles Herald* (December 22, 1906), 1.

6. "Strung Up a Second Time," *Alexandria [DC] Gazette* (December 24, 1906), 1.

7. "Bungle at Houston, Mo., Hanging," *Boston Evening Transcript* (December 22, 1906).

8. "Hanging of Youth a Gruesome Bungle," *Reading [PA] Eagle* (December 22, 1906), 8.

9. Ibid.

10. "Murderer of Five Hangs Twice," *San Francisco Call* (December 22, 1906), 10.

11. "Hang Boy Twice," 1.

12. "Hanging of Youth," 8.

13. "Miscellaneous," *Yellowstone News* (Billings, MT) (December 22, 1906).

14. Ibid.

15. Ibid.

16. "The Rope Broke," *Lawrence [KS] Daily World* (December 22, 1906).

17. Ibid.

18. "Newsy Bits," *Lewiston [ME] Saturday Journal* (December 22, 1906).

19. Annulla Linders, "The Execution Spectacle and State Legitimacy: The Changing Nature of the American Execution Audience," 36 *Law and Society Review* (2002), 618.

20. Chris Greer, in a smaller study than our own, asserts that the coverage of botched executions "positioned the news reader in a way that constrained a deeper 'witnessing' of the violence involved in state killing, and did much to ensure that the integrity of the institution, if not the method, remained intact." Chris Greer, "Delivering Death: Capital Punishment, Botched Executions and the American News Media," in *Captured by the Media: Prison Discourse in Popular Culture,* ed. Paul Mason (Portland, OR: Willan, 2006), 98.

21. Ibid., 99.

22. See Judith Shklar, *The Faces of Injustice* (New Haven, CT: Yale University Press, 1992).

23. Edwin Emery and Michael Emery, *The Press and America: An Interpretive History of the Mass Media,* 5th ed. (Englewood Cliffs, NJ: Prentice-Hall, 1984), 256–57.

24. Christopher Daly, *Covering America: A Narrative History of a Nation's Journalism* (Amherst: University of Massachusetts Press, 2012), 122.

25. John Stevens, *Sensationalism and the New York Press* (New York: Columbia University Press, 1991), 76.

26. Emery and Emery, *Press and America,* 281.

27. Ibid., 259.

28. Ibid., 295.

29. Stevens, *Sensationalism*, 100.

30. "War Hero Dies in Death Chair," *New York Tribune* (September 4, 1915), 12.

31. See Austin Sarat et al., "Gruesome Spectacles: The Cultural Reception of Botched Executions in America, 1890–1920," *British Journal of American Legal Studies* 1 (Spring 2012), 6.

32. Linders, "Execution Spectacle," 611.

33. "Murderer Snell Dies on Gallows," *Atlanta Constitution* (June 30, 1900), 3.

34. "Benjamin Snell Executed," *St. Louis Republic* (June 30, 1900).

35. "Benjamin Snell Hanged," *Washington Times* (June 30, 1900), 4.

36. Ibid.

37. Ibid.

38. "Snell Put to Death," *Washington Post* (June 30, 1900), 2. Emphasis added.

39. Ibid. Emphasis added.

40. "Benjamin Snell Hanged."

41. "Paid 'The Wages of Sin,'" *Boston Daily Globe* (June 30, 1900), 7.

42. "Execution of a Giant," *Los Angeles Times* (June 30, 1900), 17.

43. Ibid.

44. Ibid., 180.

45. "Antonio Ferraro Executed," *New York Times* (February 27, 1900), 14.

46. "Ferraro Makes No Struggle," *New York Tribune* (February 27, 1900).

47. "Frightful Execution," *Tacoma Times* (December 29, 1903), 1.

48. "Six Contacts Used to Kill," *Washington Post* (December 30, 1903), 3.

49. "Six Shocks Necessary to Kill Negro," *Washington Times* (December 30, 1903).

50. "Buckled in Death Chair, Negro Defied Lightning," *Atlanta Constitution* (December 30, 1903), 1.

51. "Negro Suffers Death Penalty," *San Francisco Call* (December 30, 1903), 1.

52. "Frightful Execution," *Tacoma Times* (December 29, 1903), 1.

53. Ibid.

54. "Negro Suffers Death Penalty," 1.

55. Ibid.

56. Ibid.

57. Robert Blecker, "Killing Them Softly: Meditations on a Painful Punishment of Death," 35 *Fordham Urban Law Journal* (2008), 976–77.

58. Stevens, *Sensationalism*, 78.

59. Daly, *Covering America*, 154. Emphasis in original.

60. Ibid., 154.

61. Ibid., 100.

62. "Minister-Sheriff Acts as Hangman," *Washington Post* (September 16, 1922), 4.

63. "Iowa Preacher, a Sheriff, Pulls Trap at Hanging," *Chicago Tribune* (September 16, 1922), 8.

64. Ibid.

65. "Weeks Asserts His Innocence Before Hanging," *Telegraph-Herald* (Dubuque, IA) (September 15, 1922), 1.

66. In the period from 1920 to 1940, fewer than 20 percent of articles on botched executions from cities having a population greater than 250,000 were written in a sensationalist style. In contrast, well over half of such articles from small towns over the same period employed sensational language.

67. By 1955, less than a tenth of the coverage of botched executions, regardless of geography, displayed any sensationalist bent.

68. "Boy, 18, Goes to Death for Murder Crying 'God Have Mercy, I'm Sorry,'" *Meriden [CT] Daily Journal* (August 21, 1948), 1.

69. "'Dead' Convict Moves After Death Shock," *New York Times* (February 3, 1923), 2.

70. "Taken from His Coffin, Killer Is Executed Again," *Chicago Tribune* (February 3, 1923), 2.

71. "Pays Twice in Chair," *St. Joseph [MO] News-Press* (March 21, 1935).

72. Ibid.

73. Ibid.

74. "Five Charges Used to Kill 'Tough Guy,'" *The Day* (New London, CT) (March 21, 1935).

75. "Novice Drags Out Deaths of Killers to 42 Minutes," *Pittsburgh Press* (August 2, 1939), 4.

76. Ibid.

77. Ibid.

78. "Two Murderers Die in Massachusetts," *Victoria [TX] Advocate* (August 2, 1939), 2.

79. As controversy grew in the 1960s, execution vigils became commonplace. Though a few high-profile cases—Sacco and Vanzetti, Julius and Ethel Rosenberg—had stirred up public outcry before, in the years leading up to the moratorium, protests became frequent occurrences at the executions of even relatively unknown convicts. Death penalty opponents staged vigils at the executions of, to name a few, Pablo Vargas, Aaron Mitchell, and Caryl Chessman. Indeed, public support for the death penalty was reaching an all-time low in the 1950s and 1960s. Early Gallup polls measuring death penalty attitudes found that about twice as many people were in favor as opposed in 1936, 1937, and

1953. By 1957, these numbers had shifted substantially: 47 percent supported while 34 percent expressed opposition, with the balance undecided about the practice of capital punishment. In 1966, opponents outnumbered supporters for the first—and so far the last—time in American history. Stuart Banner, *The Death Penalty: An American History* (Cambridge, MA: Harvard University Press, 2002), 240.

80. "5 Murderers Are Executed," *Washington Post* (May 14, 1960), A3. Yet this decline in public support did not directly cause the decrease in the number of executions carried out. A reduction in capital sentencing, led primarily by Northern juries, played some role, but Banner argues that the steady decline in executions starting around 1950 resulted largely from judicial intervention. He describes a "procedural revolution" between 1951 and 1965, which allowed more convicted murderers to appeal their sentences. Even though few appeals resulted in ultimate success, the delay between a conviction and an execution stretched longer and longer: "the death row population doubled between 1955 and 1961 and doubled again between 1961 and 1969." Ibid., 246–47. By 1970, then, the death penalty was both less popular than ever before and threatened by an increasingly confident legal challenge.

81. "Sex Slayer Executed," *Newburgh [NY]-Beacon News* (May 13, 1960), 1.

82. "Rape Killer Executed," *New York Times* (May 13, 1960), 18.

83. Michael Schudson, *Discovering the News: A Social History of American Newspapers* (New York: Basic Books, 1978), 5–6.

84. Ibid., 156.

85. Ibid., 9.

86. "Dies Screaming in Gas Chamber," *Chicago Daily Tribune* (April 7, 1956), 1.

87. Ibid.

88. "Puts Up Fight Before Dying," *Spokane Daily Chronicle* (April 29, 1932), 1.

89. Garland, *Peculiar Institution*, 261.

90. "Attorney Charges Evans Was Tortured by Alabama in Botched Electrocution," *Washington Post* (April 24, 1983), A5.

91. "Lawyer: Killer 'Burned Alive,'" *Philadelphia Inquirer* (April 24, 1983), A1.

92. "Two Attempts at Execution Kill Dunkins," *Gadsden [AL] Times* (July 14, 1989), 1.

93. "Crossed Wires Bungle Killer's Electrocution," *Rome [GA]-News Tribune* (July 14, 1989), 1.

94. "19-Minute Execution: First Surge Not Fatal," *Miami Herald* (December 13, 1984), 1A.

95. "2,300 Volts Help Quench Lust For Revenge," *Orlando Sentinel* (Octo-

ber 20, 1985), H3.

96. "Use of Electric Chair Under Fire," *Times-Union* (Warsaw, IN) (October 17, 1985), 24.

97. David T.Z. Mindich, *Just the Facts: How "Objectivity" Came to Define American Journalism* (New York: New York University Press, 1998), 7. Chris Daly criticizes the seesaw model harshly: "In practice, this view holds that journalism is neither the pursuit of ultimate truth nor an outlet for the journalist's own personal expression. Instead, the proper role of journalism is to find out what *other* people are doing and saying. In this framing of the role, the journalist is not obligated to get to the bottom of things. It is enough to gather tidbits." Daly, *Covering America*, 297, emphasis in original.

98. Kathy Fair, "Woman Leaves Executed Killer a Message: 'Tell My Husband Hello,'" *Houston Chronicle* (December 14, 1988), A25.

99. "Texas Executes Drifter Who Killed Three Women," *New York Times* (March 13, 1985), A15.

100. Mary Bounds, "10 on Texas' Death Row Want Sentences Carried Out," *Dallas Morning News* (March 14, 1985), 44a.

101. "Texas Executes Drug User Killer by Lethal Injection," *Atlanta Journal and Constitution* (August 21, 1986), A8.

102. "Death Penalty," *Orlando Sentinel* (June 25, 1987), A16.

103. Kathy Fair, "White Was Helpful at Execution," *Houston Chronicle* (April 24, 1992), 31.

104. "Use of Electric Chair Under Fire."

105. Margaret Talev, "Medina Dead When Mask Flamed Up," *Tampa Tribune* (April 1, 1997), 1.

106. Ibid.

107. Sydney Freedberg, "Bloody Execution Leads to Stay for 2nd Inmate," *St. Petersburg Times* (July 9, 1999), 1A.

108. "Medina Dead."

109. Greer, "Delivering Death," 95.

110. In its decision declaring electrocution unconstitutional under its state constitution, the State Supreme Court of Nebraska cited stories of horrifically "botched" electrocutions as motivating states to change their execution methods. It acknowledged its own reliance on newspaper accounts in some instances to determine whether electrocution had effectively served its purpose or if electrocutions were botched and the prisoner remained alive after initial execution attempts. See *State v. Mata*, 275 Neb. 1, 44 (2008).

111. Adam Liptak, "Trouble Finding Inmate's Vein Slows Lethal Injection in Ohio," *New York Times* (May 3, 2006), A16.

112. The three-drug protocol employs an anesthetic, a paralytic, and finally potassium chloride, which stops the heart. The most controversial part of this

formula is the second drug, the paralytic, usually pancuronium bromide. The other two drugs would kill the condemned on their own, so the paralytic is not necessary to bring about death. The paralytic would, however, cause severe pain to the condemned were the anesthetic not entirely effective. Total paralysis, moreover, would effectively prevent a suffering inmate from signaling that anything had gone wrong. It is, after all, designed to mask the violence of the killing act.

113.   Ron Word, "Doctors, Death Penalty Foes Focus on Mistakes in Florida Execution," *Press-Register* (Mobile, AL) (December 17, 2006), A1.

114.   Kevin Begos, "Execution Puts Crist to Test," *Tampa Tribune* (December 15, 2006), 1.

Index